MAKING
MUSIC VIDEOS

MAKING
MUSIC

LARA M. SCHWARTZ

FOREWORD BY BRETT RATNER

BILLBOARD BOOKS AN IMPRINT OF WATSON-GUPTILL PUBLICATIONS/NEW YORK

VIDEOS

Everything You Need to Know from the Best in the Business

Executive Editor: Bob Nirkind
Designer: Kapo Ng @ A-Men Project
Production Director: Alyn Evans

First published in 2007 by Billboard Books,
an imprint of Watson-Guptill Publications,
Nielsen Business Media,
a division of The Nielsen Company
770 Broadway, New York, NY 10003

All photos taken by Dean MacKay unless otherwise noted.

Library of Congress Cataloging-in-Publication Data

Schwartz, Lara M.
 Making music videos / Lara M. Schwartz.
 p. cm.
 Includes index.
 ISBN-13: 978-0-8230-8368-8
 ISBN-10: 0-8230-8368-3
 1. Music videos—Production and direction. I. Title.
 PN1992.8.M87S39 2007
 780.26'7—dc22
        2006035692

Printed in the U.S.A.

First printing, 2007
1 2 3 4 5 6 7 / 13 12 11 10 09 08 07

CONTENTS

FOREWORD

I had dreamed of being a director from a very young age. The directors I admired at the time were feature directors—Hal Ashby, Martin Scorsese, the Coen brothers—guys who had made the movies I grew up loving. Music videos were never a part of my dream, but eventually became a big part of my life.

I loved watching them. At the time, Michael Jackson's videos were, of course, the best. Next came Madonna. Then the big rock videos were the most popular. And eventually rap videos took over MTV. But I never wanted to be a music video director. Although I loved them, directing music videos was never part of my game plan because, at that time, there were very few video directors making the transition to feature films.

I wanted to make features. I had heard stories about Steven Spielberg stalking the lot at Universal, Spike Lee maxing out his credit cards, and the Coen brothers using all the money they had to make their first feature film. Nobody ever heard of a music video director being recognized for his talent and offered a feature film.

In 1992, I was two years out of NYU film school, and I was trying to decide what I was going to do with my film career. I had already made many short films since the age of eight. My friend Russell Simmons, who had started Def Jam, offered to have a screening of my student film, *Whatever Happened to Mason Reese*. The only people who came, aside from my mom and my friends, were rappers. A few months later, Russell and I attended a Public Enemy concert, and Chuck D approached us and said to Russell,

"We want Brett to direct our next video." Despite the fact that I was standing right next to him, Russell asked, "Brett who?" Chuck then said, "Brett. Your friend, Brett. White man, Brett. Brett Ratner." Russell was so proud that somebody he had been hanging out with was being recognized for his work by one of his artists.

Russell's company Def Jam wrote me a check for $25,000 for the budget, which I deposited into my personal bank account. I took a few friends from NYU with some film cameras and followed Public Enemy as they toured with U2. I spent two months editing my first video. The day the video aired was a very important day in music video history—MTV decided to put the director's name on the video. No longer was the director anonymous.

The video aired, and, all of a sudden, every artist started calling Russell and asking, "Can we get Brett to do our music video?" My career took off. What was most exciting was that I was getting paid to learn. Every time I got a bigger budget, I would rent another new piece of equipment that I didn't have access to in film school. I figured out how to use the tools of my craft. Being a music video director was my version of grad school.

I experimented with every aspect of filmmaking. For example, I began to understand why to use a steadi-cam versus a dolly for a particular shot. Then I started doing music videos that told stories, with a beginning, middle, and end, while always staying true to who the recording artist was—similar to what I would later do with the characters in my films.

Displaying the director's name on music videos changed the face of the entire medium. Now that a name was attached to a piece of work, music videos started to improve. Bad videos slowly disappeared, and exceptional directors started to emerge. All of a sudden, names like David Fincher became associated with Madonna, Michael Bay with Meatloaf, and Mark Romanek with Michael Jackson. There was always somebody new breaking onto the scene, and it seemed that every month would introduce us to the next great talent—Chris Cunningham, Jonas Ackerland, and Hype Williams. Music video directors were finally getting recognition, and most music videos were looking even better than the movies being shown in theaters. They were like minimovies, with the most cutting edge photography, camera work, and storytelling. Music videos began defining pop culture—not only the music, but the fashion and the design. Guys like Fincher and Bay became the coolest feature film directors, which opened the eyes of Hollywood, and the doors for people like myself, Spike Jonze, Michel Gondry, as well as for the next generation of music video directors who aspire to become the great filmmakers of our future.

Music videos are now a medium where true talent is taken seriously, and where a director can go from a music video one day to a $100 million feature film the next. This practice continues to grow stronger—great filmmakers regularly emerge from the world of music videos, not just from film schools or the DGA training program.

Being hired as a feature director is no longer contingent upon making a long-form story. Achieve a successful career in music videos, and Hollywood will come to you.

But how does one actualize the dream of succeeding in the world of music videos? *Making Music Videos* is the perfect teaching tool, explaining how to create music videos, and how to break in to the music video business, an industry that can be an end unto itself, offering a long and sustainable career, or one which can be used as a stepping stone to a thriving career in feature films and television.

Lara was a novice producer when I launched my career as a music video director. At that time, there were no structured manuals with practical applications about music video production. It was simply trial by fire. Since then, the music video industry has matured and it is no longer possible to "wing it." *Making Music Videos* has everything necessary to create artistic, marketable, and memorable music videos. I recommend this book as required reading for anyone starting out as a filmmaker today.

Brett Ratner
Hollywood, CA
September 2006

INTRODUCTION

At their most basic level, music videos serve as short film clips designed to enhance the experience of hearing songs by engaging a second sense: sight. At their best, they successfully marry two key components: music and visual imagery—both equally important, inherently intertwined, and fundamentally influencing and inspiring the other.

Different from feature films, music videos do not focus on character development or the relatively slow unwinding of a story or plot. Instead, they aim for instant gratification. By adding compelling and often titillating images to an existing song, music videos strive to get a quick emotional response from their audience. This response, it is hoped, leads to album sales and increased popularity for the artist or artists involved.

Woven into the fabric of world entertainment since the launch of MTV in 1981, music videos established a visual style that has dramatically overtaken our nation, and the world. They make and break trends in fashion, make-up, hairstyles, sports, music, movies, video games, and advertising in both television and print. Videos influence how we dance, how we dress, what music we listen to, what jewelry we wear, what kind of car we drive, what sports we play, what foods we eat, and what beverages we drink. Music videos represent marketing within marketing, the ultimate promotional machine.

But what do we really know about music videos? How are they produced and by whom? Who pays for them and who's involved in the creative process? *Making Music Videos* will answer

these questions, and many others. This book will familiarize you with the process of creating music videos from inception through execution, as well as provide an insight into the personalities of the professionals working in the industry.

There are two parts to the music video process. The first part involves the initial conception of the music video project, during which the record label and artist solicit directors, review their proposed visual treatments, and select which director and treatment best fits the song. The second part involves the actual making of the music video. The two parts of this book are set up similarly. In Part One, "Developing the Music Video," the chapters cover the commissioning of a music video, the responsibilities of the director and the director's representative, the responsibilities of the production company team, the treatment-writing process, the budgeting process, and the preparation of contracts. In Part Two, "Creating the Music Video," the focus shifts to hiring the crew, preproduction, shooting the music video, postproduction, and the final wrap.

Ninety-three industry professionals—directors, record label commissioners, executive producers, director's representatives, producers, assistant directors, director's of photography, production designers—were interviewed for this book, and throughout it they provide an insider's perspective of how music videos are made. A dynamic cross-section of the music video community was chosen so that the video productions discussed within these pages range from low budgets to high budgets, from New York to Los Angeles, as well as span genre boundaries in order to provide a deep and nuanced understanding of all aspects of the music industry. The book opens with Expert Testimonials introducing all of those who were interviewed.

Accompanying the text are forty-seven color photos that illustrate some of the activities and equipment involved in the creation of music videos. The appendices at the back of the book include the Point Zero Bid, the most widely used budget format; an example of a video treatment; the IATSE union rules, the basic union agreements for music videos; and Teamster Rules and Guidelines, used for music video production.

After reading this book you will understand the standard language and procedures involved in making music videos and have the technical knowledge necessary to produce videos of any budget and intricacy. While essential for anyone interested in making music videos, including music and film students, this book will also speak directly to music industry professionals, freelance producers, production managers and coordinators, directors, and music video enthusiasts.

It's important to keep in mind that every record label and production company has its own personality and that "consistent," "standard," and "normal" are relative terms in the music video world. *Making Music Videos* provides as close a description as possible of the "standard" operating procedures of an art form that changes as quickly as the music video itself. Although it's fair to say that in the past ten years videos have grown up in terms of their stature and influence within the mainstream film industry, they remain more mercurial and unstructured than most other forms of film production. As such, they offer a huge learning curve in real time; many filmmakers—not only film students but also those making a living in the industry—fine-tune their skills and have fun by experimenting on music videos, something more difficult to do in other forms of film or video making. Although videos have become more conservative and less open to experimentation in recent years, by the sheer nature of the speed at which they are created—the period between the initial conception of the video through delivering the finished product often being a month or less—they continue to strengthen and stimulate creativity through spontaneity and allow and encourage directors and producers to push the limits of their imaginations.

"The reason I've been drawn to music videos is there's so much diversity of people I get to work with, different experiences, traveling here one day and shooting nights in the rain, and the next day you're against a green screen or whatever," says director Roman Coppola (Phoenix's "CQ" and The Strokes' "12:51"). "There's just a new experience with each video. It's very much a learning type of thing."

Andy Warhol once claimed that fine art and commercial art were no longer distinct. Forty years later, pop culture combines art and commerce, each a part of the other more than ever before. In Warhol's terms, music videos epitomized pop culture. With this in mind, we dive into the process of explaining how music videos make the journey from the directors' minds to viewers' eyes, taking into consideration three major aspects: art, finance, and marketing music.

For Mark,

Thank you for always paying such close attention. You're my everything.

EXPERT TESTIMONIALS

NAME	TITLE
Baca-Asay, Joaquin	Director of Photography
Barber, Bryan	Director
Bayer, Samuel	Director
Bohas, Molly	Director's Representative
Bray, Kevin	Director
Care, Peter	Director
Cavallo, Helen	Executive Producer
Cole, Cayce	Executive Producer
Coppola, Roman	Director
Curl, Rachel	Producer
Danko, Ericka	Executive Producer
Daughters, Patrick	Director
Dayton, Jonathan	Director, "Dayton Faris"
Dewart, Caleb	Producer
Dick, Nigel	Director
Eddy, Clark	Editor
Ehrlich, Nicole	Creative Services and Broadcast Media Dept; Geffen Records
Erasmus, Nicholas	Editor
Estrella, Michael	Assistant Director
Faris, Valerie	Director, "Dayton Faris"
Ferrari, Verenne	Director's Representative
Finkelstein, Lorin	Senior Director, Music Video Commissioner; RCA Records
Finkenstaedt, Catherine A.	Executive Producer
Giraldi, Bob	Director
Green, William	Producer
Greenwald, Julie	President; Atlantic Records
Gregory, Heidi	Director's Representative
Haase, Janet	Executive Producer and Director's Representative
Hahn, Joe	Director

NAME	TITLE
Hamri, Sanaa	Director
Harder, Phil	Director
Hardin, Jil	Producer
Harvey Hatfield, Retta	Vice President of Video Production; Universal Music Group Nashville
Hussey, Dave	Colorist
Jones, Noble	Director
Kahn, Joseph	Director
Kahn, Michael	Assistant Director
Kaplan, Jill	Independent Music Video Commissioner; Formerly at Atlantic Records
Karr, Dean	Director
Klasfeld, Marc	Director
Kleinbaum, Janet	Senior Vice President of Marketing and Video Production; Jive Records
Kluthe, Doug	Executive Producer
Kohr, Mark	Director
LaBuda, Tommy	Director's Representative
Landis, John	Director
Leon, Beau	Senior Colorist and Partner of Postproduction Facility
Little X	Director
Lockwood, Danny	Vice President of Video Production; Sony BMG Music Entertainment
Masick, Tim	Colorist
Mc G	Director
Mesina, Lenny	Offline Editor
Meyers, Dave	Director
Miller, Kate	Senior Vice President of Film and Video; Capitol Records
Mouaness, Oualid	Producer
Nispel, Marcus	Director
Osborne, Joe "Oz"	Assistant Director

NAME	TITLE
Panzer, Jeffrey A.	Independent Video Commissioner; Formerly Emperor of All Videos/Music Executive at Universal Music Group
Perel, Larry	Executive Producer
Poliquin, Matthew	Postproduction Producer
Poveda, Billy	Executive Producer
Ratner, Brett	Director
Rivera, Sabrina	Director of Video Production; Sony BMG Music Entertainment
Robertson, Dustin	Offline Editor
Rolston, Matthew	Director
Sarno, Devin	Vice President, Visual Content; Warner Brothers Records
Sarno, Kelly Norris	Executive Producer
Scott, Laure	Director's Representative
Shilo	Directors Collective
Siega, Marcos	Director
Silverman, Susan	Independent Music Video Commissioner; Primarily with Atlantic Records
Skinner, Randy	Independent Video Commissioner; Formerly Vice President of Video Production; Virgin Records
Sosin, Shana	Former Executive Director of Business; Music Video Producer's Association
Tortolla, Livia	Senior Vice President of Marketing and Artist Development; Atlantic Records
Uliano, Joseph	Executive Producer
W.I.Z.	Director
Wakefield, Jay	Head of Production
Webb, Marc	Director
Whittaker, Teri	Production Designer

CONTRIBUTORS

NAME	TITLE
Boocheck, Rob	Director, "Tomorrow's Brightest Minds"
Clark, Andrea	Executive Director of Creative; Music Video Producer's Assoc
Gibbard, Benjamin	Artist, "Death Cab for Cutie"
Griffin, Meg	Executive and DJ; Sirius Satellite Radio
Harmer, Nicholas	Artist, "Death Cab for Cutie"
Harpootlian, Wade	Director, "Tomorrow's Brightest Minds"
Malloy, Brendan	Director, "The Malloys"
Malloy, Emmett	Director, "The Malloys"
McGerr, Jason	Artist, "Death Cab for Cutie"
Miguel, Grace	Formerly Creative Services and Broadcast Media Dept; Geffen Records
Nesmith, Michael	Former Artist, The Monkees, and One of The Fathers of the Modern Music Video
Simmons, David	Director, "Tomorrow's Brightest Minds"
Smith, Justine	Director's Representative
Sutherland, Kate	Producer
Walla, Christopher	Artist, "Death Cab for Cutie"

PART ONE
DEVELOPING THE MUSIC VIDEO

CHAPTER ONE
COMMISSIONING THE VIDEO

Although the music business changes with alarming speed, one thing remains constant: The record label's paramount responsibility is to its artists' music production and, subsequently, to the marketing and sales of the music. Each label seeks out recording artists they feel will appeal to a wide audience, which, in return, will allow the label to sell a lot of music. The label then negotiates a recording contract with the particular artist. The contract outlines the artist's responsibilities to the record company as well as the record company's responsibility to the artist, including items such as royalties and what the record company will do for promotion. The record label specializes in helping their artists develop the highest possible sales potential through marketing the artists and their music via the Internet, radio play, and television video networks and shows, and then selling their music through a vast array of audio and visual distribution outlets, such as retail stores, Internet and iTunes, ring tones, and video compilations.

The record label-artist relationship is codependent. The reason an artist signs with a record label is three-fold: First, the label advances the artist money to pay for recording their music, as well as for album artwork and various marketing campaigns such as videos, commercials, fliers, and in-store appearances. This up front money, earmarked for the artist's development and production, may also go toward basic living expenses while the artist works on his or her album. In return for this cash advance, the label retains specific rights and percentages on future

sales of the music. Prior to the 1990s, labels rarely got involved in more than simply the sale of the recorded music. These days, however, it's becoming increasingly prevalent for them to negotiate deals that involve merchandising and touring. For example, in 2002, British superstar Robbie Williams signed a deal that made him a partner in merchandising and touring with his record label EMI. And in 2005, Korn entered into a similar deal with EMI.

The second reason an artist will sign with a label is due to their vast array of contacts in the music industry and distribution outlets, as well as their acumen in the formal business arena. Labels develop and market professional musicians, akin to a mentor taking a student under their wing. Artists are often young and unfamiliar with music business practices, so a record label can serve as a guide for the actual operation.

The third, and often unspoken, reason an artist signs with a label is its prestige. Julie Greenwald, the president of Atlantic Records, sums up the relationship between the label and the artist saying, "Record companies are completely reliant on artists putting out their albums. And artists rely on us to properly roll them out."

Artists often mistakenly believe that labels exist to promote their creative vision. This is only true as long as the artist's vision conforms to the label's overriding goal of achieving significant financial gain through music sales. The bottom line is that record companies want to sell as many products—by as many of their artists—as they possibly can. Since MTV went live in 1981, music videos have played a huge part in that process. Therefore, the process of commissioning and creating music videos begins with the record company.

THE RECORD COMPANY'S ROLE IN THE VIDEO PROJECT

Although creating music videos is a team process, each record company operates differently. While every department within a label has a specific role in the process of creating the music, marketing the music, and getting the music to the consumer, certain departments are more involved in the video process than others. Every record company has an Artist & Repertoire department (A&R). A&R executives seek out new talent and sign them to a contract to record exclusively for their label. In return, the artist receives the guidance and financial backing of the A&R person and his or her team, in addition to sharing in the profits the artist makes for the label. In a nutshell, the record company agrees to advance to the artist a specific amount of money, which is negotiated by the label and the artist's attorney and/or manager. This allows the artist to write, produce, and record his or her music. Some A&R people get involved in the video process and some do not; it depends on the persons, the relationships, and the label.

Once signed to a label, the artist is then assigned to a product manger, who essentially functions as the artist's in-house manager. The product manager takes responsibility for the day-to-day management and welfare of all the artists on his or her roster, guiding the artists through all of the stages of the cycle. As such, the product manager often takes a very active role in the video process, since it is an important part of marketing and branding the artist.

The artist must be properly developed and "rolled out." Developing the artist includes advancing and nurturing his or her music and image. Every department at the record company collaborates in this process, pushing the agenda of their particular division—but also working together to accomplish it. For instance, the New Media department has its own concerns, which inherently overlap with the Publicity Department's. The record company also draws on the expertise of each department to roll out the artist. Rolling out is traditionally an advertising technique whose goal is to cover as many markets as possible, while also increasing distribution and product sales. Videos play a major part in an artist's roll out.

What make a great music video?

"A great video is something different, something that you haven't seen before. It stops you in your tracks."
—Randy Skinner, Independent Video Commissioner; Formerly Vice President of Video Production; Virgin Records

"A great video starts with a really good or a great song whose images will provoke you to think and to use your imagination. It gets the viewer to react to something, to make them feel good, because we're not coming up with the cure for cancer or AIDS doing this job. A great video should make you think and make you feel something. It has to be interesting and compelling—stuff that isn't the same garbage that you see from beginning to end."
—Jeffrey A. Panzer, Independent Video Commissioner; Formerly Emperor of All Videos/Music Executive at Universal Music Group

The marketing department leads the process of creating the roll out campaign, taking into account each department's input and concerns regarding the particular artist. Marketing coordinates all of the other departments insofar as the overall plan of promoting and branding the artist. As the leader of this process, it is common for the marketing department to house the video department as well as the other departments fundamental to the marketing process, such as publicity and promotion. It is generally through marketing that the single for the video and the budget for the video are determined and, in turn, handed down to the video department.

Since the music video process is integral to the overall marketing scheme for each artist, it is not uncommon for label presidents to take a very active roll in the videos. Julie Greenwald, at Atlantic Records, oversees all the aspects of the video process, from budgeting to the actual shoot. Andy Slater, the president of Capitol Records, also maintains hands-on involvement in the entire video making process.

People outside the label may also be involved in a music video project, depending upon the project. For example, if a guest artist, signed to another label, performs in a song, the artist may be asked to perform in the video. If that is the case, the guest artist's representatives, such as his or her personal manager or record company product manager, may get involved in the production of the video. Or, if the video is for a movie soundtrack and movie footage will be cut into the video, the executives from the movie studio, as well as the director of the movie, may get involved in the production of the video. As you can see, each project has its own parameters.

UNDERSTANDING THE RECORD LABEL'S STRUCTURE

As the popular saying goes, it takes a village to raise a child; the same applies to developing an artist. For example, Atlantic Records holds "futures meetings," in which the A&R person, product manager, and department heads from promotion, publicity, sales, marketing, new media, and international gather to discuss an artist or band they just signed. The meeting allows each member of the team to assume part ownership of the project. The heads discuss why they signed the artist and the primary demographic to which the artist appeals; create a campaign to effectively introduce the artist; and define what visual materials are needed in order to market the artist. Rather than relying on more traditional marketing tools like focus groups, Livia Tortolla, senior vice president of marketing and artist development at Atlantic Records says, Atlantic bases most of its marketing plans on intuition, with a little help from a street research team. The brainstorming sessions at the futures meetings help fertilize the soil from which a full-blown marketing campaign will soon sprout, which inevitably include videos as an integral part of the sales strategy.

THE A&R DEPARTMENT

At some labels, the A&R person who signs the artist is very involved in the video process. Video Commissioners, employees responsible for producing the video at the record label—I will go into more detail about their responsibilities later in the chapter—generally welcome input from the A&R person, since he or she has spent the most time with the artist. After "discovering" and signing the artist, the A&R person will match him or her to a producer and keep tabs on the artist throughout the process of recording the album. A&R, in conjunction with the artist and his or her manager, will approve the songs and how they are recorded, and agree on a collection of music, mixed and mastered for delivery, within the advance's budget. The A&R person can offer valuable insight to the video commissioner, in regards to what the song may mean to the artist, which can then help the commissioner select a director and formulate some creative ideas. In some cases, however, the A&R person isn't involved as much, in which case the product manager assumes the role of advising the video commissioner.

THE PRODUCT MANAGEMENT DEPARTMENT
The product manger looks out for the artist's best interests as a whole from inside the label machine, by basically shepherding the artist through the record company to get the best of what the record label has to offer. In the early days of music videos, many labels didn't have video departments, and product managers took charge of the video process.

THE MARKETING DEPARTMENT
A large chunk of a record label's budget for an artist goes toward marketing. The label's marketing department creates an overall strategy for each artist it has signed, which includes coordinating music videos, promotion, publicity, and any other campaign to sell the music. Videos are an integral part of each artist's overall marketing plan. As Janet Kleinbaum, the senior vice president of marketing and video production at Jive Records, explains, videos are the biggest and most expensive tool used in marketing the artist.

Since the days of *American Bandstand*, imaging and performance have grown to be, arguably, on par with an artist's music. His or her career depends on it. The music video has become the key medium for an artist to establish an image. Some genres, like hip-hop and R&B, have become driven by the music video, which has supplanted live performance as a means to expose an artist's image to the public. As such, music video is often called a promotional video or, in Europe, a promo.

Music videos blend various aspects of the artist's personae and the song, as well as other factors integral to sell music nowadays, in one fell swoop. They also offer another way for artists to express themselves and their creative vision. In addition, they give viewers a visual memory of a song and allow them to get to know an artist, while boosting the artist's image and brand at the same time. A music video even has the power to change a person's opinion about a song he or she may have previously disliked. A good video clip can also drastically reduce the need for touring.

Music videos are only effective marketing tools if (1) they enhance the artist's music and image, and (2) if they are accessible to the appropriate audience by being placed in the correct marketplace. To properly market an artist, the record company must know the target market they want to reach. For example, Atlantic Records president Julie Greenwald feels that it is crucial for her to go to clubs several days a week to keep up with the artists and their fans. An acolyte of the Internet, she points out that artists can make any kind of video they want and know they will be able to get exposure with it online. She also realizes, however, that relying solely on the Internet is a dangerous game; artists need to be seen on video outlets that go far beyond the Internet. A quality video should find a home on a cable video channel, as well as in clubs, bars, stores, and restaurants that rely on music videos as part of their ambiance.

What do you love about music videos?

"I love the fact that I get to work with artists. I'm the luckiest person in the world. I was in D.C. the other day, watching this baby band that we have, and I watched him [the singer] do a cappella version of a few of his songs. It was so magnificent and so beautiful, and just so compelling. I'm sitting there watching this and going, 'Gosh, I can be a part of this guy's career. He's letting me be a part of it, and it's just going to be such an amazing journey.' That's amazing. Jay Z, when he came to us, he had *Reasonable Doubt* under his belt, and then I worked on like seven other album projects with him and he let us in. He let us into his life, both professionally and personally, and we had real relationships. We all vacation together in Italy, and just when do you get to do that? I watched Sum 41 go from being this unknown little band to performing on *Saturday Night Live*. And I'm a part of changing peoples' lives. They buy houses, they get married, and then they have kids, and you know their children and their grandchildren are going to be taken care of. It's amazing."

—Julie Greenwald,
President, Atlantic Records

"What I love about this job, about being a video commissioner—which is a weird term—is that it's really creative, and I don't have to be overly involved in sales or marketing. The video department has a lot of leeway, because it's such an unpredictable sort of animal. It's sort of its own entity within the music industry. I love the marriage of creativity and marketing. It's where art meets commerce."

—Kate Miller,
Senior Vice President
of Film and Video;
Capitol Records

"I love making stuff, and I love music, and I love creative people. I like a high volume of work. It's probably the best gig in town. When I started, I just wanted a job where I could wear what I wanted—I swear—be who I wanted to be, and be around young, like-minded people."

—Lorin Finkelstein,
Senior Director,
Music Video Commissioner;
RCA Records

The Electronic Press Kit (EPK) is another visual tool used to market artists. EPKs are generally short five- to twelve -minute video highlights that offer a broad, comprehensive view of the artist's personality; tour footage; behind the scenes footage; lifestyle moments; interviews with family, other artists, and talk show hosts; still photos; album artwork; and, of course, interviews with the artist. All the material is then edited together into a mini-documentary. EPKs are designed to provide an in-house overview of an artist for record label employees, as well as a glimpse into the artist's persona for the media, radio, and other potential sales outlets, such as Virgin Megastore, Best Buy, etc. EPKs tend to be much less creative and expensive, than music videos, and require much less production.

Although not as important as they once were, the evolution of the EPK into enhanced CDs and DVDs, dual discs, high-concept mini-movies, and a host of other new media marketing tools has become a visual "value added" incentive to boost music sales. EPKs give the artists additional exposure, which, in turn, makes it easier for a record label's departments to do their jobs and sell the artists. According to Nicole Ehrlich, who is part of the Creative Services and Broadcast Media Department at Geffen Records, "We make all different kinds of tools (art/commerce) such as television specials and shows, commercials, long forms, live shows, DVDs, webisodes, podcasts, movies, short films, and more. We try to include the right lifestyle products and tie-ins to offset the costs or give us more exposure. With the help of all these different types of media tools we hope to engage not only the artists' fan base but also conquer new audiences. This, in turn, will then help effect radio play, visibility, concert attendance, touring, buying music, buying videos, press, merchandise, new media interaction—and the list goes on."

THE MUSIC VIDEO DEPARTMENT

At most labels, the music video department usually falls under the purview of the marketing department. But, as I mentioned before, the responsibilities of all the departments at a record company many times overlap. At Atlantic Records, Warner Brothers, and Capitol Records, the video department falls under the aegis of the marketing department. At Geffen Records, how-

What makes a great commissioner?

A great commissioner:
- **Thinks outside the box.**
- **Constantly searches for new talent.**
- **Doesn't just rely on the same old standards.**
- **Pushes the medium forward.**
- **Recognizes talent.**
- **Knows what director is right for a particular artist or piece of music.**
- **Is realistic in his/her goals and expectations, and matches those with the right team.**
- **Sticks to the idea.**
- **Trusts the director and team.**
- **Keeps calm during trying circumstances.**
- **Makes informed suggestions.**
- **Stays faithful to the director's abilities.**
- **Maintains loyalty to the artist's image.**
- **Has a balanced awareness of the creative, financial, and technical processes as they relate to music videos.**
- **Understands the production process from the beginning to the end.**
- **Does the best job possible in helping producers with the overall process rather than washing his or her hands of responsibility in difficult situations.**
- **Willingly watches reels, returns phone calls, and takes creative risks on new talent and new ideas.**

ever, the setup is different. The video department is part of the Creative Services and Broadcast Media Department, which is a standalone department within the company. And yet at another label, such as Universal Music Group Nashville—which encompasses Mercury, MCA, Lost Highway, and DreamWorks—the video production is its own department. Jive Records has the least typical flow chart of responsibilities, since the video production department is set up as part of the marketing team and not all of the marketing report to Janet Kleinbaum. She has specific projects that she handles from a marketing standpoint, while many other artists on the label may have their marketing handled by different executives. However, the entire video production department reports to Kleinbaum, who reports directly to Barry Weiss, the CEO and president.

THE VIDEO COMMISSIONER

Within the music video department, there are music video commissioners, which, as I previously mentioned, are responsible for producing the videos for the label. The title Commissioner is not universal. Independent video commissioner Randy Skinner, formerly the vice president of video production at Virgin Records, explains that, "Commissioner is a term that came out of the UK, and that's what they were always called there. We never called ourselves commissioners [here in the US]. That sort of came along fairly recently."

Nicole Ehrlich explains that there aren't really titles at Geffen, she is simply in the Creative Services and Broadcast Media Department. Kate Miller is officially the senior vice president of film and video production at Capitol Records. The semantics are such that she oversees managers on her staff, as opposed to being a commissioner and having junior commissioners reporting to her. Independent video commission-

er Jeff Panzer, formerly the head of the music video department at Universal/Motown Records, had the most unusual title on his business card. He was officially the Emperor of all Videos. However, for the sake of ease and consistency, we will call everyone who is in charge of producing music videos from the label side a commissioner. Generally there is one commissioner who is the department head, and the less senior commissioners who answer directly to that person.

A commissioner's role is similar to that of an executive producer in the feature film world. The commissioner brings the money from the record label and oversees the entire project, making sure that the label's interests are being met. Hopefully, on any given project, the artist's interests and the label's interests line up. "I heavily involve myself in the development of the concept," say Danny Lockwood, Sony BMG Music Entertainment's vice president of video production. "That includes imaging of the artist and the positioning of them in the marketplace."

Because commissioners work very closely with the artists throughout the entire process of making a music video, many established artists like to work on multiple projects with the same commissioner over the course of their careers. Janet Kleinbaum explains, "I always get an artist's input. Some [artists] have a lot to say, some have very little to say, but you can't do this without their input. How can you show up for a photo shoot and not discuss what their hair's going to look like? You can't do that. It has to be their personality coming across on screen. It has to be what's right for them. And a lot of them obviously have very clear-cut ideas about who they are and how they want to be portrayed."

It all comes down to an artist's image: what the artist wants to project, what the company wants the artist and the video to project, and

Snapshots from the Set

"Nirvana's 'Smells Like Teen Spirit' was my first job. The band hated me. I was very intense. I certainly can take some responsibility for being—what's the word—stubborn. I was stubborn about what my vision was going to be, and I think they were a punk band that had never made a music video. Everything I was doing with the video kind of turned them off. As that shoot day went on—that day that made my career—we fought more and more. I got into a fistfight with one of the kids at lunch. Kurt disliked me so much that he refused to sing the song, and I had to go up to the record label and say, 'Please let Kurt sing the song a few times. I promise you you'll have a great video.' Then Kurt went out and sang the song four times, probably one of the best performances I've ever gotten out of anybody. i really feel that all his rage was sort of directed at me, and because I was holding the camera—I DP [act as a director of photography for] all of my own work—I kind of got that intensity directed towards the viewer, and that turned out to be a great thing. I think all that tension on the set helped make a great video.

The other part of the story is when the kids destroyed the set at the end of the video; it was totally an unscripted moment. These kids were drunk, pissed off, and hated me. They were there all day, and we had them there for free. They begged me to come down and destroy the set, and I said, 'Fine. Destroy the sets.' They started destroying the sets, and I looked through a camera and said, 'Oh my God; that's amazing.' And I turned the camera on, and that's the whole end of the video."

—Samuel Bayer, Director

"I'm an improvising director. I was directing a Redman video back in the day, and Redman came up to me and said, 'Man, we need a white bitch that comes up and buys some weed from us in the video.' And I said, 'But it's three o'clock in the morning. There are no white bitches in Harlem right now.' And he pointed over beyond me and said, 'Well what about THAT white bitch?' I said, 'That's my mom.' He said, 'So what? Get your mom to get in the car and buy some weed from me.' And that's how my mom ended up being the white bitch in the Redman video buying some weed."

—Brett Ratner, Director

The Video Commissioner's Responsibilities

The video commissioner is responsible for:
- **Familiarizing him or herself with the artists on the label.**
- **Understanding the record label's big picture, as well as the artist's needs.**
- **Imaging the artist and positioning him or her in the marketplace.**
- **Liaising between the in-house record label staff working on the project, as well as between the production company and the artist and/or his or her management.**
- **Matching the artist with the right director and treatment.**
- **Evaluating the budget submitted by the production company.**
- **Supervising the selection of key crew members (DP, Producer, 1st AD, Editor, etc.).**
- **Approving wardrobe fittings, locations, choreography sessions, etc.**
- **Supplying the correct version of the song for the sound package.**
- **Overseeing set execution.**
- **Attending the telecine session to ensure the artist and video look as flattering as possible.**

how the director and commissioner can best balance their artistic visions. " I don't think you can really force an artist to be something that they're not," Kleinbaum says. "You can kind of point them in a direction, because if you try and it comes off as being corny or false, the consumer picks up on it immediately."

Each commissioner works with a specific roster of artists, and frequently specializes in a specific genre, since every kind of music has its own nuances. Video commissioners must know these subtleties. They ultimately answer to the artist and the artist's manager, the label's product manager and marketing department, and any additional people connected to the artist or the project.

The commissioner also ensures that everyone working on a video project in-house is on the same page. Sometimes, depending upon the label, the commissioner may work directly with the head of marketing, or the art department, or even the president of the label. Once he or she is given the budget and information, he or she will meet with the artist and the artist's team to discuss concept ideas, as well as thoughts concerning who they would like to direct the video. The commissioner must be up to speed on the current music video directors, as well as who represents them, with which production company they're signed, and their budget range. Once these topics are decided, the commissioner begins the process of soliciting the directors.

Susan Silverman, a freelance commissioner who works primarily for Atlantic Records, says, "I truly believe that the record company representative/commissioner is the person holding it all together, the glue. Your artists need to feel good, safe, trusting in your hands. After all, you're going out there to the community, representing them, their music, and their vision. They need to know that you've got their music and best interests at heart, that it isn't about money, and that, creatively, you're speaking on their behalf. I take that aspect of my job very seriously, and it's normally the first step in getting everything off to the right start."

The commissioner supplies the proper digital recording of the song, which usually is in a digital audiotape (DAT) format, to the video producer, so that he or she can put together an audio package. This package contains the music video's song in different formats to be used at specific points of the production process with the various types of equipment (see page 149 in Chapter Eight for more details). The commissioner must also make sure that the production team has the proper song, even the proper mix of the song. Using the correct music is imperative for both the shoot and postproduction.

BUDGETING A MUSIC VIDEO

To begin the music video process, the song and the budget for the video are handed to the commissioner from upper level management at the record label. Every music video budget has two crucial development stages: (1) when the label determines the total amount they will spend to make the video, and (2) when the production company representing the video director breaks the budget down into line items, detailing exactly where they intend to spend every dollar. In this section, we will focus on stage one, the criteria a record label uses to decide on a video budget.

Initially, senior management at the label establishes the budget. For example, at Atlantic Records the label president and the head of marketing determine the music video budgets. President Julie Greenwald explains that she first tries to estimate how many units the CD will sell on its worst day on each album project. Based on that estimate, as well as on various aspects of the artist's career, she comes up with an amount of money to spend on music videos that fits into the bigger picture of the overall marketing budget for the CD. Some of the factors she might consider include:

- The number of previous hits the artist has had
- How elaborate the vision for the video is
- The value of the video in promoting the artist
- Expected airplay
- Past history of airplay
- The genre of music
- How many CDs the video's exposure might sell

In addition, MTV assumes a substantial role in this decision, since it is the benchmark for all music videos and an important gauge of what's popular. Although MTV plays a lot fewer videos now than they once did, it still continues to lead the way as a venue for them. To get MTV airplay, an artist's video must have certain production values and aesthetic elements, such as: highly stylized lighting and/or set design; extravagant locations; expensive outfits for the artist; fancy cars; beautiful, and exquisitely clad, cast members or dancers; and high-end visual effects, to name a few. Genres like hip-hop, rap, and R&B need MTV airplay more than others. Some rock bands may focus more on touring and getting their video on Fuse or online, in which case they don't need to spend as much on a video clip.

Livia Tortolla says that Atlantic Records is up front with its artists, explaining to them in detail that there is a finite amount of money in their budget. She reveals, "Some artists don't believe that. They think it's bottomless, but you've got to sit down and say, 'No, to initially launch your record, this is the pool of dollars that we have. And we think that these are the areas where it's most important, what do you think?' Then we really have a conversation."

Another important aspect of the music video budget that may need to be spelled out for the artist is that they ultimately pay for the video out of their royalties. In most recording artists' contracts, the cost of making a video is a recoupable expense. Livia Tortolla confirms that although it depends entirely on the deal, the first video on an album is usually fifty percent recoupable by the artist, and any follow up videos are usually 100 percent recoupable. The record label foots the initial bill for both.

Creating a budget becomes a combination of speculating about profits along with a gut instinct as to what the video could do for the artist's career and the company's bottom line. Although Julie Greenwald tends to approach the process conservatively, she also says, "Every once in a while there's a project that comes along where you say, 'Fuck it, I'm going to throw the entire building behind it and if I burn down the building, I burn down the building.'"

Given the state of the recording industry since the turn of the millennium, independent video commissioner Jeff Panzer, formerly "The Emperor of All Videos," at Universal Records, says his budgets have been cut in half over the past several years, although expectations remain the same or may become even higher. Generally speaking, he said his budgets in 2006 ranged from $40,000 to a very rare six-figure budget.

"We did a rock video for the band 10 Years for $15,000 in 2005. $40,000 would be an R&B group called Philly's Most Wanted. And Nelly, Lil' Wayne, Baby (Birdman), and Lindsay Lohan were the higher ticket budgets that go somewhere into the six figure range, which is generally reserved for multi-platinum artists," explains Panzer.

At Sony, Danny Lockwood says that it is not uncommon for them to commission videos for between $10,000 and $30,000 these days. When their sales drastically dipped in 2000, though, their video budgets were also slashed. At Sony's sister company, RCA, the budgets seem to be larger. Senior director, video commissioner Lorin Finkelstein says that although he recently did a video for $86,000, his budget range tends to be between $100,000 and $400,000. But he points out that RCA has only four or five artists on whom they will spend more than $250,000.

At Warner Brothers Records, music video budgets have also become quite modest, according to Devin Sarno, vice president, visual content; Warner Brothers Records. As he generally works with newer rock bands, his video budgets tend to range from $10,000 to $100,000. It has become unusual for the company to spend $150,000 to $200,000 on a rock band.

SELECTING A DIRECTOR FOR A MUSIC VIDEO

Once the single and the budget are established, the commissioner must begin the process of soliciting directors. Since music video channels began giving credit to the directors in the early 1990s, including their names alongside the artist's and song title, artists have become savvy critics of which directors are the best, or, at least, the most popular. Therefore, the process often begins with an artist insisting on a well-known director such as Samuel Bayer who directed Green Day's "American Idiot," "Boulevard of Broken Dreams," "Holiday," and "Wake Me Up When September Ends"; Melissa Etheridge's "Come To My Window"; Blind Melon's "No

Rain"; and Nirvana's "Smells Like Teen Spirit," or Paul Hunter, who directed Gwen Stefani's "Hollaback Girl"; Will Smith's "Switch"; Snoop Dogg featuring Pharrell's "Drop It Like It's Hot"; and Notorious BIG's "Hypnotize." Generally, any director whose work gets heavy rotation on MTV's *Total Request Live* is a likely candidate. The artist may not know exactly how he or she wants the video to look, but they know the director's work from MTV. It often becomes the commissioner's job to rein in the artist's ideas and to educate the artist and management, often bringing other talented directors to their attention.

For example, an artist may have decided on hiring Paul Hunter as the music video director; however, Paul may be too expensive for the artist's budget, forcing the commissioner to come up with an alternative director who is also popular but won't break the bank. Sometimes mediating between the artist and the budget can be a difficult task.

Once the artist and the commissioner come up with a short list of prospective directors, the label calls the directors' reps and explains a bit about the project to them. The label then forwards the video's song; any information about the artist and the video, such as press kit; the basic idea for the video; a possible location they would like to shoot; a general budget; and a due date for the director's treatment. Each rep, in turn, gives the material to the prospective director. The director needs this information to write a one- to three-page descriptive treatment (also called a *concept*) of his or her vision for the video. Some directors have a treatment writer do this work, although most prefer to write their own treatments.

"My job is to match the artist with the right director," says independent commissioner and former Atlantic Records video commissioner Jill Kaplan. "This entails providing the reels for the directors I feel are appropriate for the project to the artist while simultaneously sending out music to corresponding directors. Thereafter, I help the artist, label, and management sift through the various treatments that the directors have submitted so we can come to a collective decision. After a preliminary choice is made, I evaluate the production company's budget to see if it is accurate to execute the job."

The commissioner reads all the treatments they receive. He or she begins to weed out the video ideas that will not work—one might be too expensive; another may take the artist's image in the wrong direction. At the end of this process and after the artist, his or her manager, and everyone involved in the video at the record label have reviewed everything, a unanimous decision as to which treatment and director to go with is made. If there is some uncertainty, they might pare the choices down to two treatments, or the video commissioner may request the budgets for both treatments. As Jill Kaplan indicated, if one budget is drastically higher than the other, it could be a major deciding factor over which director gets the job. Other factors might include if one of the potential directors has a better track record of hit videos, or if one seems "hungrier," therefore providing more "bang for the buck."

"You have to think visually," says Janet Kleinbaum. "When you read a concept, you have to see it in your head. And you also have to be able to identify the difference between what you think might be a good director and who's just not going to be able to bring it to the table. But you also have to be able to have an overall marketing vision, because you have to represent the business side, not just the art side. You have to understand what your company needs."

If both budgets come in around the same price, the commissioner may set up a meeting between the artist and each potential director. "Many artists have very specific ideas about either elements of what they want to be in a music video, or the entirety," adds Kleinbaum. "Some will spend hours on the phone with a director; others will say 'Oh, this is what I like, see you Tuesday.' Everybody has a different way of doing it, and part of our job is to figure out their methods and then fill in the blanks."

Often, the final choice of a director is influenced by whom the artist feels the most comfortable with or whom he or she likes the best. Although rare, sometimes the record label may give the video project to a director without going through the entire solicitation process. Generally, this happens when dealing with very popular directors, or with directors with whom the artist has previously worked. Top artists, who command a lot of power—as well as a sizeable budget for a specific video project—may sometimes "single bid" a popular director. This means that the artist will solicit only one director for the video project rather than having him or her bid against other directors. In the case of new artists and bands, many times they are so under the radar that they are able to hire a friend to direct the video. Once the director gets the job, the process of preproduction begins.

THE ARTIST-COMMISSIONER RELATIONSHIP IN THE VIDEO PROJECT

As discussed above, an artist's input in his or her video varies. It may depend on whether the artist is new or already established, how much the label has allotted for the video budget, or if the artist is interested in the filmmaking process. Some artists love the process and want to be completely collaborative with the commissioners and the directors. There are also those who will tell you that they simply play music, period. They would rather have everyone else focus on the video. Video commissioners must gauge their guidance in relation to the artist's input. Each video has its own balance of personalities. "I am there to make sure the artist is happy, looks great, and delivers the best possible performance," says Jill Kaplan. "I act as a liaison between production and artist/management for all details leading up to the [video's] shoot."

Much more goes on behind the video scenes than what goes on the screen. The video commissioner is in the thick of it. "After the job is awarded," Jill Kaplan explains, "I oversee selection of key crew members, and act as a liaison between production and artist/management for all details leading up to the shoot...I am involved in the selection of the offline producer, DP, editor, and the glam squad [workers who attend to the artist's glamour, such as the hair stylist, make-up artist, and wardrobe stylist]."

Nicole Ehrlich says, "I love what I do, so I really get into everything. I try not to step on toes, but I am such a passionate person when it comes to my artists and 'making things.' No production team knows my artist better than I, and no production team will know what the label needs to sell records for the artist better than I. So even though I trust who I hire, I still keep a tight ship and get involved in everything from band travel; band equipment and gear; getting the right track/version of the song we need for the sound package; coordinating wardrobe fittings; going over locations and location pictures; casting; looking at any visual references; sometimes overseeing choreography sessions; hiring glam squad; etc. In green screen videos, we have anamatics to approve and storyboard approvals. Sometimes there are props that we all have to agree on—cars are an easy example. Then there's nitty-gritty stuff, like making sure we get the artist's food preferences."

"Sometimes I feel like I'm a production assistant," Danny Lockwood adds. "Other days I feel like a lawyer drafting out legal agreements for actors and actresses. Other days I could be working and giving sketches to directors of how I see certain things happening. But it just depends on a given day."

On the day of the shoot, all of the pre-production elements come together. The video commissioner takes on the responsibility from the label's perspective and ensures that the shoot runs smoothly, keeps it on schedule and budget, and gets the necessary footage that best serves the artist. "My main concern on the shoot day is making sure we shoot everything in the treatment and that my artist looks amazing," Nicole Ehrlich says. "Most of the time I'm watching what's being shot from behind the monitor. I'm there to speak out if we're not getting something.

For example, if I need to see a guitar solo, a wide shot of the band, a close-up of a cymbal crash, or a take without hair covering the artist's face, I let the director or first assistant director know, and I never go around them. Usually, the director and I have a mutual respect, and we appreciate each others input and needs. On set, if it's a low budget job, or any budget for that matter, I'll help out in any way I can, even moving things."

"Every job presents its own set of production problems," Danny Lockwood explains. "You're always working against time; you're always working with not enough money, not enough people, not enough manpower."

For all the reliance on music video as a multifaceted tool in the music business, some of the directors really believe that video killed the radio star. They forget that the people on the soundstage are not actors, they're primarily musicians. "I have a lot of input into how the artist comes across on camera," says Lockwood. "A lot of people, even a lot of directors, except for the really good ones, forget that the people in the video are musicians, not readymade, telegenic actors. And sometimes an artist doesn't really deliver a song in the most appealing kind of saleable way, and so I try to work closely with our artists as far as that goes."

"I make sure the artist is on time and goes through make-up, hair, and wardrobe," adds Ehrlich. "I make sure the artist has food and all their equipment is right. Our days and nights are very long and it can be exhausting, especially in a performance video. I try to keep my artists motivated and keep their energy up. I help to keep my artists as sober as possible, because the shoot days are so long that alcohol or other drugs usually gives me a shorter shelf life with them. It also makes them look puffy and older on camera. I am also the liaison between the artist and director. If the band isn't feeling a set-up or they have an idea and I feel like they're on the right track, I'll bring the director into the mix. If I know something is hot and the artist isn't feeling it, I'll try to make them feel it by showing them the [VTR] playback because you can't always tell how something looks when you're in front of the camera. I always say, if worse comes to worse, you don't have to use it but at least try it."

After the shoot, a new process begins: postproduction. This involves taking the raw footage from the day of the shoot and combining it into the video that everyone will hopefully see. The commissioner, of course, gets involved with the postproduction process. Ehrlich explains, "First I go to the telecine to approve the looks for the video. Telecine is where the raw footage is viewed and color corrected. I send management and other label employees some picks from the session to get them excited for what's to come. Then I go to the edit and usually make sure, before we send out the first rough cut, that we get a tight performance and the artist looks dope. I try to go to the edits for each rough [cut] to speed the process along. If we have animation or green-screen aspects, I approve things along the way with the management, band, and label. I always try to go to the online because that is where my final product is output. It is where I make sure that everything from perfect synch to all the right shots are in the cut. Unfortunately, even when you have the final product and everyone in our camp has approved it, the networks sometimes have standards issues or need cut-downs before they'll add the piece to their line-up. At the same time, I also create and complete any television specials on the artist for the networks such as MTV and Fuse."

Kaplan says, "I hold the artist's hand through the entire process," keeping the artist and management in the loop at all times. This may be the commissioner's most important job. And to do it smoothly, the commissioner must be in constant communication with the main players at the production company—the director, the director's representative, the executive producer, and the producer—throughout the video process.

CHAPTER TWO
THE DIRECTOR AND THE DIRECTOR'S REPRESENTATIVE

Music video directors act as quarterbacks in that they oversee the entire video process from conceptualization to realization. Constantly making choices that run the creative gamut, they must decide on important components such as where and what the location will be, the set and props, the color and tone of the lighting, the placement of the camera, and the pace of the final edit. Directors are consulted, and have a say, on the artists' wardrobe, make-up, hairstyle, and style of performance as well. They generally have a strong creative vision and an equally strong conviction to take the video to its completion without wavering from their vision. In addition, they must also work well with others, since they have to interact with a large team on a day-to-day basis.

The most important responsibility of the director's representative, also known as the rep, is to get the director hired on music video projects and to keep the director working as often as possible. A rep's responsibilities are similar to that of an artist's manger or agent. Each production company has a rep that pitches (sells) its directors for possible video projects, always trying to advance his or her director's career.

THE RESPONSIBILITIES OF THE DIRECTOR

As I briefly introduced in Chapter One, the music video director drives the video-making process.

Usually signed to a production company, the director makes music videos exclusively for the company. Although some directors work for other production companies to make commercial advertisements or even feature films, the music video director has an obligation to produce through one production company. For example, director Noble Jones (Donnell Jones featuring Jermaine Dupri's "Better Start Talkin'" and Goo Goo Dolls' "Better Days") is "repped" by Curious Pictures in New York City for commercial work and by Revolver Films in Canada for music videos.

Some directors prefer to be repped by different companies, whereas other directors prefer to be under the same "roof," so to speak, for everything. Although Jones has kept both tracks of his career separate to date, he says "I'm currently trying to find someplace that really kind of feeds into everything," meaning that he'd like to eventually be at one company that produces both music videos and commercials.

The director typically earns a standard ten percent of the budget for his or her work on a music video, which is based solely on *below the line* expenses, which are the physical production costs juxtaposed with *above the line* expenses, which include the production company's fee, the director's fee, and sometimes the producer's fee (depending on the operating procedure of the production company), as well as the costs for talent, insurance, postproduction, and travel.

What makes a great director?

A great director:
- Has creative vision, drive, and ability to push the limits and expectations of an idea.
- Captures the essence of the artist and the soul of the song, revealing them in a captivating way onscreen.
- Has excellent communication and delegation skills.
- Understands the fine balance between artistic expression and client expectation and obligation.
- Articulates his or her vision onscreen while maintaining the integrity of the artist and being respectful of any budgetary constraints.
- Makes choices without wavering.
- Has confidence and a signature style.
- Understands how to problem-solve and prioritize.
- Is a terrific salesperson.
- Can get people excited about ideas.
- Is prepared and knowledgeable about the process on set.
- Is pleasant to work with and be around.

The Director's Responsibilities

The director is responsible for:
- Conceptualizing the video.
- Writing the treatment.
- Designing the video's look.
- Describing the video's vision.
- Distributing pertinent information.
- Leading with a creative perspective.
- Maintaining creative integrity.
- Setting and transferring the look from film to tape.
- Instructing during the edit.
- Building a successful career.

CONCEPTUALIZING THE VIDEO

The director's idea for a music video and its presentation are the deciding factors when it comes time to pick a director for a project. Once the director receives the track slated for the video from the video commissioner, the director brainstorms as to what visuals will be appropriate, keeping in mind both the artist and the target audience.

As director Roman Coppola describes, his process of coming up with video ideas "happens many different ways. I often will just keep an idea list of things that come out of something I've seen in a magazine, an image that might spark an idea; or something will pop into my head randomly that doesn't tie to any song, just something that's on my mind. Then the band will say, 'Hey, what do you want to do?' and I'll say, 'I was just thinking about Kung Fu movies,' or whatever, and it applies to that song somehow. I very rarely try to consciously understand what the song is about. I really try to stay away from that, because I find that it can be misleading, and tends to lead me in a direction of boring ideas. So when I'm aware of a band that wants to work with me, I'll think about my impression of who they are and what their spirit or vibe might be. Before even listening to their music, I'll open up that file in my brain that conjures up to me what they're about and what types of ideas they might be looking for. And I try to have a few potential ideas before I even hear the song. Then I'll listen to the song and hopefully one of those ideas will cling to it somehow."

WRITING THE TREATMENT

Once hired for a music video, the director writes his or her visual idea in the form of a treatment, which is a one- to three-page document that describes the director's concept. "I'm responsible for the idea and communicating that to the band and label," says director Phil Harder (Rob Thomas' "Ever the Same" and Hilary Duff's "Beat of My Heart"). "My idea—or treatment—is my bread and butter. Many get rejected, and I just keep writing until I land a job."

Directors usually get a week or less to submit a treatment to the record label. On occasion, the first round of submitting treatments yields the desired outcome—getting hired. In many cases, though, the process of writing and rewriting treatments can go on for several days or weeks, and still may not yield a job in the end.

Although most directors prefer to write their own treatments, some hire treatment writers to write their conceptualized ideas. More often than not, directors use these writers when they are too busy to write themselves. (See Chapter Four starting on page 62 for a detailed breakdown of the treatment-writing process.)

Directors often bid on several projects at a time, coming up with ideas and submitting treatments for a variety of videos simultaneously. To keep on the cutting edge of current trends in music videos and popular culture, they spend a lot of time researching and looking for ideas, new art forms, techniques, and talent, which they can incorporate into their work.

Although the treatment-writing process can continue indefinitely, once the video commissioner approves a treatment and awards the video project to the director, he or she, along with the record company and the artist's management, determine the shoot date(s). Along with the other parameters of the project, such as budget and delivery date, the information is written into the contract. The record label and the production company execute the agreement, binding the director to the video project.

From the signing of the contract, the video process usuallly takes approximately one month, with the director at the helm from beginning to end. "Once a job is awarded," says Director Phil Harder, "it all comes down to bringing the idea to the screen, which gets more into the craft of the music video. There is a lot of diplomacy through the entire process, and I try to be as honest as possible with the label, because I have faith in the project and the band has put faith in me by selecting my idea."

DESIGNING THE VIDEO'S LOOK

Once the video is awarded to the director, preproduction begins. From this point forward the director's written treatment creatively guides the entire team. Since a treatment can be interpreted

---

What makes a great music video?

"A great video is when the song and the visuals connect."

—Little X, Director

"I'm always happiest with the videos that have a degree of subversiveness about them. The videos are commercials, and usually they're pretty mainstream, and that's fine and good; but it's great if you can get something on the air that people can see that also bends the rules a bit and that you can have some fun with."

—Devin Sarno, Vice President, Visual Content; Warner Brothers Records

in as many ways as there are people reading it, the director must make strong choices to shape the look of the video. The director must have a clear sense and understanding of every aspect of the video's creative design, including, but not limited to, the coloration, composition, art direction, wardrobe, and action, as well as the artist's mannerisms and affectations. The director provides this information to the team early so that everyone is on the same page.

Director Matthew Rolston (Mary J. Blige's "Be Without You" and Natasha Bedingfield's "I Bruise Easily") explains, "I'm completely involved in every single detail of the way the artist is presented and every detail of every frame of film, from the hair and make-up, to the colors to the fabric of the wardrobe, to the way it's going to work with certain effects like wind, water, or rain."

DESCRIBING THE VIDEO'S VISION

The director maintains constant communication with the producer, director of photography, and label commissioner (through the EP, rep, or producer), keeping everyone abreast of what his or her vision is. Director Dean Karr (Dave Matthews Band's "Crash Into Me" and Marilyn Manson's "Sweet Dreams") says, "In preproduction, I am involved with storyboarding, crew meetings, tech scouting, casting, location scouting, art department, prop shopping, and hair/makeup decisions."

If the video contains special effects, the director may need to spend time upfront describing the intended look with the postproduction team, discussing potential techniques to ensure getting adequate coverage, such as shooting enough film to allow for the creation of visual effects or making sure that the film conforms to the technical necessities in order to seamlessly integrate the special and/or visual effects.

The director compiles a shot list and reviews what each scene needs to achieve so that the assistant director, or AD, can create a realistic shooting schedule and disseminate the necessary information to the rest of the crew. Since the AD functions as the director's mouthpiece for the crew and the talent on the shoot day, the assistant must have a clear idea of the director's vision. "After a job is awarded," says Harder, "I get into storyboards. I do quite a few conference calls. I'm constantly on the phone with the producer, DP [director of photography], location scout, set designers, props, wardrobe, makeup, hair, casting, etc. I need to make decisions on every item, down to the mic stand and microphone. I sketch out sets and graph shots or look for pictures or film clips that help describe my ideas. All these elements are put together in the mad dash to the finish line. The preproduction makes or breaks the shoot."

DISTRIBUTING PERTINENT INFORMATION

The director must also work closely with the director of photography, or DP, to set up the actual shots as well as direct the artists' performance. "The most important directing skill to learn, above all else, is sensitivity, the ability to communicate with the other humans," says W.I.Z. (Chemical Brothers' "Out of Control" and Shakira's "Te Dejo Madrid"). "When I understood and embraced film as a collaborative medium, I was one step closer to getting what I wanted."

The video commissioner will attend the video shoot, offering suggestions about specific shots he or she feels the video requires from the record label's standpoint. The director needs to take heed of the commissioner's recommendations while not compromising his or her vision. The director has to ensure that the commissioner has a clear understanding of what is being committed to film. The producer, or executive producer, helps to navigate and sometimes mitigate the commissioner 's recommendations or comments so as not to disrupt the video-making process.

Throughout the shoot, the director stays in constant contact with the producer, ensuring that the overall workflow progresses on time, on budget, and in line with the expectations of both the record label and artist. Throughout the chaotic process of shooting the video, the director must remain calm and focused and lead the crew to achieving the creative vision, making the best possible video. "I try to stay focused on what's important to the story and band performance," says Harder, "and avoid getting bogged down in details that don't matter." (See Chapter Nine starting on page 166 for a detailed breakdown of the shooting process.)

LEADING WITH A CREATIVE PERSPECTIVE

The director often spends time prior to the shoot day(s) with the artist or band, getting to know them, making sure everyone is on the same page, building excitement about the shoot, and rehearsing. On the day of the shoot, the director guides the artist through his or her performance. "I am vocal with my talent and get the most out of the band's performance to lens," says Dean Karr. "Being a musician also, I know what to cover, and I know when the band is doing a good job or when I need to cattle prod them into giving more."

"Throughout the shoot day, I keep chumming with the band," explains Harder. "The bands are always cool. In the past few years I haven't experienced problems from the musicians, and most of the time the bands have great ideas and give very constructive input into the process because they know their music and image better than me."

Of paramount importance, the director must remember and acknowledge the clients on the project. A fine balance needs to be struck between passion for the project, its creative merits, the personal vision that drives it, and the best interests of the record label and artist. If a director makes a bad video, it's not the end of the world—for the director! If artists make bad videos, they can seriously damage their careers, potentially stopping them before they have a chance to develop. The director must always keep in mind just how high the stakes are for the artist.

What do you love about music videos?

"Music videos are the most exciting medium that anyone could be a part of, because it's a great way to be creative and it's a great place to fail and learn from your mistakes and also to excel. Also, it's a great stepping-stone to cross over into other mediums."
—Brett Ratner, Director

"Creative music videos have a major influence on commercials, movies, and filmmaking in general. I love making financed short films—music videos—and going as crazy as I can with my ideas, and then moving on to another job. Only music videos let a filmmaker do that."
—Phil Harder, Director

"I love the artists and the people that I've worked with. Being able to listen to music and to make visuals is so inspiring. I just think it's fun, and it's a great thing to do to expand your horizons and creativity."
—Sanaa Hamri, Director

MAINTAINING CREATIVE INTEGRITY

Throughout the process of creating a music video, the director works closely with the producer to ensure that the vision of the video as outlined in the treatment is followed within the constraints of the allotted budget. While the director is the creative leader of the team, the producer is the fiscal leader.

Since the aesthetic details and the budget directly correlate, the director and producer must communicate constantly to keep both in check. "I work very closely with the director from inception to the completion," says producer Oualid Mouaness (Elton John's "Answer in The Sky," directed by David LaChapelle, and Ashley Simpson's "Pieces of Me," directed by Stefan Smith). "I usually support them [the directors], and sometimes question them in order to understand where they are going, and sometimes argue with them if they are asking for something that is outside the realm of the budget. The idea is to approach everything from all angles until we are sure we are maximizing our resources."

SETTING AND TRANSFERRING THE LOOK FROM FILM TO TAPE

During postproduction, the director works with the telecine artist, also called the colorist, often along with the aid of the director of photography. The colorist is a technical craftperson who operates the telecine machine, a device that transfers motion picture film images to video. During this process, the telecine artist tweaks the look and the coloration of the video according to the director's instructions by adjusting the light and saturation of different colors as the images on film are being converted to video.

INSTRUCTING DURING THE EDIT

Once the telecine process is finished and the film images are transferred to video, the director

Snapshots from the Set

"I was shooting a 50 Cent video and had asked the art department to get a kit car Porsche, which is a fake Porsche that looks real for the stunt. As we were driving it through a window, I did not think to ask again. Three days later I got a bill for twenty-two thousand dollars for a paint job. It was a real Porsche with some kit car extras added. I could have killed them."
—William Green, Producer

"While shooting a hip-hop video in LA, a large plexi tank of water was being used to shoot underwater shots of the artist. The artist kept putting the shot off, but ultimately agreed to enter the tank. While the cameras were running, the artist plunged into the tank and sank straight to the bottom. He was embarrassed to tell anyone that he couldn't swim."
—Doug Kluthe, Executive Producer

works closely with the offline editor to piece the video together through the rough-cut process. This involves taking the scenes and shots captured during filming and placing them in the order they should appear in the video, without any computer-generated visual effects.

While some directors edit their videos themselves, most prefer working with an offline editor who has the technical proficiency to work nonlinear editing equipment, as well as the artistic eye and sense of rhythm to put together a moving image collage using the footage shot for the video and the director's treatment as a guide.

During the offline edit, the video image quality is fairly low, because the process is intended to organize the shot structure and rhythm of the piece using scenes from the footage as building blocks to construct the video in a no-frills manner. The director adds the frills—high quality video images and computer effects—in the online edit. (To learn more about this process, see Chapter Ten on page 186.)

The director continues to oversee every aspect of the edit process until the "picture is locked," meaning that all the parties involved, including the record label and the artist, approve the final video and demand no more changes. At this point, the director generally oversees the online edit, the final edit using the master tapes, and an edit decision list (EDL), which is a digital map generated from the offline edit. The EDL sets which portion and how much time from each specific shot will be inserted into the finished video. (For more information about the EDL, see page 197 in Chapter Ten.) The online edit uses the high-quality video images and the computer digital effects discussed in preproduction, resulting in a high-end video ready for distribution. When finished, the online edit concludes the video-making process.

BUILDING A SUCCESSFUL CAREER

Most established directors built their careers based on some sort of strategy. Sometimes they developed their strategy early on, and sometimes they realized how they did it in hindsight. Most directors say that they discovered their personal strategy through the learning process of making music videos. The most common strategy involves the careful selection of artists and songs they chose to work with. However, when a director first begins his or her career, he or she generally doesn't have the luxury of picking and choosing video projects. As the director becomes more established, the careful selection

of video projects can help advance his or her career. "I got tired of doing a video and not getting seen. I said, 'You know what, I'm only going to do videos for records that are hits!'" says Brett Ratner (Mariah Carey's "We Belong Together" and Madonna's "Beautiful Stranger"). "So I would speak to the record company and say, 'OK, which record is your priority? You're doing a video for the first single, but is the second single really the one that you're going to blow out of here? Which is the one that you're putting the most promotion into?'"

In other words, it's tough to build a career on videos that never get seen. According to Ratner's strategy, becoming a successful director has as much to do with choosing video projects and marketing oneself as it does with creativity on the set. Picking a hit song that the label is behind can be integral to establishing one's reputation as a director. Director Marcus Nispel (George Michael's "Killer/Papa Was a Rolling Stone" and Puff Daddy's "Victory") concurs, explaining, "In looking back, I'm actually curious if you get more videos because your last one was a truly great piece of film or because your last one was in the top ten. It seems to hardly matter if you're good or bad at it, as long as you keep on going in the top ten. That's where you get the most gigs."

THE RESPONSIBILITIES OF THE DIRECTOR'S REPRESENTATIVE

As mentioned earlier, the main goal of a director's rep is to keep his or her directors employed. Molly Bohas, the rep at the production company Anonymous Content (Johnny Cash's "Hurt," directed by Mark Romanek and Nine Inch Nails' "Only," directed by David Fincher), explains "My job is to get my directors videos and get them working with the best possible artists."

Some reps plug away in-house, working exclusively for a specific production company, representing only the company's roster of directors. Other reps ply their trade on a freelance basis, handpicking a roster of directors affiliated with different production companies. In either case, the director's rep works closely with the director and the executive producer at the director's production company.

Some reps work for two or three directors. In some cases, the reps only offer services to the director for music videos, whereas other reps represent their directors for anything music related, such as DVDs and live concerts. Regardless of how many directors a rep may work for, independent rep Laure Scott (R.E.M.'s "Losing My Religion," directed by Tarsem and Madonna's "Take A Bow," directed by Michael Haussman) points out, "Representing talented directors is very important. You have to have good talent to get good bands. It's a Catch-22."

What makes a great director's rep?

A director's rep:
- Maintains a talented roster of directors.
- Is persistent, passionate, competitive, and hungry.
- Exhibits strong sales and marketing skills.
- Is well-liked and trusted.
- Understands the delicate balance of calling the commissioners often, looking for work, and being a pleasure to speak with.
- Appreciates the directors he or she is selling and always keeps in the director's goals in mind.
- Can articulately explain why the director is right for the job.
- Knows which director is right for a particular style.
- Knows the commissioner at each label and is also familiar with the label's roster to know which of their directors would be a good fit with which artist.
- Cares about the directors with whom he or she works.
- Consistently delivers treatments for videos that can be made within the assigned budget.
- Possesses knowledge of production and the record industry.

The Director's Representative's Responsibilities

The director's representative is responsible for:
- Forming and nurturing important relationships.
- Staying on top of video projects.
- Introducing the director to potential clients.
- Networking.
- Building and maintaining an impeccable reputation.
- Updating the director's reel.
- Encouraging and guiding the director's creativity.
- Realizing the director's current and future goals.
- Supporting and clarifying the director's creative ideas.
- Advancing the director's career.
- Possessing a knowledge of production costs.
- Supplying a proper support team.

For landing a director for a music video project, it is standard practice for a director's representative to earn five percent of the video's budget, based on the below the line expenses. Some in-house reps make a lower commission, but collect a retainer fee each month, similar to a salary, from the production company. The rep's fee usually comes out of the production company's mark-up, not out of the production budget.

FORMING AND NURTURING IMPORTANT RELATIONSHIPS

To properly do their jobs, reps must establish strong relationships with video commissioners at the various record labels. They need to know the current trends in the music scene, and strive to have their directors make videos for the most successful and popular artists. Reps must reach out to music industry professionals with the hiring power and then form working relationships with them to forward their directors' careers. "It's imperative that my relationships are flawless and that each label commissioner has a great experience working with me and my roster of directors," says independent rep Tommy LaBuda, (Death Cab for Cutie's "Soul Meets Body," directed by Jon Watts and Rob Thomas' "Ever The Same," directed by Phil Harder). "For me it's about the big picture and the experience. Obviously, the product needs to be amazing, but I feel that the overall experience, from beginning to end, is almost as important as the final product. This breeds more follow up business."

"You need to think ahead, or think beyond just calling the major labels," adds Heidi Gregory (The Foo Fighters' "D.O.A," directed by Michael Palmieri and All American Rejects' "The Last Song," directed by Charles Jensen), an independent rep who works primarily with directors formerly at A Band Apart and Lotus Filmworks. "You have to research, go through the magazines, and find the indies—even talk to other people in other areas of the business."

STAYING ON TOP OF VIDEO PROJECTS

Reps must be aware of all the developments in the music and video industries at all times. The more informed and knowledgeable a rep is, the more likely his or her director will be in on the ground floor of a project. "Having a knowledge of the commissioners' projects is important," LaBuda says. "I work with the commissioners in supplying them with innovative ideas from my roster of directors that might fit for their artists and make for an incredible video."

Maintaining an awareness of past, present, and future music videos being shot and stay-

Advice for Aspiring Directors

"I think a young director should definitely call the labels on his or her own. Sometimes the labels will even recommend production companies or reps for them to call. I also think it's a way to start a personal relationship with the labels rather than going through a rep all the time. It surely doesn't hurt to try."

—Heidi Gregory, Director's Rep

"I would definitely advise striving directors to learn a technique and to make sure that they're technically capable as well. If possible, shadow either a director or a cinematographer, and really learn the ins and outs and the politics of the industry so you can work it to your advantage."

—Sanaa Hamri, Director

ing familiar with the people who direct the videos, direct the photography, produce, art direct, and edit are just as important. As LaBuda points out, "I have to be on the pulse of music; knowing what releases are coming is crucial."

Knowing as early as possible the record companies' new release schedules can give a rep a head start on the competition when it comes to pitching his or her directors. Molly Bohas says she reads all of the music industry trade magazines to keep up on all of the new releases as well as industry information.

INTRODUCING THE DIRECTOR TO POTENTIAL CLIENTS

If a rep signs a new director, he or she may take the director to meetings with the record label's commissioners so that each can assess the other's personalities. After all, the entertainment industry is fueled by personal relationships. "When it comes to launching new directors, it's not just about meeting everybody, it's about looking at the work and saying, 'Who is going to respond to this? Who is going to give the opportunity to the kid?' and just building the relationship with the right commissioners," says independent rep Verenne Ferrari (Madonna's "Human Nature," directed by JB Mondino and Janet Jackson's "You Want This," directed by Keir McFarlane). "Just give the director a chance, because what it comes down to is you taking a risk. So you're going to need to really believe strongly in this director's work."

Additionally, reps often bring their directors to live performances by new artists to meet the artists, labels, management, and competitors.

NETWORKING

The never-ending battle to get work for their stable of directors often forces the rep to find avenues and create relationships beyond the record labels. For instance, a rep may build a relationship with the soundtrack department at a feature film studio, since the department often takes an active roll in creating a music video for a song in a movie soundtrack. A rep may also follow unsigned bands and artists on independent labels to get their directors into artists' and managers' consciousnesses before the performers make it big. "A rep is always 'on,'" Molly Bohas says, "repping at all times, kind of like an actor, and you have to take all the rejection too, day in and day out."

"The most important aspect in working with record label commissioner is being respectful of his or her time. Keep it moving! Your clients will appreciate you more if you are not a stalker and you have a feel for their time," director's representative Tommy LaBuda adds. "Having knowledge of their projects is important as well. I work with the commissioners in supplying them with innovative ideas from my roster of directors that might fit their artists and make an incredible video."

It's important to operate effectively while working on multiple projects. Bohas explains, "I don't think you can calculate the time frame spent per project. Sometimes we grovel over jobs for six months before we actually get the job. In that time, it's calling every week, continuing to follow up, and making sure the single doesn't change for a third time, or I'm making sure the job hasn't come off hold again so they don't happen to forget to put us back in on the mix."

BUILDING AND MAINTAINING AN IMPECCABLE REPUTATION

All reps must communicate and meet frequently with video commissioners to get the artists and labels excited about their directors. The rep keeps the commissioners abreast of their directors' latest work. The most effective reps know their business and pursue work for their directors, while still respecting the video commissioners' time—a delicate balance at best. Beyond that, a rep's "rep"—that is, reputation—must remain unimpeachable. One of the major assets a representative brings to the table is credibility.

UPDATING THE DIRECTOR'S REELS

Beyond his or her own credibility, the most important tool in any rep's arsenal to capitalize on hard-won relationships within the industry is

---

Do you need a great song to make a great video?

"That's a big problem. Because a lot of times I'll show great videos of a bad song, and the commissioner's like, 'I can't watch the video because the song sucks,' or, 'Turn down the volume.' So there's already negative energy, and that definitely causes a problem. A lot of times I feel like a label will want to hire a good director to make the visuals exciting for a bad song so at least it will get attention that way. Commissioners will tell you a lot of times that they expect the director to sell the artist, to market the artist."

—Laure Scott, Director's Rep

"Yes, you can. A good video will help that song get played more, definitely. It helps to have both, and I think that they can both help each other. I think if you have a strong song and the video's not really strong, it's going to get played no matter what. But on the other hand, if the song's not that strong but the video's amazing, it's going to help that band out as well."

—Heidi Gregory, Director's Rep

---

the director's reel. The reel, a compilation of the director's best work, represents much of what the industry knows about a specific director. For new directors, the reel, which is actually a DVD, can run no more than ten minutes, and usually begins with a brief, enticing montage followed by short snippets of the best videos they have done. Established directors often open with a montage as well, but typically place several full videos on their reels, since they are not as concerned with keeping their reels abbreviated. Reps help their directors put together the best show reels, update them frequently, and regularly send them to potential clients or present them at meetings.

ENCOURAGING AND GUIDING THE DIRECTOR'S CREATIVITY

In many ways, a director's rep fills the role that a manager might for an artist. Similar to an artist manager's responsibilities, the rep's main role is to keep as many obstacles as possible from interfering with the director's creativity. A rep may need to act as a sounding board for the director's ideas, or as a personal counselor for the director's woes that might stand in the way of work. In addition, the rep has to keep the director professionally happy, busy, and well paid. "With my roster of directors," says LaBuda, "I try and make myself available 24-7. Having unlimited access to the person that is attempting to guide your career is crucial. We discuss strategies, go over treatments, target artists to work with, and try and maintain a friendship through all of this."

REALIZING THE DIRECTOR'S CURRENT AND FUTURE GOALS

Reps work with the directors' production companies, particularly with the executive producer, to guide their directors' careers. The rep and executive producer need to know the director's strengths and weaknesses, aspirations, and the kinds of projects they should not even bring to the table. For instance, director Sanaa Hamri (Prince's "Musicology" and Mariah Carey's "Crybaby") will not entertain directing a video that has explicit lyrical content, markets drugs and alcohol, or suggests that underage kids frequent clubs, so her rep, Molly Bohas from Anonymous Content, will turn down these types of videos from the record label. Reps also do their best to keep the director from getting typecast, but rather apply the director's reputation to a genre that works best. If a director excels at creating videos for female R&B singers, he or she will most likely have difficulty landing a video for a rock and roll band—no matter how badly the director may want it. Directors that get pigeonholed in country music find it especially difficult to cross over into other genres. Reps face these kinds of issues every time they pitch one of their directors. According to Janet Haase, previously the rep and executive producer at the production company Villains (P. Diddy's "Diddy," directed by Brett Ratner and Linkin Park's "Breaking the Habit," directed by Joe Hahn), to do the job right, a rep must "understand all the facets of the director they are selling and always keep in mind where that director wants to be."

SUPPORTING AND CLARIFYING THE DIRECTOR'S CREATIVE IDEAS

The director's rep obtains the music for which the director writes the treatment, guides the director through the writing process, and helps the director pitch creative ideas, while keeping the parameters of the video established by the label, such as budgetary constraints, on the forefront of the director's mind. The rep may even help the director write the treatments, offering creative suggestions, editing the treatment, and, in some cases, going as far as writing the treat-

ment if the director does not have the time. A candid relationship between the director and the rep is important. "I work to be as honest as possible with them [directors] about how they can improve their treatments and how different clients will or won't respond to the type of treatment they have written," Bohas says. "I also make sure that they follow the brief that was given."

"I feel like I'm the older sister trying to keep the directors a little more under control," says Heidi Gregory. "They might go really crazy and have this wild idea, and I'm like, 'OK, that's good, but why don't we cut this out or do this?'"

ADVANCING THE DIRECTOR'S CAREER

The rep and executive producer strategize and creatively collaborate on upcoming projects, making sure they solicit all the possible outlets that might lead to the kind of work a director needs to stay busy and move forward. "We constantly communicate—kind of like a checks and balance system—making sure all our bases are covered at all the time," Bohas explains regarding her relationship with Sheir Rees-Davies, the executive producer at Anonymous Content. "If I send out a treatment that I think is too ambitious, I make sure that she reads it and helps me see where we can trim off the fat and pare down the idea to make it more affordable for the given budget. We also make sure that we have exhausted all possible outlets for our directors with the jobs that are currently out there. We both put feelers out to double team people and to make sure we are up for all the jobs that are out there by doing so."

The collaboration between the rep and the executive producer is employed primarily when trying to land a project for a director. "Once the job is awarded," Gregory says, "I step back and it becomes the executive producer's job. At that point, it's all about the budget, and the producer comes on and they start producing the job."

POSSESSING A KNOWLEDGE OF PRODUCTION COSTS

Once the rep succeeds in getting the director a track to "write on" (create a treatment), the rep must have the answers to basic budgetary questions that may impact the director's creative process. Reps need to know how to break down a treatment and estimate approximately how much an idea might cost to produce. If a record label tells a rep that the budget is $100,000, and the rep allows a director to submit a treatment for a $250,000 idea, it reflects poorly on the production company, the director, and the rep. Occasionally, an excellent—albeit overly expensive creative idea—comes across so well that a rep will submit a treatment significantly more costly than the original budget quoted by the label. When this happens, the rep will forewarn the video commissioner as to what to expect so that the commissioner understands the treatment will cost more than the budget will allow, but might be worth it.

SUPPLYING A PROPER SUPPORT TEAM

The rep, executive producer, and producer always try to surround the director with the best possible support team. "I take a very active role in aligning my directors with producers that will fit with their personalities," says LaBuda. "I work through the budgets in conjunction with the individual EP's at each production company. Once the job has booked, I serve as a liaison, if necessary, between the director and label." When showing a director's reel to a potential client, the rep may highlight specific players on the director's team, such as the DP or production designer, if they are considered top-notch.

Once the rep lands the director the job, some reps take an active role in building the team for the video, matching the director with a producer that fits the director's style or employing a director of photography that might enhance the creative idea. Often, the rep will go to the set to supervise the production process and ensure that both the director and the label get what they need and want. However, once the director signs the contract for the video, the rep has completed his or her primary responsibilities in the video process and may supervise from a distance, mainly overseeing client relations with the label and the artist. Beyond that, the time comes for the rep, as LaBuda puts it, "to move on to the next conquest."

CHAPTER THREE
THE PRODUCTION COMPANY

Most music video directors work for, or with, a production company. As noted in the Chapter Two, once directors sign on with a company, they create videos exclusively for the company, even though some may work with different companies on different kinds of projects such as television commercials or feature film work.

The executive producer, or EP, oversees the entire production company and its directors, always ensuring that the company makes money. This, of course, involves guiding the careers of the directors. The more popular a director becomes, the more money the company will make.

Sometimes one person at a production company will take on the dual role of being both the director's rep and the executive producer. This is especially the case in smaller companies, since both jobs have overlapping duties. Janet Haase, formerly both the rep and executive producer for the production company Villains, explains, "Since my role is twofold, I deal with the label commissioner from beginning to end, from the pitch to the delivery of the project."

THE PRODUCTION COMPANY'S
RESPONSIBILITIES

The production company is responsible for:
- **Providing administrative and monetary support.**
- **Building their directors' careers.**
- **Ensuring proper business practices.**

Where the executive producer oversees individual projects in the context of the production company's "big picture," the producer gets down into the trenches, working hands-on with director, the EP, the production team, the technical crew, and others involved in the project to realize the director's vision as best as possible within the allocated budget.

THE RESPONSIBILITIES OF THE PRODUCTION COMPANY

The production company plays a key role in the overall process of music video production, so much so that its representative (usually the executive producer) and the director both take on legal and fiscal responsibilities for delivering the various materials that the treatment states in the contract between the production company and the record label. The production company serves as the conduit through which the video project runs from start to finish. The production company's representative oversees all of the creative aspects of the project that is spearheaded by the director.

Most music video production companies also produce EPKs, enhanced CDs, CD ROMs, and DVDs. Some even produce commercials and feature films as well. Due to the current financial climate of the music video business, many companies simply cannot survive solely on videos.

Production companies generally work with seven to twenty music video directors at any given time. Some of the larger ones have more, and some smaller companies have fewer.

PROVIDING ADMINISTRATIVE AND MONETARY SUPPORT

The production company provides office and administrative assistance to the directors and producers on each video project, which prevent the director from being distracted by mundane business responsibilities such as accounting, budgets, and contracting the film crew. "The production company houses the production," says Kelly Norris Sarno, the executive producer of Revolver Film Company (Christina Aguilera's "Fighter," directed by Floria Sigismondi and Goo Goo Dolls' "Better Days," directed by Noble Jones), "which means allowing producers and production manager's to use their phones, photocopiers, and anything else required to help the production run smoothly."

Additionally, the production company provides monetary support, such as supplying accounts with various vendors and providing a video's payroll. As Sarno also points out, "The production company will front the necessary finances required until first payment from the label arrives." The production company may also offer the director much needed financial support with a bonus or retainer. However, this is generally reserved for popular, highly reputable directors who ensure that they will bring a lot of work to the production company because of their prominence in the music video industry, or for a new director who exhibits promise toward quickly becoming a superstar director and who has already created a buzz in the industry.

Insurance

Proper insurance policies are a necessary part of the administrative support provided by the production company. The production company must have the following insurance coverages:

LIABILITY

To protect against claims alleging that one's negligence or inappropriate action resulted in property damage or bodily injury.

EQUIPMENT

To protect the production company if any of the rented or purchased equipment on-set gets damaged or destroyed.

PROPERTY

To protect against most risks to property, meaning "one's own things," such as theft, fire, and some weather damage.

VEHICLES

To protect against losses involving the use of automobiles. Additional coverages within vehicles includes liability, which covers bodily injury, property damage, and medical payments, and collision, which protects against physical damages to the vehicles. The basic production insurance policy covers all the vehicles on a specific project for the duration of the job, including prep, wrap, and shoot. Usually, this insurance policy also functions as the secondary insurance for any of the workers' vehicles. If a crew member's car gets hit while he or she is working for the production company, his or her own insurance is considered the primary insurance. If necessary, such as if the worker doesn't have enough insurance to cover all of the damages, the production company's insurance then kicks in.

WORKER'S COMPENSATION

To protect employees who may get injured or disabled in connection with work, the primary worker's comp policy is that of the payroll company. The production company's worker's comp constitutes the secondary policy. If a gaffer falls and breaks his leg and files a worker's comp insurance claim, the payroll company handles all of the details, logistics, and expenses through its policy. But if an unpaid intern falls and breaks her leg, the production company will have worker's comp built into its insurance policy that will cover the intern's medical expenses.

NEGATIVE COVERAGE

Negative coverage insures the film negative, covering any loss of film negatives or videotapes resulting from faulty stock, faulty processing—developing, laboratory work, or editing—faulty cameras or recording equipment, accidental exposure to light, and accidental erasure of videotapes and soundtracks. If the lab accidentally destroys the exposed film, the production is covered for the cost of the shoot, enabling a reshoot without additional costs. Most insurance policies include negative coverage.

If it's a fairly small operation, the production company's insurance may offer minimal coverage, which is usually half of a million dollars' worth of equipment on any given shoot. A larger company will want coverage for at least one million dollars' worth of equipment per shoot, if not more. For all but an enormously high budget music video, this should be sufficient. On occasion, a vendor requires more insurance coverage than the existing policy, and usually an insurance company can easily change the policy to accommodate production needs. In the music video world, this happens all the time, and even the insurance companies are prepared for quick, on the spot changes.

Until fairly recently, short-term insurance policies were helpful if a company wanted to produce only one or two videos in a year. These policies were also useful for a production company from another country just needing coverage in the United States for one project. However, this has changed in recent years, and it is now difficult to get a short-term or smaller policy. Most insurance agencies either do not offer them, or they cost a great deal of money.

Keep in mind that every insurance policy has a deductible that must be met before it covers expenses. This means that if the company makes an insurance claim, they must meet the deductible before any monies exchange hands. The amount varies, depending on the policy.

BUILDING THEIR DIRECTORS' CAREERS

Directors greatly benefit when they work with excellent production companies. A well-known and trusted production company can use its reputation and finances to build a director's career.

> ### What makes a great music video?
>
> "I think a great video is one that enhances your enjoyment of the track and teaches you something new about the artist, whether the artist is in it or not. There are so many things that a video can do, and that's what's cool. It can dazzle your senses, it can move you, it can make you want to get up and dance."
> —Danny Lockwood, Vice President of Video Production; Sony BMG Music Entertainment
>
> "A great video is innovative, smart, and at the same time fulfills the marketing needs for the label."
> —Shana Sosin, Music Video Producer's Association, Former Executive Director of Business

Once a production company and its rep gain the trust of the record industry, record labels will consider them first for projects and will also be willing to take chances on its new, up-and-coming directors.

Just as it benefits a director to work with an excellent production company, it benefits a production company to have top, high-priced, in-demand directors. First and foremost, the production company can then charge the full mark-up on every video project they produce that is directed by the in-demand director (oftentimes times, a production company does not make their full mark-up, or any mark-up at all, when producing a video directed by a new or lesser known director), and secondly, great videos by "core" directors will shine the spotlight on the entire production company, offering glory by association. Therefore, if a production company believes in a director and uses its resources to support and help him or her build a career, there's a good chance a monetary pay-off will be the reward in the end.

For taking care of the business end of the music video market, the production company takes a "standard" mark-up of fifteen percent of the "below the line" budget. These days, most production companies do not usually get the full fifteen percent, often pulling in less profit on certain video projects to reinvest some of the mark-up into the cost of production in order to build the director's reel—thus adding value to the video. This boost in *production value*, as it's called, helps elevate the director's work, which, in turn, builds the director's reel and makes the director more desirable to both artists and video commissioners. Taking a reduced mark-up (profit) has become fairly standard in the music video industry, and is often expected by the record label commissioners on certain projects.

ENSURING PROPER BUSINESS PRACTICES

The production company takes responsibility for all legal issues associated with their music videos and ensures the proper business practices are adhered to. They must pay their bills in a timely manner and follow all federal and state laws. They also must ensure that they have the proper insurance policies.

With the support of both a full and part-time administrative staff, a successful production company must document every production detail and keep all the records and receipts, such as record label contracts, budgets, purchase orders, time cards, petty cash logs, talent/casting releases, and location releases, together until the final audit of the video project at the end of production. It is referred to as *maintaining the wrap book*. (See page 203 in Chapter Ten for a more in-depth explanation of the wrap book.)

THE RESPONSIBILITIES OF THE EXECUTIVE PRODUCER

Although the executive producer, or EP, supervises all the activities at the production company, he or she has two primary concerns: (1) maintaining a good relationship with the directors and (2) monitoring the bottom-line to ensure the company makes money.

The executive producer occupies the top ring of the music video production hierarchy, short of being the owner or a member of a company's board of directors. A full-time position, the executive producer usually receives a salary for the job, as opposed to a commission, percentage, or project fee. Some companies use freelance executive producers, usually when the production company has an abundance of work and needs someone to manage the overflow or when it needs coverage while their full-time EP is on vacation.

Like almost every position in the music video industry, an EP's role overlaps and varies. "The executive producer position is nebulous, because all EPs are different," Joe Uliano, the EP at the production company MERGE@crossroads (Bruce Springsteen's "Lonesome Day," directed by Mark Pellington and Metallica's "I Disappear," directed by Wayne Isham) explains. "Everybody does it his or her own way. Some people really do sales, and some people are creative. I think all of us, no matter what, have to be business savvy."

Executive producers take on two disparate, but equally important, roles. One is to be, as Cayce Cole, executive producer of the production company The Director's Bureau (The Strokes' "Last Night," directed by Roman Coppola and Fatboy Slim's "Praise You," directed by Richard Koufey, Roman Coppola, and Spike Jones) says, the "mouthpiece or ambassador for the directors and the company." The other is to oversee each music video project the production company undertakes, keeping a sharp eye on the bottom line so that the company makes a profit. Consequently, an EP always has an eye out for new talent to bring into the company.

"I try to guide the directors to make the best choices that will help them bridge into other directing avenues," explains Helen Cavallo, former executive producer at the now defunct production company A Band Apart (John Mayer's "Bigger Than My Body," directed by Nigel Dick and Foo Fighters' "Resolve," directed by Michael Palmieri), "whether that be television or film, or other videos and commercials. I am constantly looking for new talent, someone with an eye to create things that we haven't seen or someone who can help us see it in a different way. For the

The Executive Producer's
Responsibilities

The executive producer's responsibilities
include:
- **Advancing the directors' careers.**
- **Overseeing project acquisition.**
- **Managing, budgeting, and scheduling.**
- **Hiring.**
- **Mediating and resolving conflicts.**
- **Overseeing the shoot and postproduction.**

company, or any company, you always want a billing director or someone with the potential to become that."

ADVANCING THE DIRECTORS' CAREERS

An executive producer helps to guide and build the career of every director the production company signs. Working in tandem with the director's rep, some executive producers keep track of upcoming releases to target specific artists and record labels for future video projects. EPs also work to surround the directors with the best and most creative teams to allow the directors to grow creatively and develop their craft, ideas, and visions. "The EP needs to understand the directors and how they work and to try and make the process smooth for them," explains Kelly Norris Sarno "That would entail hiring people, such as the producer, who you feel best understand their [the directors] artistic visions and who can work with their personalities. It's a delicate balance dealing with various personalities. The director needs to feel secure and protected, as well as represented in the best light possible."

"The director and EP have a very close relationship," adds Doug Kluthe, veteran executive producer (Godsmack's "Straight Outta Line," directed by Dean Karr and Everlast's "White Trash Beautiful," directed by Dean Karr), "the EP is the center of the hub of the world for the director."

The EP often works with directors from the beginning of a project to the delivery, developing a strategy to take their careers to the next level, from executing the treatments to working with clients and crews. The EP may offer suggestions and guidance to facilitate the creative process and ensure the most compelling ideas are turned into a great video. The EP must develop an innate understanding of how the signed directors work in order to make the production process as smooth as possible.

To avoid cutting into the working time of the director, the executive producer, along with the director's rep, will often oversee the development of the director's reel to make sure it creatively represents the director as effectively as possible. Together, they will determine the number of videos to feature, how the videos should be sequenced, and whether or not to include a montage of the director's previous work. The production company then assumes the responsibility for dubbing the reels, labeling them, keeping an updated inventory, and sending them out to perspective record label clients.

OVERSEEING PROJECT ACQUISITION

As mentioned, the executive producer keeps an eye on every music video that passes through the production company, from the creation of the concept all the way through postproduction. Once the record label has requested that a director "write on" a specific track, the EP may work with the director and the director's rep to help develop an idea that will impress the record company and artist while remaining within the allotted budget at the same time. The EP also makes sure the director hands in the treatment on time.

In regard to working with a director's rep, Kelly Norris Sarno explains, "As the EP, I like being kept up to date on various upcoming projects, pushing them [the reps] to go after particular jobs I feel would be best suited for your particular director; I push the rep to think outside the box and understand the process, and I make sure that the rep doesn't cross the line of following up on a director or actually being too persistent that the director feels overwhelmed."

MANAGING, BUDGETING, AND SCHEDULING

Once the contractual details are ironed out, the executive producer and director—on behalf of the production company—sign the contract, and it falls to the executive producer to create a budget for the video project. Some executive producers prefer to have the producer create the budget, however, the EP will never submit a budget to a record label without reviewing it first. "I am responsible for overseeing the job, making sure that the client is happy as well as my director," says Kelly Norris Sarno. "I do not put in a budget without going through it and making sure that all angles are covered. I sometimes set up deals for postproduction, make sure deadlines can be met, and review the contract before it's signed by myself and my director."

Sometimes an EP will reduce or remove the production mark-up from the budget to allow a more expensive idea to reach fruition, provided the resulting video on the director's reel would bring the company more work—for which they can take the full mark-up. Once the company lands the project, the executive producer may also review the contract from the label to ensure that they can deliver everything within the contract.

Snapshots from the Set

"Joseph Kahn directed the AZ/Foxy Brown/Nas video 'Do or Die.' We were shooting at the Algonquin Hotel in New York City. The guests were complaining that youths were running through the halls trying to get into the guests' rooms. Just as the hotel manager was telling us we had to keep our people on set, an extra in the video pulled out a gun during a take, creating havoc. The manager immediately pulled the plug on us, and called in the NYPD riot police to clear the room and remove us from the premises. We regrouped at an entirely new location and shot a one-take video that wrapped just as the sun was rising."
—Doug Kluthe, Executive Producer

"I shot a video in Poland in 1991 for an artist called Cary Clail and the On U Sound System. We bribed the army to let us film their tanks driving down the street with him singing. We had them [the tanks] all day, and kept having them go back up one-way streets in Warsaw; no one said a word; we had no permits, nothing. A crazy experience."
—William Green, Producer

HIRING

Even through the budget process, an executive producer may concurrently begin to check the availability of producers, directors of photography (DPs), production designers, and assistant directors (ADs), either directly or through their respective agents. It usually falls to the executive producer to hire a competent producer who will complement the director. In addition, the EP will help to fill other essential crew positions, especially if a new, up-and-coming director will lead the project. Even after the company wins the contract for the video project, the EP may continue to help during the hiring process. "We might encourage our directors to work with new DPs, new stylists, a new choreographer, or someone that they wouldn't have otherwise," says Ericka Danko, formerly an EP at the production company HSI (Usher's "You Don't Have To Call," and John Mayer's "Clarity," both directed by Little X). "And we talk them through it, and we say the reasons why."

MEDIATING AND RESOLVING CONFLICTS

Often, the creative ambition of a video outstrips the available budget. In production parlance, it is called *underbidding*. Part of the balancing act the executive producer performs involves working closely with the producer and the production team to make sure that everyone honors both the budget and the project's creative goals. An underbid video can cause a schism between the creative goals and the budget, which can lead to strained relationships between the producer and director.

The division often causes a director to try and squeeze more money out of an already limited budget from the producer. Since the director is the leader and visionary, the producer must do everything in his or her power to realize the director's requests—no matter how difficult or, at times, outlandish they may be.

When the demands veer into the realm of unreality, the EP will need to step in. The intervention might involve explaining the financial realities to the director or changing how the director and producer relate to each other. It may fall to the EP to become stern with the director, which the producer may not feel comfortable doing. The executive producer, as the head of staff at the production company, is the producer's boss, which we'll look at a bit later in the chapter. Most often, the two maintain a relationship based on confidence—with the executive producer trusting that the producer will supervise the shoot and report any information regarding the budget, creative aspects of the project, and client relations.

OVERSEEING THE SHOOT AND POSTPRODUCTION

If scheduling permits, the executive producer usually attends the day of the video shoot, but only gets involved if necessary. The EP ensures that the client is satisfied with the shoot, acts as a liaison between the director and the client, stands by for any emergency that may arise, and backs up the producer. The executive producer has to keep one eye toward the finish line, making sure that things do not deviate too far from the original plan. If they do, he or she has to evaluate and then negotiate production and budgetary obstacles. "On set, my job is time management, helping to stick to a realistic schedule and not wasting opportunity," says Larry Perel, the EP at the production company Arsenal, Inc. (Semisonic's "Closing Time," directed by Chris Appelbaum and The Killers' "All These Things I've Done," directed by Anton Corbijn).

Keeping production on course, on time, and within budget is paramount in the music video world. When the video enters the postproduction process, the executive producer will help select the best team and facility while continuing to serve as a liaison between the director and the client, making sure everyone meets their deadlines, and helping to coordinate all aspects to everyone's satisfaction.

THE RESPONSIBIILTIES OF THE PRODUCER

As noted in Chapter Two, the director quarterbacks the video project while the producer coaches it, calling the plays from the sideline, and making sure all the players follow the game plan. The producer has the responsibility of bringing the director's creative vision to life through planning, scheduling, budgeting, hiring, and managing the video's production. The amount of the producer's creative input depends on his or her personality, as well as on the relationship with the director. "I work in conjunction with the director to find the balance, feasibility, and executability of the creative [vision] within the budgetary restrictions," explains producer Oualid Mouaness, "meshing the creative and the technical in order to achieve the best possible outcome in achieving the director's and the artist's vision of what the video should be. I have assumed many responsibilities as a producer. Primarily, the skill is linked to getting the best possible result and quality of work out of all the individuals involved in researching ideas as well as budgeting and scheduling."

"As producer, you are responsible for everything," adds William Green (Outkast's "Hey Ya," directed by Bryan Barber and The Rolling Stones' "Streets of Love," directed by Jake Nava). "If the video goes over budget, your fault. If it looks bad, it's your fault. If the artist won't get out of the trailer, your fault. No one likes the AD, your fault. You have to keep an eye on everything and keep the powers that be in the loop."

The term "producer" has many meanings in the film and video world. On a feature film or a high budget commercial, lots of people get called producer, such as: the executive producer, line producer, unit production manager, and post-production supervisor. Many of the tasks of these producers fall on the music video producer, everything from dealing with the financer—the label—and shielding the director from the label commissioner, like an executive producer, to helping the director and assistant director organize the set, like a unit production manager, to scheduling post-production, like a post supervisor. In the music video arena, the producer's job most closely resembles the line producer, the person in charge of organizing the production, dealing with the budget, hiring the crew and vendors, and working with the director to realize the video's creative vision.

The producer must follow the budget, line by line, to ensure the video project's execution and completion within the allotted amount of money while also working with the director to determine how best to realize the video concept laid out in the treatment. With the treatment as the creative guideline and the budget setting the limits, the director and producer work together to hire a technical crew. The producer needs to stay on top of any compromises or changes, have them approved by the director, executive producer, and the record company, and accomplish all the preproduction tasks for the shoot day, such as:

• hiring the crew
• hiring the art department
• hiring the equipment

- ordering the film
- securing the set location
- completing the casting
- supervising the wardrobe
- arranging transportation
- getting necessary approvals from the director, EP, record label, and artist's manager

The producer delegates much of the above responsibilities to the production team, which includes the production manager, or PM, and the production coordinator, or PC. "I'm responsible for coordinating the execution of the director's vision while balancing the interests of the record label, the artist, the production company and the director—interests that are not always in sync," says producer Caleb Dewart (Justin Timberlake's "Cry Me A River," directed by Francis Lawrence and The Malloys' video for Metallica's "St. Anger"). "The production company wants to make as much money as possible while keeping the client happy; the director sometimes wants to make a piece of art; the artist just cares about how they look; and the produc-

The Producer's Responsibilities

The producer is responsible for:
- **Shepherding the video project.**
- **Maintaining the integrity of the creative process.**
- **Establishing and nurturing a relationship with the director.**
- **Overseeing the budget.**
- **Encouraging open communication.**
- **Managing morale and expectations.**
- **Troubleshooting.**
- **Supervising postproduction.**

What makes a great producer?

A great producer:
- **Is excellent with budgets and crunching numbers—and adept at hiding money in a budget.**
- **Brings a project on or under budget, delivers a quality video, and provides the director with the necessary tools to make a treatment come to life.**
- **Understands the balance of managing and protecting the finances on the job while still giving the director the freedom to create.**
- **Knows how to decide between what is and isn't necessary.**
- **Makes both the record label and production company happy, respecting the client's needs and desires while also looking out for the best interests of the production company and the director.**
- **Multitasks and manages the wide variety of personalities and egos involved in a video's shoot.**
- **Never complains to the commissioner.**
- **Communicates well and keeps everyone informed.**
- **Pays great attention to detail, has a calm demeanor, and solves problems easily.**
- **Negotiates well.**
- **Is interested in every aspect of the production company.**
- **Allows the production crews to do their jobs.**
- **Is tough yet fair, diplomatic, and thorough.**
- **Possesses a background in production.**

tion company wants to spend as little money as possible, while getting the most commercial product possible."

Since music video producers are usually not part of the production company's staff but are often hired as independent contractors, they do not have the authority to approve additional spending. This falls to the executive producer, who often looks to the producer to be the watchdog, keeping tight control over the budget. The line producer is the middleman, the bad guy to the EP if the shoot goes over budget, and is the killjoy to the director who wants to spend more money realizing his or her vision.

A producer is traditionally paid a standard five percent of the below the line budget. If the directors and the production company form a good working relationship with a producer, it makes sense to continue the alliance; therefore, most producers work primarily for one or two production companies. It also saves time and stress, as the producer knows the inner workings of the production company, which vendors they use, and how the directors like to work. Green sums up a producer's responsibilities by saying, "It's all about getting the director what he or she wants, making the production company their mark-up, or not losing the mark-up, and keeping the client happy and informed. As a producer, you have to keep your head and be ready for the worst-case scenario. Something always happens, so you have to be firm and fair and make sure crew know that you are both of them, and be able to discuss the treatment and ideas with the director. Instead of just saying 'no,' come up with a solution or a back way for them to think about. At the end of the day we are just making music videos, so it's okay to have a laugh and some fun as well."

SHEPHERDING THE VIDEO PROJECT

From the inception of the video until the final delivery, the producer must find a means of pleasing everyone. "My job is part babysitter, part accountant, and part diplomat," explains independent producer Rachel Curl (Foo Fighters' "Resolve," directed by Michael Palmieri and Backstreet Boys' "Just Want You To Know," directed by Marc Klasfeld). "I am equally responsible for keeping the director happy and executing his or her vision as I am for staying on or under budget and maintaining the morale of the crew. It's a tricky balance."

"Before the job is budgeted, I generally speak to the director about the specifics of his or her vision," Caleb Dewart says, summarizing his role in the overall process. "Usually, we're trying to hit a specific dollar amount for the bid, and we spend quite a bit of time trying to come up with creative solutions to deal with the severe financial limitations of the job that are in direct opposition to what the director is trying to achieve. Once the job awards, I'm overseeing the logistical and financial coordination of the job—hiring the crew, making deals with vendors, location scouting, set building, and more."

"During pre-pro [preproduction]," Green explains, "I communicate with the client, the director, and all the relevant heads of departments, trying to see what problems will arise early on. You try to be a voice of reason for every department as well as helping your director get his or her vision, and sometimes that means battling the record label, as they have a different take. Sometimes what a director writes in a treatment can be misconstrued in many ways."

"Preproduction is the most important stage of the job," says Rachel Curl. "A good prep will make the shoot go smoother, and will save you the pain of having to play catch-up if one thing goes wrong, which always happens—even when you least expect it. Preproduction is like putting the pieces of a huge puzzle together, or organizing an extremely messy house. When I come onto a job, there is just an idea, and the director and I need to figure out how to execute it. My main goal in pre-pro is to work with the director to execute his or her idea. This involves many meetings, scouting locations, wardrobe fittings, drawing storyboards, designing sets, creating a shooting schedule with the AD, etc. Before the job books, I am usually involved in the budgeting process, collaborating with the executive producer. Once the job is awarded, I immediately book my production team, the production manager and production coordinator. I then book all department heads, including the DP, AD, production designer, wardrobe stylist, etc. The director ultimately chooses all creative crew, but I do the actual negotiating and booking. The record company is often involved in the decision making for some creative crew, in particular the glam squad. Again, I can't stress enough the importance of a good prep. In my opinion, you can't over-prep a job. Unexpected things always come up, so the more prepared you are the better you will be able to handle the curveballs.

"On set I'm usually worrying about how much money we're spending and how much overtime we're going to incur if we're moving too slowly and if the schedule we've come up with is entirely too ambitious," Dewart continues. "If we get behind in our schedule, I'm talking to the first AD and the director about what we can do to make up time—which generally involves the director cutting shots from their shot list."

The time a producer spends on a project may vary wildly. Generally, a producer begins with the initial budgeting of the job and sees it through to completion, which takes about a month. A very low budget job or major rush job can take as little

as two weeks, while a video that requires a lot of visual effects, animation, intricate editing, or other intensive effects may take up two months or longer. In some cases, these videos require a postproduction supervisor (see Chapter Ten starting on page 186 for a full job description of postproduction supervisors), letting the producer off the hook for the last stages of the project. On the flip side, if the label or artist doesn't like a video, the process can drag on for months. When this happens, everyone expects the producer to remain on the project until the end, and often for the original flat fee.

MAINTAINING THE INTEGRITY OF THE CREATIVE PROCESS

Since the producer strives to follow the treatment according to the director's vision—while staying on budget—the relationship between the director

Do you need a great song to make a great video?

"Yes, but nobody's going to say it's a great video. Name a really crappy song with a good video. But you could name a lot of really great songs with crappy videos that still got a lot of airplay and got a lot of exposure, and it didn't tank the single. I think the power of the song definitely helps make the music video that much easier to pull along."
—Billy Poveda, Executive Producer

"I think you can have a great song with a lousy video and succeed, but if you have a lousy song and a good video, you won't succeed. It's like putting a beautiful ring on a crippled finger—it doesn't make the crippled finger look better, it just highlights the problem."
—Marcus Nispel, Director

and producer often has its share of challenges, with the director constantly pushing the producer to squeeze more out of the budget, and the producer often having to draw the line. To work well together, they must trust and respect each other, realizing that they both seek the same goal—to produce the strongest video possible within the parameters that have been set for the project. "I work very closely with directors," Dewart says. "There is so much problem-solving that has to go on that I think it's essential that producers have a clear understanding of what the director is trying to do."

ESTABLISHING AND NURTURING A RELATIONSHIP WITH THE DIRECTORS

As mentioned, most producers regularly work with the same two or three directors, and some directors work exclusively with one producer. In such a case, the freelance producer functions much like an executive producer would. When a director and producer know each other's styles, quirks, likes, and dislikes, it makes both of their jobs easier and more comfortable, and, in turn, simplifies the entire video process. In a high pressure, fast-turnaround process like making music videos, working with someone you know well makes the job easier for all involved.

"The director and producer are a team, setting the tone for rest of the crew," Rachel Curl observes. "While my job is to collaborate and execute the director's creative vision, I also have to keep spirits up for the crew and protect the financials for the company. There is a responsibility between the director and producer to uphold leadership and preserve the morale of the crew. However the collaborative process works between the two, it is extremely important to maintain a united front. Once a director and producer work together over time, there is an unspoken communication that happens. The partnership is often compared jokingly to a marriage."

OVERSEEING THE BUDGET

Some videos require that the producer "bid the job," which means creating a line item budget for the specific video project. At other times, the producer has to deal with a pre-existing budget from

Advice for Aspiring Directors

"Just keep working and studying. Get a video camera and shoot something. Especially with the technology now, there's no reason why you can't show somebody that you've got some talent. No one's just going to say, 'Here's tens of thousands of dollars.' You don't need a big budget. Just get a video camera and show people, 'Look what's coming out of my head and what I understand about this thing.'"

—Little X, Director

"I would hope that people wouldn't want to become the next Matthew Rolston or the next 'anybody.' Rather, [I hope] that they would want to become a fully realized version of themselves. Create a style, which is simply a thing that you like. Gravitate toward those things and learn about them. That's your style. It's a way of educating yourself that is a great pleasure. Delve deeply into things that you love and adore. That's very important."

—Matthew Rolston, Director

the production company. Either way, the producer, being the person in charge of the budget, approves each hire and every purchase.

If the video looks like it might go over budget, the producer must bring everyone up to speed on possible "overages"—additional money that is above and beyond the contracted budget amount—that are needed to properly complete the video according to the director's treatment. The producer must make budgetary decisions with the help and guidance of the director, executive producer, and record label commissioner.

ENCOURAGING OPEN COMMUNICATION

The producer keeps the executive producer and video commissioner in the loop at all times. For example, certain aspects of the production, like the glam squad and casting, often require the commissioner's approval. "When working with commissioners," Oualid Mouaness says, "it is imperative for me to make clear the point that we are working toward the same goal and that we have a clear understanding of the creative and the technical processes involved. I think of the commissioner as the creative producer from the label, who is protecting the vision that was agreed upon."

"The producer is the point person for whom all information should run through, and from which all information should be dispensed. We're meant to be the answerers of 'who,' 'what,' 'where,' 'when,' and 'how much can I spend' for the entire crew," explains Jil Hardin (Usher's "Rhythm City Mini Movie," directed by Little X and Alicia Keys' "You Don't Know My Name," directed by Chris Robinson). "It is a balancing act to maintain an unencumbered space for directors to express their genius and voice, while also sufficiently addressing the comments without jeopardizing the limited time you have to shoot and thus the status of your budget. Sometimes being

a producer feels like being a glorified babysitter or guidance counselor. Anyone and everyone that has a problem comes to you to complain about it and looks to you for a resolution."

MANAGING MORALE AND EXPECTATIONS

While the producer has concrete responsibilities, the job also requires some harder to define aspects, especially when it comes to maintaining morale on the set. As Jil Hardin explains, "If you respect, support, and take care of your crew, the majority of them will reciprocate or acknowledge your efforts by giving you a bit more hustle when time is running out, more of a discount

What do you love about music videos?

"I think videos are great to do because they can be stepping stones for your career, but also they're great opportunities to experiment and just dive into filmmaking for a couple days and try out all these different things that you wanted to try out."

—Joe Hahn, Director

"What I love about music videos is that they are a bastion of creative filmmaking. As a producer, I have the opportunity to support that by finding the right director to bring the client's piece of music to life."

—Catherine A. Finkenstaedt, Executive Producer

"I love that you can do anything. You can do whatever you want. It's rock and roll. If you want to shoot a bunch of puppets, you can do that. I definitely appreciate that aspect of it."

—Marc Klasfeld, Director

on equipment when the budget gets too high, or work through lunch and waive a couple of extra meal penalties when you really need to finish up that last shot before changing set ups. It sounds simple, but it's often a virtue that is lost when the pressure's on and the hours are long. The energy of the crew directly affects your experience during production and the outcome of the project itself.

"Personally," she adds, "I feel it is the responsibility of the producer to set and maintain a high standard of moral conduct and consideration for the crew and whomever they interact with throughout the course of the production. As the producer of a particular project, you become an extremely influential representative of the production company, the director, the label, the artist, and ultimately the music video and film community. The position is fraught with obstacles and hurdles that rely on your guidance for a swift and amicable resolve, with as little cost as possible."

TROUBLESHOOTING

All the preproduction precautions in the world cannot keep the unexpected from happening. Throughout the entire process, the producer works to prevent problems. On set, he or she often acts a troubleshooter, maintaining the shooting schedule with the assistant director and director. The producer must ensure that the director has everything required for the shoot. Acting as liaison between the client and the director, the producer acknowledges the label's concerns throughout the shoot while shielding the director from unnecessary interruptions.

SUPERVISING POSTPRODUCTION

Once the video is shot, the process still has a long way to go, as do the director and the producer.

The shoot gathers the raw elements as described in the treatment, which are then combined in postproduction.

"For postproduction," Caleb Dewart says, "I spend most of my time on the phone coordinating the finishing of the project with the editor, the postproduction facility, the director, and the label. Many jobs have extensive post—either special effects or cosmetic clean up. I manage the approval process during post, getting directors to sign off on work that is then passed on to artists and labels for final approval."

"During post," adds Oualid Mouaness, "trying to stick [to] a timetable usually proves very difficult. Postproduction is the most mercurial part of the process where the final look, types of effects, and texture is decided."

If the production company hires a postproduction supervisor (postproduction producer), he or she will have significantly fewer responsibilities during this last stage of the project. Often the budget does not allow for a postproduction supervisor, which leaves the producer to organize and oversee this final stage of creating the video. The steps in the postproduction process that the producer needs to oversee include:

- Developing the film.
- Transferring the film to tape.
- Doing an offline edit, in which the editor takes the raw footage, or "dailies," from the shoot and arranges it to the song.
- Creating the rough draft, or "rough cut," of the music video.
- Mastering the final video in the online edit.

Once the director is happy with the cut, the label and artist watch it and make comments. Eventually, they all agree on a final rough cut and do what is called an "online edit," the last step in the postproduction process when the final, high-quality version of the video is assembled. The producer hires the editorial crew, purchases the supplies, schedules time in the postproduction facility, budgets the overall process, and makes sure that everything happens on time. The producer also makes sure that everyone who needs to see a copy of the edit receives one, and then collects and passes along any comments about the cuts. "I oversee the telecine with the director," says William Green, "make sure that the label knows which way you are making the film look, make sure the edit goes out on time, and to the relevant people [managers and commissioners], make sure everyone's notes are addressed—and there are a lot of people now—and get them put in the video without the director having too many issues. Or, if he or she does have a lot of issues, going back and explaining why, and hopefully getting the video delivered on time. If you are crazy busy, get a postproduction supervisor to stay on top of all of the running around and sending cuts out, and you can just deal with the calls. However, a lot of the times something goes wrong, and you, as producer, end up having to fix anyway."

CHAPTER FOUR
THE TREATMENT-WRITING PROCESS

The process of making music videos starts with the director's treatment, also called the concept. In this one- to three-page document, directors convey their vision of the song, vividly describing what they intend to capture on film and put on screen.

Once the record label commissioner has solicited a few directors for a music video, the music track is sent to the directors' representatives. Each prospective director must then come up with an idea, or treatment, of how to visually present the song. The treatment chosen by the label and the artist will evolve, and the concept takes a life of its own.

The way a song is visualized and expressed in the treatment differs from one director to the other. The director's success is determined by how he or she translates his or her treatment to the video. Accomplished directors understand that they must creatively interpret the song using a mix of artistry and marketing in relation to the artist's personality, image, and song.

Usually, the director develops the idea for the treatment, but sometimes the artist will offer some inspiration or a sense of the emotion he or she would like to convey in the video. More often than not, artists have a better idea of what they *don't* want, and leave it up to the director to apply his or her visual style to the video. On occasion, the director will hire a treatment writer to transfer the director's vision, inspiration, and ideas to paper. However, most directors prefer to write their treatments themselves.

Beyond the director's reel, the treatment is the only means a director possesses to get hired by a record label. Sometimes a director may pitch his or her idea to the artist in person or over the phone, but normally, being awarded the video project relies on the written treatment. Only a very select number of enormously accomplished directors have the benefit of not submitting a treatment to a label. In such circumstances, the commissioner, artist, and manager choose the director simply on his or her merits. This is called "single bidding." Most directors must submit treatment after treatment in order to keep working. They know that the treatment will determine who is awarded the contract.

THE EIGHT CATEGORIES OF MUSIC VIDEOS

Before the writing process begins, the director needs to know the guidelines set by the record label. The label may say that the artist would like to make a performance video, act in a storyline, shoot in a specific location, or shoot the video within a limited window of time. It helps to know any such parameters and expectations before proceeding into the creative brainstorming process, since the director must account for any restrictions the budget or schedule may require.

Music videos fall into the following eight categories. These categories are not official, but they represent the various styles that video directors need to keep in mind when writing a treatment.

PERFORMANCE

As the name suggests, performance videos feature the artist or band performing, and often take place in various locations with the performers wearing different outfits in each shot. Some examples include Coldplay's "Speed of Sound," directed by Mark Romanek; Green Day's "Boulevard of Broken Dreams," directed by Samuel Bayer; and Augustana's "Boston," directed by Paul Fedor.

CONCEPT

The artist or band neither perform nor, many times, appear in concept videos. These videos portray only stories or images, never performances. Some examples include Beastie Boys' "Sabotage," directed by Spike Jonze and The Prodigy's "Smack My Bitch Up," directed Jonas Ackerlund.

STORY

A story video features a narrative, with a beginning, middle, and end, which is intercut with footage of the artist or band performing. The artist may or may not be a character in the story. Some examples include Hoobastank's "The Reason," directed by Brett Simon; Ludacris, featuring Mary J. Blige's "Runaway Love," directed by Jessy Terrero; and Daughtry's "It's Not Over," directed by Dean Karr and Jay Martin.

GAG

A gag video relies on visual tricks. They can be shot live, also known as executing the visual effects "in camera," such as using dolls that look like the band for the performance rather than the band itself, or using special prosthetics to visually alter the artist or lead actor in the videos. Or, the visual tricks can be postproduction effects, such as giving the artist or lead actor an unrealistically long tongue, or setting the video in a location impossible to real life, such as outer space. Some examples include Sum 41's "Hell Song," directed by Marc Klasfeld and Ludacris' "Get Back," directed by Spike Jonze and Missy Elliott, featuring Da Brat's "Sock it 2 Me," directed by Hype Williams.

DANCE

As the name describes, a dance video features choreographed dancing. Some examples include Gwen Stefani's "Hollaback Girl," directed by Paul Hunter and Destiny's Child's "Lose My Breath," directed by Marc Klasfeld.

ANIMATION

An animated video features animated images, in which the artist and band may or may not be depicted. Some examples include Gorillaz's "Feel Good Inc.," directed by Jamie Hewlett and Gnarls Barkley's "Crazy," directed by Robert Hales.

PARTY OR CLUB

A party or club video features scenes that take place in a dance club or at a party. Some examples include Nelly's "Hot In Herre," directed by Little X and 50 Cent's "In Da Club," directed by Philip G. Atwell.

FILM CLIP

A film-clip video is used when a song is featured in a movie soundtrack. The video will contain clips from the film that are intercut with the music video. Some examples include "Hero" by Chad Kroeger featuring Josey Scott, directed by Nigel Dick, from the movie soundtrack of *Spiderman,* and Eminem's "Lose Yourself," directed by Eminem, Paul Rosenberg, and Phillip G. Atwell, from the movie soundtrack of *8 Mile.*

The eight categories oftentimes overlap in music videos, resulting in most videos featuring various aspects from each category. Examples are Michael Jackson's "Thriller," directed by John Landis and Usher's "Caught Up," directed by Little X. These videos are a mixture of story and dance with a performance by the artist.

Outkast's "Hey Ya!," directed by Bryan Barber, mixes performance and gag, as Andre 3000 of Outkast portrays all of the musicians in the band through a motion control device (see page 157 in Chapter Eight for further information on motion control).

The Used's "All That I've Got," directed by Marc Webb, blends performance, live action, and animation by depicting a young boy wandering around in a storybook.

Crystal Method's "Name of the Game," directed by Marcos Siega, combines story and gag by featuring a day in the life of a kid whose entire head is a huge nose, and Wax's "California," directed by Spike Jonze, mixes concept and gag, showing just one shot of a man on fire running in slow motion with no visual performance by the band.

Missy Elliot's "We Run This," directed by Dave Meyers, mixes performance, gag, and film clip. The video incorporates footage from the movie *Stick It,* a film about an elite gymnastics team and their competitions, and the gag is Missy Elliot doing intricate gymnastic moves in the video footage as well as in the actual movie footage.

TECHNIQUES FOR CREATING THE MUSIC VIDEO TREATMENT

The treatment begins with the song. Many music video directors feel they must like the song to write a treatment; many others will write whether they like the song or not.

Two necessary ingredients inform the creative process of writing a treatment: (1) coming up with a specific and hopefully unique idea, and (2) expressing that idea by writing it in treatment form. Every director has a different approach to both.

Every director has a unique technique for brainstorming treatment ideas, and they don't always flow smoothly. Some videos take several brainracking days. Others just come as a flash when hearing the song, a "gift-from-God" idea, as director Mark Kohr (Shakira's "Eyes Like Yours (Ojos así)" and Green Day's "Time of Your Life") describes it. Many directors use similar methods to catch this creative lightning in a bottle. The

Techniques for coming up with the music video idea include:

- Recycling Ideas
- Beginning with the Lyrics
- Finding a Solution to Questions
- Finding the Hook
- Finding the Feel of the Music
- Identifying the Artist
- Single Bids and Pre-existing Relationships
- Artist Collaboration
- Using Movies as Inspiration
- Using Books and Comic Books as Inspiration
- Developing Creative Routines
- Being Spontaneous

process is mercurial and difficult to fully capture; however, the following describes the various ways in which directors come up with their ideas.

RECYCLING IDEAS

Some directors recycle ideas for video concepts. "I usually just go into a bag of ideas that I have and I figure out something from there," Marc Klasfeld (Destiny's Child's "Lose My Breath" and Avenged Sevenfold's "Bat Country") says. "It's probably different every time. I have so many developed ideas that I usually try to take something that I already have and fit it into another song's treatment. Or once in a while something completely new hits me and I'll just write it at that moment. But usually that sort of inspiration is few and far between. It just depends on where the inspiration is at that particular moment."

"I have a ton of these ideas wrapped up inside," Joseph Kahn (Kelly Clarkson's "Walk Away" and Backstreet Boys' "Incomplete") adds. "I'm just waiting for the right moment to bring out the right one that will actually, legitimately, be the great video."

Of course, the idea might need tweaking out of the bag. "A lot of times it's the combination of just being inspired by the song and then combining that with ideas that I've had that have been kicking around in my head," Marc Webb (All American Rejects' "Moving Along" and Yellowcard's "Lights and Sound") explains. "I'll give you an example, actually. I'm finishing up this Hot Hot Heat video, and I'd written this idea two or three years ago where a guy's inside a house and all of a sudden he's walking through. He's alone in this house and he runs into a Polaroid camera and the camera flashes and as the picture develops he sees that he's in the same space, but the space is filled with people. He looks around and there's nobody else around

him. I always liked that hook, but I just incorporated that idea into this other idea that we did for Hot Hot Heat for this song called 'Middle of Nowhere' where everybody kind of disappears, which is more of a motif of the song 'Middle of Nowhere,' and I just kind of incorporated those elements. So sometimes it's a very simple thing, like you think of it all simultaneously, and sometimes it's a long, brutal process where you stay up all night and tear your hair out. You piece it together bit by bit. And those are usually the worst videos. And sometimes you just kind of assemble a collection of things based on a very simple theme. I like my ideas to come from a very simple place, and then elaborate on those."

BEGINNING WITH THE LYRICS

Some directors begin with the lyrics of the song. Sanaa Hamri describes this process:

"First thing, I look at lyrical content to make sure that I want to even be involved. And if the lyrical content is good enough, and the artist is somebody that I want to collaborate with and help their career, I start listening to the music in my car and at home and I start letting random images come to my head, kind of uncensored. Sometimes labels and artists have desires that they want in the video, and I, of course, take that into consideration. I build it around what their requests are. So if an artist says that they want to shoot this entirely on a beach, then I work from those parameters of being on a beach. If I don't have any parameters, then I just come up with something and I write whatever I feel necessary."

FINDING A SOLUTION TO QUESTIONS

Some directors look at the process of coming up with an idea for a video as finding a creative solution to many questions, like a puzzle. Mark

Kohr says he views himself as a "bottomless pit of creative answers and solutions" when it comes to the treatment-writing process. "I've always felt that what's wonderful about music videos is that you get music which has an incredible equation that you need to solve. You have music that has emotional content and words, both of which affect how the listener feels. And the equation necessary to solve is what visuals to add to the music in order to point out and heighten that emotional content. Then you have the record company: what do they want to achieve? You have the band: what do they look like, how do they move, have you seen them act, do they even want to act, what will they be most comfortable with? And then you have culture: what's going on at the time? You get all that stuff and condense it down to an answer, which is supposed to be a page and a half long [the video's treatment], and that page and a half is supposed to be something great. And then you have money and time. And you have weather and a location. So you condense it down more and say, 'OK, I can shoot this for this much money in this much time.' There it is: your answer to that elaborate equation."

Sometimes the director doesn't exactly have to solve a puzzle or answer a question so much as figure out the best way of following orders. "I actually work best under assignment," said Marcus Nispel, "and then I try to rearrange the furniture. A good example is the Bush video for "Greedy Fly," where they came in and essentially wanted me to do a rip-off of *The Shining*. And I was like, 'I don't want to go down trying to outdo Kubrick.' So I asked, 'How can we do a story like *The Shining*, which essentially builds a schizophrenic, and turn it around to make it ours?'"

FINDING THE HOOK

Some directors find one truly original idea—a "hook"—for the artist and the song, and then work with it as the center to create a whole concept. The director's treatment will center on a defining idea that makes the video stand out. Often it has nothing to do with lyrics.

"Song lyrics are stupid for the most part," said director Marcos Siega (Weezer's "Beverly Hills" and Blink 182's "What's My Age Again?"). "Especially pop songs. And you just kind of snap to the rhythm. So what I do is I listen to the song once, get a feel for the tone, then I just kind of play it on repeat to really feel the movement...Then I say 'I've got it. There's a guy with a giant nose,' and people would look at me like, 'What?' and I'd be like, 'Yeah, think about it.'"

"I would tell Lanette, my rep, 'You just saw a video for 311 and then you saw a video for Nine Inch Nails, then you saw a video for Rancid, and they're performance videos and they're cool, but now you just saw a video with a guy with a giant nose. Which one are you going to walk away remembering?' And she was like, 'You're right.'"

"If you look at my computer you'd see I have six hundred treatments that never got made. Labels would look at them and go 'OK, you're smoking crack.' But I've done videos where the lead is a marionette. I've done a video where the lead is just a giant nose for a head. I've done a video where the lead is a blow-up doll. I've done a video where the guys are naked. That was my process. What is the thing that people are going to remember?"

Since record companies regard videos as four-minute advertisements for the songs and the artist, some advertising theory goes into conceptualizing them. As Siega pointed out, a director can't forget or underemphasize an artist's unique selling point, something that makes both the artist and the video memorable, something special.

"You need to look for the element that's going to make the video special. Eighty percent of it could be girls shaking their asses, concert, club, whatever," explains director Dave Meyers (Missy Elliot's "We Run This" and Pink's "Stupid Girls"). "The thing that's going to allow a director to grow is that in each video there's an element, a hook. If the director does a great narrative that doesn't really touch anybody, or they do a great club video that's just sort of run of the mill, then they're like everybody else. Even if it's well shot or whatever, who cares?"

Marc Webb used an unusual video technique in his Switchfoot's "Dare You to Move" video:

"A lot of that was based on a technique, the technique of a lot of people lying in the same position. To me, the climax of that was so important and it was based on technique, all of these, what I think of as versions of the same guy throughout his history meeting up at the same time. To me, the only way you communicate that is through this parallel framing. What's special about that video, the technique facilitates the emotion, which I think is sometimes a difficult thing to do, but when it works it works really well."

FINDING THE FEEL OF THE MUSIC

Another approach a director can use to create a treatment is how the music "feels." Some music has a particular ethnic or socio-geographic sound as a reference point, and a director might take off from that. "Led Zeppelin has a very Middle Eastern kind of influence to a lot of their music at times," Nobel Jones pointed out, "and that's naturally going to inspire your visuals to a certain degree, or at least a play on that. So you have to listen to how the music's done. If it's done with a Spanish bent, if it's done with a darker tone or a brighter kind of thing, or maybe a contrast on that."

Snapshots From The Set

"For 'Say Say Say,' Paul McCartney took me for a walk in the woods, got me high, and made me promise not to let him dance next to Michael Jackson, because he was smart enough to realize that he would come off second best. So there's a little teeny bit of movement in 'Say Say Say,' but that's why the story's frolicking, that's why it's kind of that Mac and Jack act."

—Bob Giraldi, Director

"Seal is just an extraordinary performer, and he understands the process. He almost made it too easy. He literally stood there and said, 'Let me see the monitor and see where my frame lines are.' He understood the concept of moving through the frame immediately. It was like two musicians playing off each other; me, operating the camera, directing, and being able to speak to him not as a cameraman, but as an artist. I'd jump from behind and talk, and then we'd go back and do it. It was a lot of fun."

—Noble Jones, Director

IDENTIFYING THE ARTIST

Some directors strive to capture an element of the artist, thus writing treatments to express both the artist's personality and message. "I try to make contact with the singer of the band and get inside his head asking 'Where were you when you wrote this song?' 'Who is it about?' or any other information he cares to give up to me," says director Dean Karr (Seether's "Truth" and Tommy Lee's "Good Times"). "When I feel I'm on the edge of something which moves me, I jump right into it. I love creating wild, surreal worlds in which to convey the band's message and make them look cooler than they ever dreamed."

In addition, some directors try to add an understanding of the artist's music from a cultural perspective. This, in turn, translates and ties into the way the record company decides to market the artist. But even beyond that, it helps shape the perception of the artist in popular culture.

"On a critical level, know your marketplace, know your demographic, know who you're making the video for," explains director Joseph Kahn. "But on another level, it's understanding the material. If you can't understand the material, you'll never be able to make a good video. That doesn't mean you have to make the greatest art in the world; it just means that whatever it [the material] is has to be truthful to whatever it is that you're trying to say. Music videos are there for sales, but you're never going to make good sales unless you understand what it is that you're selling. The actual process of coming up with the idea comes from a million different ways, but it's also tied in with one big overriding thing: it's a marketing tool. You have a responsibility to the artist to make sure that this video is going to air in a way that it's going to sell more records. So, ultimately, I always reference it from the point of view of, 'Is it a fair use of the artist's money to invest in an expensive director like me for an idea that will help their career?' So that's an over-riding pact."

Another factor a director must consider when writing a treatment is where an artist stands in his or her career. Beginning artists, veteran artists, superstars, and artists attempting a comeback all require entirely different treatment approaches. "I think the first video [for a band] usually introduces the band or the performer," says director Marcus Nispel. "It's very simple. It's performance-oriented, maybe something from a live show, where you just see them honest-to-God. Then the second or third [video], you can take sort of a departure. The really big glossy ones you don't want to do until a little bit later, because you always want to start authentic, get to know those people. So what's successful for a band at the beginning of their career is not necessarily going to work for them at the end of their career. You've got to amp up and then surprise. Look at Madonna. In her first video, she was completely accessible, reminded you of any girl you ever saw in a club, and then she went through different changes and reinvented herself. That's, I think, when it gets much more involved. I usually prefer doing the second or the third [video] or the comeback one. Change the perception."

"A lot of it has to do with timing," director Joe Hahn (Alkaline Trio's "Time to Waste" and Linkin Park's "Breaking the Habit") adds, "which goes back to being able to see the whole scope of the situation. Because a lot of it has to do with where the artist is at the moment, what he or she needs out of it, and what the label needs out of it. It's chemistry. It's like going out on a date. Either you have that chemistry or not."

SINGLE BIDS AND PRE-EXISTING RELATIONSHIPS

Established directors may acquire jobs via their reputation, their friendships with the artists, or their track records working with the artists on past occasions. This can lead to a single bid, or to an established director submitting a treatment in a way that wouldn't happen for a newer director.

For instance, the band U2 chose Joseph Kahn to direct the video for their song "Elevation" as a single bid, due to his reputation and pre-existing body of work. Kahn spent a week with the band on tour, watching their concerts from different vantage points to analyze performance angles, which he then discussed with Bono. After establishing a relationship with the band, Kahn was also single bid on U2's "Stuck in a Moment" video.

Once directors get established, they can focus on getting to know the artists to bring out their personalities. Often, newer directors don't have the advantage of spending time with an artist prior to the shoot. Brett Ratner says, "Most of the time you get a record. You listen to the record, you think you know the artist, you write a treatment, and you shoot the video. You meet the artists on the day of the shoot or the day before. I've spent time with the artists. I got to know them. I got to know what qualities they have that I can bring out in the video so that when you watched [the video] you were seeing the inside to this artist... When I did a Madonna video, it looked like Madonna. When I did a Mariah video, it looked like Mariah. When I did a D'Angelo video, it looked like D'Angelo. I wasn't imposing my kind of style on the artist. I was trying to deliver for them a true interpretation of what the song was."

Sometimes, an off-the-wall treatment submission can put a director in the driver's seat, but only if the director is already established. "I was sitting in the office, and I didn't really have an idea," Siega recalls when remembering how he landed Weezer's "Island in the Sun" video. "Someone wanted to order from Baha Fresh. I gave him twenty bucks and said, 'Get me a Baha Fresh gift certificate'. He brought back the gift certificate and was like, 'What do you want this for?' I wrote Jordan Schur—the president of Geffen—on the gift certificate and sent it with a note that said, 'Weezer will play at a Mexican wedding.' That was my treatment."

Siega's rep thought he was crazy, but the next day he got a call from the Rivers Cuomo, the lead singer of Weezer, who said that he loved the idea. Siega had already directed Weezer's "Hash Pipe" video, so they had an established relationship. They awarded the video to Siega. Without an established relationship, they probably wouldn't have considered his minimalist treatment.

ARTIST COLLABORATION

Collaborations between the director and the artist are quite common. An artist may want to collaborate with a specific director on a treatment and single bid the particular director for ideas. For example, Missy Elliot consistently single-bids Dave Meyers, and Outkast consistently single-bids Bryan Barber. These artists have a solid working rapport with those directors, and enjoy the collaborative process. But collaborative treatments don't always come through single bids. For example, an artist and video commissioner may have a kernel of an idea that they give to several directors along with the music and instructions for creating the video's treatment. One of the directors may come up with some intriguing ideas based on the idea that piques the interest of the artist. At this point, the artist might want to have a brainstorming session with the director to

further collaborate, which may lead to hiring the director for the video project.

Many of Roman Coppola's video ideas come about in collaboration with the artist or band. "I had a really good collaboration with Daft Punk," he says. "The idea for 'Revolution 900' was very much a collaborative idea. I had conceived the premise of doing an instructional video, the idea of having a recipe in there and framing kind of a story within a story, going back in time. But I had written something else, and they kind of pushed me and said, 'That's not right, but how about setting it in the milieu of a rave party, since that's what the song's about, and I had kind of resisted because it was too obvious. In any event, that was an experience where I threw something out, they threw something back, and it worked very well as a collaboration."

Artists often have strong ideas about how they want to present a song. Some bands have a very strong visual sense. A lot of musicians have either studied or worked in the visual arts in addition to their musical endeavors. When the band R.E.M. formed, lead singer Michael Stipe was an art student at the University of Georgia. Director Peter Care (R.E.M.'s "Aftermath" and Bruce Springsteen's "Secret Garden") discovered Michael's art background when he worked with the band on the video for "Radio Song." "I think I did the longest treatment I ever did for a music video in my life in order to get the job, but the treatment wasn't that kind of bullshit stuff, like 'I will make the band look amazing, this is going to be the greatest video ever.' It was just a list of ideas. The band makes all the decisions together, but Michael Stipe is obviously the voice, so I said to Michael, 'Look, I'm going to do this thing. I'm just going to put a bunch of ideas down that come to me when I listen to your music, a few things in there that I wanted to do

What makes a great music video?

"It's the creation of the best visual interpretation of the song that's true to the artist's vision."

—Brett Ratner, Director

"A terrific video for me is something that conveys a response, whether you're laughing, or you're astonished by it for some reason, or you're sad, or whatever. [It's] kind of the same reason why people go to movies. They need to be entertained and want to be told a story. I think once you get that reaction out of people, that's a great video."

—Joe Hahn, Director

when I was a film student that I never did, and you just mark off the ones that you want to do and the ones you don't want to do.' He faxed it back with lines through some ideas, and then that became the video, which was "Radio Song." And I was just like a pig in shit, because I was so happy. One, this is a band I really was excited about filming. Two, I could really talk to Michael Stipe directly.... And it worked out really, really well, and that just broke the ice. They came back to me four or five times after that, as well. Their music generally moves me; something comes out of me, and they're able to make me ten times better than I would be able to be on my own."

Director Matthew Rolston is frequently called on to collaborate with an artist and record label. He has developed a unique visual sense by maintaining a parallel career as a highly acclaimed fashion photographer. He explains how diverse each collaborative experience is saying, "Lenny Kravitz, who I've known for years and done various videos and still shoots for, calls

me up personally on the phone and says, 'I want you to do this for me, and I don't know what I want. Call me back.' Now, he's not calling a dozen directors. He literally called me. Contrast that with a young artist—I'm not going to name any names—but someone young that's more of a, shall we say, artist that was created by a committee. Now, that's valid; that's not a value judgment. I might not hear from that artist at all. I might talk to management and to the label head, not even video commissioners—who have various, very powerful ideas that they want for that artist. They might have a storyline involved or a narrative of some kind. Or they might want me to look at the album package that's already in existence and play off of that visual, which someone else created, on some level. And then that artist might show up on the day of the shoot and say, 'OK, what am I doing?' I try to talk to everybody involved that has a voice in the thing, and then write something that I feel will satisfy all."

USING MOVIES AS INSPIRATION

Many music video directors aspire to directing films, and many more have studied filmmaking. Therefore, it's no surprise that a lot of directors favor cinematic sources to reference. "Ben Folds Five was an interesting one," director Kevin Bray (Whitney Houston's "One of Those Days" and Jessica Simpson & Nick Lachey's "Where You Are") remarks on how he came up with the video treatment for Ben Folds Five's "Brick" video. "That came from *Powers of Ten*, the Eames movie. A microscopic look at us becomes a whole other universe. It just kind of endlessly loops and loops and loops. And that had something to do with the idea of conception, because the song was about a girl, and a boy taking his girl to get an abortion on Boxing Day. I used images of water and the boy and his girl playing in the water. The video represents a whole bunch of different kinds of abstractions of the womb."

Directors don't only reference their own favorite films; sometimes they reference a favorite film of the artist for whom they're creating the video. Bray used a scene from one of the artist Meshell Ndegeocello's favorite movies, Bertrand Blier's *Going Places*, when he wrote the treatment for (and subsequently made) the video for "Leviticus: Faggot." Bray was taken by the image of a bunch of teens hanging out on the street by the office of DNA, the production company to which he was signed. "Every day you kind of saw them down there," Bray says. "I probably had my chin in my hands and was just listening to the song on my Walkman and staring down on the street. The song was called 'Leviticus: Faggot,' and it was about a boy who had been beaten up because of being gay. There is a scene in Blier's movie where a group of guys are racing around, and one is pushing the other one in a grocery cart, just like grown men playing with abandon, which you never see. Starting with that image and taking off from there, a bunch of images just started to come together: a group of boys in tank tops in Santa Monica; somebody pouring a bottle of Evian over their heads on the street on the corner of Santa Monica and Vine. The theme of Meshell's song and the scene from Blier's movie were the inspiration for that video."

USING BOOKS AND COMIC BOOKS AS INSPIRATION

It's common knowledge that throughout history, books have influenced music, theater, painting, and certainly filmmaking. Needless to say, they also serve as an important inspiration for music videos. Discussing his work on the band Blink 182's "Always" video, director Joseph Kahn says, "I love reading pop physics books, and one of the pop physics books I was reading [at the time of the video treatment] was talking about string theory. In order to explain certain theories of the universe, they had to come up with a whole new form of math, explaining how the universe probably works on eleven dimensions. The thing is, you can't see the other seven dimensions because they're folded into space. That made me start thinking about how filmmaking is this sort of perception of four dimensions on a two-dimensional screen that moves within a three-dimensional space: three dimensions of space and one dimension of time, like relativity. So I was thinking, can I hint at another dimension, can there be an extra dimension, a fifth dimension, a sixth dimension, whatever? And by going into that extra dimension, can you come up with a solution that you can't do in four dimensions. I just kept seeing this sort of twisting object in my head, and I came up with this whole idea of doing this split screen, where the top is in the present, the middle is in the past, and the bottom one is in the future, all represented by one person that splits into three. So that's what that video was all about. Ultimately, when people watch it, they're not going to be thinking 'five-dimensional edit'; they're going to be thinking 'That's a cool video about a girl cheating on her guy.'"

Comic books serve as one of the biggest inspirations for cinema. Like comic books, video treatments must convey the visual sense of what the writer, or, in our case, the director, sees. Storyboards, which are sometimes attached to treatments, offer the same kind of graphic panel treatment as a comic book. Not surprisingly, a lot of directors love comics. Director Joe Hahn, also the DJ in the band Linkin Park, says, "I'm a big anime fan. I don't want to shoot similar styles of performance all the time, so I try to come up with a lot of different things to do. I think the first animated video I did was CG, [computer graphics] for [Linkin Park's] "Point of Authority" on the remix album. It showed the band performing as our decapitated heads on top of poles with robotic parts stuck to our heads, kind of moving around. For [Linkin Park's] "Breaking the Habit" [inspired entirely by anime] I had a story in mind. I wanted it to be about people, how all these people relate, and how people have problems. But in the end, there's always something you can do about it, as long as you strive for something better. I really wanted to have this climactic feel to it. The video ultimately builds up to us playing on the roof in a fence. That's kind of like our way of saying this is our song that we made, but it's also our way of saying, 'We hear what you're saying; we understand what you're saying. Even though we can't deal with each other on an individual basis, these are things that everyone goes through.' A lot of it's under the surface."

Do you need a great song to make a great video?

"Yeah, you can have a great video without a great song. Happens all the time. Remember the song 'Video Killed the Radio Star'? The video will propel the song all the time. I think marketing and pumping imagery into twelve-year olds is going to aid a song, regardless. I'm not saying it's a good way. What are you marketing? You have to be responsible."
—Sanaa Hamri, Director

"No, often our videos will create record sales for even the worst song."
—Dean Karr, Director

DEVELOPING CREATIVE ROUTINES

Many directors come up with ideas through routines of invention and brainstorming they've created for themselves. With the demanding schedule that most directors face when creating treatments—often they turn in three to four treatments a week during the weeks they don't have a shoot—it's only natural that some have developed a means of putting treatments together so that daily stress won't affect their work. Although it helps to keep their treatments in perspective, they must then find ways to prevent their vision from going stale. Veteran director Nigel Dick (Sheryl Crow and Sting's "Always on Your Side" and Nickelback's "Savin' Me") explains, "You get into a routine of coming up with methods of inventing ideas constantly. It becomes a process that becomes a technique rather than the way you do it initially, which is purely emotional and purely related to what your ideals are and where you want to go. There comes a point where it'll become rather like a factory, like a sausage machine. You know, the first sausage you make is fantastic; it never tasted so good. Then you want to make a better one, and the third one is awful, so you find out how not to make an awful one. Then, eventually, you start turning out these perfectly formed sausages, and then after a while you start realizing they all look the same. So you have to start putting in different ingredients. And, of course, as creative people, we're never supposed to make the same sausage twice."

Originality, balanced with what will get the video into heavy rotation on MTV, becomes crucial. Certainly, a director must cultivate an awareness of what's hot in the video universe, knowing what they want to do as much as what they *don't* want to do. After all, directors won't get anywhere if they just copy successful directors such as Mark Romanek, Michel Gondry, or Spike Jonze.

"I turn off all the lights," says McG (Sugar Ray's "When It's Over" and Smash Mouth's "All Star"), "and I listen to the music over and over until the images just start to come. And then I begin to pound it out, talk about it, and be very cognizant of what's on MTV and what's been done, trying not to be repetitive yet also go into new places. I try to do my own thing."

Location also has an effect on the director's treatment routine. Directing team Dayton Faris (Red Hot Chili Peppers' "The Zephyr Song" and Macy Gray's "Sexual Revolution") tend to come up with their treatment ideas while in the car. They credit the movement of the automobile. "Driving in our car," begins Valerie Faris, "listening to the song . . ."

" . . . over and over," Jonathan Dayton completes the thought. "There's something about being in the car and having the world move around that prompts our best work . . . Just getting out of your normal surroundings and feeling the world."

BEING SPONTANEOUS

Quite often, directors come up with ideas for videos from everyday life, as director Kevin Bray did when he juxtaposed the guys hanging out on Santa Monica and Vine with the film *Going Places*. His work with Whitney Houston draws on down-to-earth imagery enhanced with drama. He said of the video for Houston's "Heartbreak Hotel," "I had an idea of a woman needing to shed the remnants of a relationship, its memories and all its accoutrements. I thought of the fur coat, an act of obscenity and opulence befitting of South Beach and Whitney. And so the image of the coat tossed in the sea came to mind. It seemed to say everything I was hearing in the song. A simple through-line, NYC and Miami, a hotel room, an act of letting go, cleaning house—so to speak. Looking back, it was the visualization of my fantasy for Whitney. It was about her getting real, loosing the diva persona and getting naked . . . So that image of her throwing the coat away, that's how that started, and I worked backward from there.

"Burberry made this beautiful camel leather jacket," Bray added about another wardrobe-inspired video treatment for Whitney Houston, which turned into the video for "My Love Is Your Love." "So there was fashion involved—like what does that character remind

A Great Video Treatment:

- Has a strong point of view and leaves the reader with a strong idea of how the director plans to execute his or her vision.
- Describes something memorable, such as a strong hook, cool visual gags, or a compelling narrative.
- Has the ability to shape an artist's identity or even change it.
- Is concise and direct; the reader can sum it up in one or two sentences.
- Includes the band or artist's creativity.
- Includes the record label's concern about sales.
- Presents a great idea in an understandable format.
- Ensures the vision carries the song.
- Falls within budget.
- Is original and unexpected.
- Connects with the song and affects the reader.
- Delivers the feeling of the song instead of solely translating the song's lyrics.
- Contains visual references that help the reader see exactly what the director wants to portray.

me of—and then it was just like this Pam Grier character in the blackout in New York wanders around in a camel leather jacket and comes across a car battery-lit party in the hood, and everybody's all copasetic."

WRITING THE TREATMENT

When writing a video treatment, the director must use words to get the idea for a music video across visually so that those reading it can see his or her vision. Treatments should be articulate, direct, concise, and have a point of view. The director needs to convey the idea of the video in such a definitive way that when it comes to actually making it, everyone can use the treatment as a written map to detail what the viewer will see onscreen as the song and video unfold.

"I think I've had so much success because when I delivered the video to the artist and the label, I did exactly what was in the treatment," says director Brett Ratner. "A treatment is not like a storyboard; it's not like a script, which is very specific with dialogue. It's a synopsis of what you want to do, but there are many interpretations of what you want to do. It's all in the director's head. I was very specific about spelling that out, so it's exactly what they wanted, what they knew they were getting."

"Writing treatments is really hard," director Marcos Siega says. "At least I think it is. I can have a great idea, but to sit down and communicate a concept on paper that anybody's going to understand and be able to see is not easy."

THE BASIC ELEMENTS

In general, American music videos contain the following elements, the knowledge of which can be very useful to new directors when writing a treatment:

- Narrative sequence (story) or *cut-a-way* shots—the interruption of a continuously-filmed action by inserting an image of something else that is usually followed by a cutback to the first action—that are intercut with the artist's performance
- Mixture of close-up, medium, and wide shots of the artist performing
- Two or more locations where the artist performs
- Two or more additional locations where the story or cut-a-ways are seen
- Two or more wardrobe changes for the artist

The basic elements above can be further broken down according to genre. Hip-hop, rap, and R&B artists tend to have their own approach that differs from that of rock or grunge bands. For instance, urban videos often feature "ghetto fabulous" elements, such as high-end cars, flashy wardrobe, and lots of "bling," whereas rock bands often downplay those elements or leave them out entirely. Videos for female artists are often beauty-driven, whereas that usually is not the case for male artists. There is always crossover among styles, and there are always exceptions—particularly in concept and gag videos—however, the basic elements of a video generally exist, no matter what the genre.

WHAT TO INCLUDE

The director needs to consider all of the details involved in his or her music video and clearly describe them in the treatment so that anyone can understand the idea. Some details a director might consider including are:

- Style or feeling the director wants to evoke
- How the artist will look, including wardrobe, make-up, hairstyle, and attitude
- The artist's performance style and how it fits in

to other details of the clip
• The story, if any, described in detail

Some directors time the song with a stopwatch, giving specific time frames to how the narrative or cut-a-ways will fit into the performance. In addition, some directors include quotes from the song in hopes the artist will be able to visualize the song and performing when reading the video treatment.

Interestingly, very few successful directors include the actual techniques they plan to use in the treatment. "You'll just scare away commissioners and artists," says director Joseph Kahn. "And that's not the point of doing music videos. No one wants to make a music video to test out a theoretical idea. People want you to do a video to sell more records."

CELEBRITIES

Some videos feature celebrities. Sometimes the actor has already hit his or her stride, and in some videos—like Bruce Springsteen's "Dancing In The Dark," for example—it helps make the actor's reputation, as it did for Courtney Cox. While the use of a famous actor could add to the selling power of the video, it behooves a director not to promise it. "All I wrote, essentially, was 'Let's get a great actress,'" recalled Samuel Bayer (Green Day's "Boulevard of Broken Dreams" and Nirvana's "Smells Like Teen Spirit") when creating the treatment for Melissa Etheridge's "Come to my Window" video. "Juliette Lewis had just done *Natural Born Killers*. She was hot. I wanted a girl that could emote and not go through that ridiculous music video kind of acting. She's obviously not a model, but she's an actress. I don't cast for the sake of a celebrity; I cast for somebody who's going to bring something to the part that you can't find with anybody else. And in the

case of Juliette, she was portraying a nervous breakdown in a mental hospital. You needed someone with depth.

"With Angelina Jolie," he added "I cast her in the Rolling Stones' "Anybody Seen My Baby" video right after she had done *Gia*. She had not won an Academy Award yet. She knocked out a bunch of stuff and was still relatively unknown, but someone had shown me her picture. I fell in love with her. She looked haunting. She had just shaved her head for *Gia*, but she was great. I didn't know she was going to be a huge star."

Generally, famous actors will only do a video for a famous and well-respected artist or band, or ones they know personally. Most directors will take the approach that Bayer describes above, casting a "really great actress" without giving specific names. Remember, the video treatment becomes part of the contract, and a director doesn't want to promise something that may be unattainable in the end.

VISUAL REFERENCES

Sometimes directors submit tear sheets, storyboards, or clips from movies as part of their treatments to serve as visual aids to help the reader see the idea. "There is nothing more frustrating than trying to relate a beautiful scenario to a group of people whose brains don't work that way and who sit at the table wondering what I just spoke about," director Dean Karr says. "Visuals do help, although I am careful not to take these visuals too literally, as I want everything I create to be special and my own."

For a new director who has not developed and established a style, visual references can introduce to a video commissioner exactly what the director envisions. An established director's reel will show the style of the director, which, in turn, helps the label and artist visualize the general style that the video will be.

TREATMENT WRITERS

Most directors write their own treatments, but some hire treatment writers. Directors who use the skills of treatment writers develop an idea for a video and then work with a writer who documents the director's thoughts in a cohesive manner. Some directors have started their careers as treatment writers or storyboard artists for other directors. Director Hype Williams ("Control Myself" by LL Cool J featuring Jennifer Lopez, and Pharrell's "Angel") hired Little X (Sean Paul's "Temperature," and "Pimpin' All Over the World" by Ludacris featuring Bobby Valentino) to draw his storyboards. Hype soon took Little X under his wing and nurtured his career. Now Little X ranks high among the established, popular, and well-regarded music video directors.

Other directors would not even consider hiring treatment writers. "I know a lot of directors are more sort of visuals driven, and their ideas aren't the most important thing to them," says director Marc Klasfeld. "I mean, I just think that everybody does something different with directing, which is cool. But I'm very into the treatment writing and the idea process. Quite honestly, it's the most fun part for me."

Nigel Dick's Seven Rules of Treatment Writing

Prolific director Nigel Dick suggests the following rules to follow when writing a video treatment:

- Make sure you know how you're going to shoot the video.
- Make sure it is possible to shoot within the budget.
- Make sure it's right for the artist's image.
- Make sure it can be broadcast on MTV.
- Make sure it's right for you—something that you can execute well and be creatively excited about and proud of.
- Make sure it hasn't been done before and that it's not boring.
- Make sure it's your best idea.

"I always wrote my own treatments," director McG says. "I never once had anyone write a treatment because I couldn't really successfully wrap my head around what someone else would write. It would have been a lot easier, and I would have been a lot more productive, but I couldn't do it."

WHAT COMMISSIONERS LOOK FOR IN A TREATMENT

Video commissioners feel that a treatment must be well written and expressive, as well as be suited to the band and the marketplace. The treatment should come alive on the page, and the reader should be able to visualize it.

"Treatments are very subjective," says Sabrina Rivera, director of music video production at Sony BMG Music Entertainment. "I like people who are creative, who really have an idea for the song. There are a lot of treatments that are just mumbo-jumbo, a whole lot of writing that says nothing. And I think the treatments that really stand out are the ones where you're like, 'You have a clear idea of what you want to do here, and you know how to write it and explain it in your writing.'"

"A good treatment has a beginning, a middle, and an end, and it images in the artist in a way that is going to compete in the marketplace," adds Danny Lockwood, vice president of video production at Sony BMG Music Entertainment. "It's just very clear about what's going to be on the screen, and not just a bunch of hyperbole that this is going to be a number one TRL video for six weeks."

"I want it to be very descriptive, so that the people who are reading it can fully grasp in their head what they're talking about," explains Universal Music Group's Nashville vice president of video production Retta Harvey Hatfield. "Sometimes concepts come in that are so vague you really can't get an idea, and they're never going to win."

Several label executives stress simplicity and brevity in expressing the main idea of the video's concept. "To me, a good treatment has always been a treatment that is explained in a line or two," says Livia Tortolla, senior vice president of marketing and artist development at Atlantic Records. "Like if somebody sat across from you and said, 'Fatboy Slim's video for "Weapon of Choice" is 'Christopher Walken dancing through a hotel.' And I'm like, 'Okay, I get it.' It's very simple in terms of what actually happens and what it means."

Commissioners look for straightforward, descriptive treatments, not flowery or common buzzwords. "I like a treatment that isn't full of statements such as 'We're going to make a really great clip and make the artist look glamorous like she's never looked before,' or 'The band will look raw and edgy, and I will take them to the next level,'" groaned independent video commissioner Jeff Panzer. "All these clichés! A good treatment does not have to be long. It can be two to three paragraphs. All I need to know is what the video will look like from the time you fade up until the time you fade down. Sometimes less is more, especially now with the economy of this business. Directors overwrite, and you tend to lose a lot of things on the shoot day that you were promised in the treatment. Then people get let down and don't understand why because they weren't at the shoot."

Most of the commissioners welcome visual references. "I love a concept that comes with visual aids," Harvey Hatfield says. "A lot of people are making it a package now; it's not just a one-page piece of paper. It's a couple of pages, and then they'll have a video reference or a photo reference, and that really helps people understand how something's going to look."

"With so many people involved," adds Devin Sarno, vice president of visual content at Warner Brothers Records, "I think you have to make things as clear as possible."

"It's helpful," Janet Kleinbaum, senior vice president of marketing and video production at Jive Records agrees, "whether it's the way they're thinking about it in terms of lighting, or styling, or location."

Having an original idea doesn't hurt either. "Treatments have to have something fresh and inventive," adds Lockwood.

"There has to be some sort of spark of originality," Harvey Hatfield insists. "I don't want to see the same old same thing every time I get a concept. I want a twist. I want something new or original."

It also helps if the director understands the song from all the angles, such as what the artist means to say, what the record company needs to see, and how the artists gets imaged and marketed. Lorin Finkelstein from RCA Records says, "The director obviously has to listen to that song and listen to those lyrics and have a genuine understanding about what this singer or song is about. I really truly feel it comes back to having things that kids get and understand. We don't need to break new ground every single time. [We need] the simplest possible thing that works. When you're reading a video treatment and you're watching videos, you're like, 'God, they're all the same.' And you're like, 'Well, wait a minute. They *are* all the same . . .' First you're like, 'I never want to make a music video where all the kids are jumping around the backyard, riding around their half-pipe and jumping off the roof into the pool.' But wait a minute. That's what fucking kids do on Saturday night. So why wouldn't you want to do that? It's taking those things into account. Coming up with things where kids can identify with them. And themes and ideas that everyone's experienced, or wish they could experience. And then some sort of little twist there."

CHAPTER FIVE
THE BUDGETING PROCESS

The director's treatment can be considered the creative map for the music video, and the budget—also called the bid—serves as the financial map. This cost analysis, in concert with the treatment, becomes the basis of the contractual agreement between the record label and the production company, stating clearly and concisely what will be produced and how much it will cost.

The schedule also plays a major role in a video's budget. Although the contract with the record label includes the dates of the video shoot, the schedule of the shoot day(s) is determined by the director's treatment and the budget. The treatment, the budget, and the schedule interrelate. All the various aspects of the treatment must tally with the financial terms of the video, which in turn must correspond to the schedule, thus allowing everything to be translated from treatment to film. (This process is discussed in greater detail on page 157 in Chapter Eight.)

The producer has to fully understand and control all three components—the treatment, budget, and schedule—in order to have a successful video shoot. Therefore, the producer adds a basic time frame to the budget. The budget represents how many days of prepping, shooting, and wrapping out will be necessary, as well as how long each of those days will be. A second shoot day can often double a budget, so all the parties involved must understand, and agree, at the beginning of the process to what constitutes an affordable and achievable schedule.

During the process of creating a budget, everyone involved in making the video works to keep the video's creative idea as close to the original concept as possible. The label attempts to keep the budget as low as it can, certainly no more than the amount initially quoted; the director tries to maintain the artistic integrity and vision of the video; and the executive producer seeks to ensure that both the record label and director are happy without putting the production company at too much risk, since it generally falls to the production company to cover any additional costs if they bid too low for the video project and the creative concept is compromised or in danger of not being achieved.

GENERATING THE BUDGET

The producer, the executive producer, or the head of production creates the budget for a music video. Occasionally, a "bidder" is hired to create the budget for the music video. A bidder researches the costs and creates the bid—the budget—that is then approved and handed off to the proper individuals who will bring the job to fruition. The services of a bidder are frequently used for commercial productions, although not as much for music video productions, primarily due to budgetary restrictions. Regardless of whether the producer creates the budget, he or she is almost always involved, because it is the producer who will ultimately be held accountable in the end.

If directors have producers that they regularly use, the producer will most often create the budget, since he or she is familiar with how the director works. The producer knows which people to hire, what equipment to rent, and how much it will all cost based on past experiences of working with the same director. A key element of a producer's job involves knowing the value of everyone and everything used in a video and then applying the costs to the budget.

"The company I work with, DNA, usually has producers do the bids," says producer Caleb Dewart. "Many companies have a bidding process more like commercial companies, where there is a bidder. Once the job is awarded, it's handed to a producer. I think that given the complexity of jobs and the severe financial limitations of jobs, it's a mistake to have someone other than the producer—who is ultimately responsible for everything—bid the job."

Executive producer Helen Cavallo takes a different approach. "My head of production and I usually make the budget," she says, "but will consult with the director and their producer to go over and make sure we've covered everything." Veteran executive producer Catherine Finkenstaedt (Sugar Ray's "Fly," directed by Mc G and George Michael's "Flawless," directed by Jake Scott) says, "Generally, I create the music video budgets and then send them to the producers to check them before I send them to the label."

Before signing off on the production company's initial budget prior to its submission to the record label, the producer checks to make sure that certain production details do not get left out and that no one has made any glaring mistakes. "I will often do the first draft and then tweak it with the executive producer, or vice-versa," says producer Rachel Curl. "Once in a while the EP does the budget without having a producer attached before the job is awarded. In this case I always review the budget before I accept a job to make sure I feel comfortable with the way it was bid."

"Most companies will do a bid and send it in to the producer to add or lose some figures before they submit it to the client," agrees producer William Green. "At the end of the day, the producer will be held responsible for that budget, and even more so if they approved it before it went in."

While not a common practice, some record labels ask for budgets along with the treatment, hoping to get a clear picture, from the very beginning, of what a video project will cost. This protects the video commissioner from being placed in a tough position and guards against the possibility of an artist getting attached to a treatment that's unaffordable. "Sometimes I have bid projects after the creative [treatment] has been awarded," producer Oualid Mouaness explains, "and sometimes a project is awarded on ascertaining that the creative is executable for a set target dollar amount."

However, most video commissioners can read a treatment and know whether a director and producer can accomplish shooting the video for the allotted budget without having an actual bid in hand. Therefore, they generally wait to ask for a budget until they are intent on hiring a specific director.

Just as the commissioner may ask a director to do a series of treatment rewrites, the commissioner might ask the biding production company to submit multiple budgets. The gamble, once again, is that neither the director nor the production company (nor the freelance producer, if that's the person creating the bid) will get paid for any of their prep work unless they are actually hired to do the project.

THE BUDGET'S FORMAT: THE POINT ZERO BID

The basic format used for music video budgets is a specialized eight-page Microsoft Excel spreadsheet called the AICP FILM PRODUCTION COST SUMMARY. The Association of Independent Commercial Producers (AICP) exclusively represents the interests of American companies that specialize in producing commercials in various media—film, video, and computer—for advertisers and agencies. Although they don't represent the fast-growing music video community, there is significant crossover between music video and commercials. In addition, since videos and commercials are both short-form film productions, they have similar budgeting needs.

Jay Wakefield, the head of production at a prominent Los Angeles-based production company called Oil Factory Inc., tailored the AICP bid, creating the Point Zero bid format as a commercial and music video template in 1993. "It was only recently customized specifically for music videos and the new union agreements with IATSE [The International Alliance of Theatrical Stage Employees, Moving Picture Technicians, Artists and Allied Crafts of the United States, its Territories and Canada] and teamsters," explains Wakefield. "The original commercial version of Point Zero still exists. I sold both versions of the program to Media Services along with the copyright." The Point Zero bid format is an Excel template that includes extensive logs that allow the user to see where the money goes. By plugging numbers into the budget, the program transfers the numbers to the necessary logs so the work doesn't have to be manually repeated for each different spreadsheet. The Point Zero bid allows for double entry bookkeeping, and the user does not need to have a degree in accounting to create it. The most updated version

of the Point Zero bid format consists of the following elements:

- Main Budget
  - Top Sheet and Production Cost Summary
- Reports and Logs
  - Wrap Report
  - Job Wrap Checklist
  - Travel and Living Detail
  - Calendar
  - Union Classifications and IATSE/AICP Rates
  - Union Rates and Benefits Specifications
  - Job Report
  - Purchase Order Log
  - Petty Cash Log
  - Payroll Log
  - Sales Log
  - Credit Card Log

THE MAIN BUDGET

This is the main budgeting document that will be most utilized and referred to throughout the project. The eight page Top Sheet and Production Cost Summary allows the production manager and producer to keep a running, working budget alongside the actual budget in order to continually compare the cost of each line item, as well as the total.

Top Sheet and Production Cost Summary

The top sheet and production cost summary of the Point Zero bid runs eight pages long, and includes the following:

- The top sheet summarizes the estimated production costs; it is the cover page of the full budget.
- The second page lists the fees for the preproduction and wrap crews (separate grip and electric crews who work on only the wrap of the video and not the actual production), as well as their predicted overtime and their payroll fee percentage.

- The third page lists the fees for the shooting crew.
- The fourth page includes the following categories:
  - Preproduction and Wrap Costs
  - Location and Travel Expenses
  - Special Props and Related Expenses
- The fifth page breaks down the set building costs listing the following categories:
  - Studio Rental and Expenses
  - Art Department Labor
  - Art Department Expenses
- The sixth page enumerates the actual shooting expenses:
  - Equipment and Related Expenses
  - Film Stock, Develop and Print
  - Miscellaneous Costs
  - Director/Creative Fees
- The seventh page lists the talent and talent-related expenses.
- The eighth page contains all postproduction expenses:
  - Postproduction labor
  - Postproduction expenses

REPORTS AND LOGS

When costs are inserted into the main budget, they are automatically transferred to the corresponding logs. The reports help keep track of the details of the project in a consistent, cohesive manner.

The Wrap Report

The wrap report is a one-page spreadsheet that summarizes the basics of the project at the end of the final video wrap. It lists:

- Amount of days and the dates of each for pre-production (Additional detail includes which days were build days, which were strike days, which were pre-light days, as well as which were in a studio and which were on location)
- Locations

- Total film shot
- Total overages
- Key individuals contact information (producer, production manager, production coordinator, and art coordinator)
- Talent contracts
- Outstanding deposit checks
- Accidents, injuries, losses, damages
- Outstanding petty cash
- Props and wardrobe to be sold
- Comments

The Job Wrap Checklist

The production team submits the job wrap checklist to inform the head of production, at a glance, exactly what is included in the wrap and what is left outstanding. It helps create conformity of the wrap book and reminds the production team of all necessary paperwork to be provided and approved.

The Travel and Living Detail

The travel and living detail is a separate page that breaks down the travel costs of each crew member. Since travel has become common in music video production and the record labels rarely pay a mark-up on these costs, the budget separates the following expenses from the rest of the costs:

• Airfare

• Per diem, which refers to the hotel cost and allowances calculated per day for meals and incidental travel related expenses

• Ground transportation, which refers to car services or taxis

The Calendar

Included in the budget is a basic calendar that that tracks the time frame of every aspect of the production process. Keeping a running calendar helps avoid overlapping appointments and scheduling mishaps.

The Union Classifications and IATSE/AICP Rates

The IATSE/AICP rates outlines each crew member's union affiliation and minimum wage rate requirement according to union guidelines. It details the hourly rate for an eight- and twelve-hour day, and a weekly schedule.

The Union Rates and Benefits Specifications

"Union classifications are set up so that if someone changes the description of a line in the budget, it can still be coded to the union class—for example, the wardrobe assistant would have the union classification of second wardrobe or third wardrobe," explains Wakefield. "When a budget is at tier level four, IATSE crew rates are based on the commercial AICP rates, so there needs to be a reference to these rates in the budget." Each tier represents a different budget level, and there are shifts in how it is governed by the union at each level.

The Job Report

The job report, calculated from the numbers in the main budget, offers quick access to key budget numbers:

• Reconciliation Report: the difference between the logs and the actual budget

• Mark-up: the fee costs as a percentage on the following delineated items:
  • Production Costs (A–K)
  • Director's Fees (L)
  • Talent and Talent Costs (M and N)
  • Editorial Costs (O and P)
  • Total of all of the above

• Insurance: calculates the insurance costs as a percentage on the same categories as above

• Detail of Additional Billings: filled in by the producer and/or production manager on receiving approval from the video commissioner/record company of any overages for which they agree to pay

• Internal Notes: filled in by the producer and/or production manager

• Rate Converter: to convert monies to US dollars for international projects

The Purchase Order Log

The purchase order log accounts for all purchase orders (PO), including:

• Purchase order number

• Payee

• Line number to which the purchase correlates in the main budget

• Date

• Amount spent

• Brief description of the item or service purchased

The Petty Cash Log

The petty cash log lists all the people who received petty cash or spent money from their own pockets and need to be reimbursed. Each person who dips into the petty cash will have itemized his or her own expenditure. This log combines all of the expenses, organizing them into one comprehensive breakdown of where the cash was spent on the video project, listing the outflow as it relates to the budget line items. The spreadsheet automatically calculates the figures and inserts the costs into the main budget.

The Payroll Log

The payroll log lists how much each crew member gets paid for the project, and includes:

- Payee (crew member's name)
- Line number to which a crew member's position correlates in the main budget
- PO
- Union Rates and Benefits Calculator
- Location Code
- Day Rate Based
- Hourly Minimum
- Daily Minimum
- Total Benefits
- Percentage of Benefits
- Percentage of Payroll Taxes/ Pension and Welfare (PT/P&W)
- Fixed PT/P&W
- Overtime
- Hourly Rate
- Days
- Day Rate
- Number of overtime hours and whether they are based on:
  - Time and a Half
  - Double Time
  - Triple Time
  - Quadruple Time

- Miscellaneous Taxable Costs
- Miscellaneous Non-taxable Costs
- Total Straight Time
- Total Overtime
- Actual due to the individual
- Description of the role that person played on the production
- Total Pension and Welfare (P&W) calculation

The Sales Log

The sales log is a listing of items sold, or deposits refunded, after the completion of the project. Often the production team will resell film, wardrobe, or props to defray production costs and reduce overall expenditure. This log includes:

- Payer
- Line number the item purchased corresponds to in the main budget
- Notes about the transaction
- Sale ID number
- Actual amount spent
- Brief description of the item or service purchased
- Total of all sales

The Credit Card Log

The credit card log is a listing of all purchases made on a credit card, including:

- Payee
- Line number the item purchased corresponds to on the main budget
- Credit card ID number
- Date the purchase was made
- PO
- Actual amount spent
- Brief description of the item or service purchased
- Total of all credit card purchases

THE MAJOR ELEMENTS OF THE BUDGET

Music video budgets have two major components: (1) the expenses that are standard percentages on any video project and (2) the expenses of the creative elements detailed in the treatment of the specific video project.

STANDARD PERCENTAGE EXPENSES

The expenses that are standard percentages involved in making a music video include:

- Production Company
- Director
- Producer
- Pension and Welfare (P&W)
- Insurance

A creative producer can find some wiggle room in each of these costs, although they are, more or less, fixed. While the record label might question the production company's fee or ask the production company to give them a reduced rate on a given project, the label rarely questions the costs of pension and welfare and insurance.

"All budgets vary due to all treatments being different," explains producer William Green. "However, there are the standard amounts that remain the same, such as director's fee, ten percent; producer's fee, five percent; and production company's fee, fifteen percent. It would be a great day, though, when the fees are actually based on the cost of the video. Most fees are based on at least twenty-five percent less than the actual budget."

The Production Company

Contrary to the overall rise of all costs in the global economy, it is not uncommon for the rates in the highly competitive music video business to drop. That said, although the standard mark-up for production companies today is fifteen percent of the budget, production companies often throw in part of their mark-up either in the beginning of the budgeting phase or at various other stages of the project, as financial considerations demand. This is especially true if the overall consensus is that the creative of a specific project is particularly good. Generally speaking, an owner, partner, or executive producer—and sometimes the head of production—in a production company has the authority to reduce the production company's mark-up.

Many executive producers willingly make less profit for a few reasons: First, it's necessary in order to compete in the music video world these days. Second, the record business frequently contracts smaller, lesser-known bands that don't have a lot of money to spend on a video, even though they generate a lot of excitement and attention in the music industry. Third, production companies often see music videos as a vehicle to launch a director into other audiovisual media, such as commercials or features—both of which generally offer a higher profit margin.

Often, in order to land a video project, a director will submit his or her treatment to the record label, despite knowing that the production company cannot realize the treatment without offering up a portion of its mark-up. "It is pretty standard, now, that the production company will not receive its full fifteen percent mark-up," says executive producer Doug Kluthe. "I really think it's more about trying to save your fee and not becoming an underwriter for the production. Many times in order to land the project, a large idea has been written by the director, and there is no way the job can be produced without the production company offering up a portion of its mark-up. This is usually agreed upon among the principles of the company (partner, head of production, EP, director) prior to submitting the idea to the label."

Production companies will put as much as possible into videos with a smaller budget by artists with a big buzz in order to create similar buzz for their director. The money has to come from somewhere. Frequently, this will mean dropping the mark-up to eight or ten percent—or less—on a project.

The production company's reputation is based on its directors. Using the philosophy of "penny smart, pound foolish," production companies tend to drop their fees to help build a director's career, keeping in mind the director's future earnings. "We all work as a team, the director, myself, and the production company, to decide what is best for the director/production company in terms of slashing the production fee," says director's representative Tommy LaBuda. "The state of the music video business today has forced production companies to do things you wouldn't have even considered five years ago. It's a shark tank. At the end of the day, it's up to the production company to decide how much of their markup they are willing to cut in order to book a project. Each project has to be assessed on a project-by-project basis; some offer bigger benefits for future work."

Production companies will even go so far as to "buy a job" for a director's reel by not making any money on the particular video project, or even spending money to properly produce it. This happens often when a company is building a new, lesser-known director's career. Thus, a production company will gamble with a particular director's creative ability and vision by compromising the profit on immediate video jobs in order to move additional money from the budg-

Advice for Aspiring Directors

"The best thing to do always is just to work. Work begets work, and you reach a critical mass. There's no one piece that's going to make you. What you need to do is just work and try to get your work out there so that people see it. I've always felt that's the most important thing."

—Mark Kohr, Director

"Just go and shoot stuff. Of course, now it's so much easier than it ever was because of digital technology. It's more important to get a feel of how images go with music and how editing goes with music. In fact, I think how you edit a music video is much more important than what you shoot, to be honest, if you had to make a choice between the two. Because I think you can make a really interesting music video with found footage, footage that you steal. Whereas if you come up with an amazing concept, but you don't have the money to shoot it and you don't know how to cut it to the music—even if you do get the money—it just lies there like a dead dog. For me, I get excited when I see young filmmakers who just go out and shoot stuff, and they edit it and maybe even build up a relationship with a brand new band. How else do you do it? Do you wait until you've got half a million dollars from No Doubt or something? I don't think so."

—Peter Care, Director

et—money that might normally be profit for the company—to the screen, thus increasing the production value.

By deferring some of the profit from production early in a director's career, the production company hopes that down the road (1) the director will be so desirable that there will be no need to decrease budgets to land good projects; (2) the quality of the director's clients will grow in stature, and the budgets will steadily increase; and (3) the director will use music videos as a mechanism to hone his or her filmmaking skills, with the goal of eventually moving into commercials or feature films, which are both more lucrative ventures.

"There isn't a lot of money in music videos nowadays," says Doug Kluthe, "but they still are great vehicles to break a director into other mediums, such as commercials or features." However, there is a risk involved in building a director within this capacity. "The investment in a director's career from the production company side needs to be mutually beneficial, because directors don't stay with one company," says executive producer Catherine Finkenstaedt. "Production companies need to be shrewd when investing in developing directors, especially in the current economic climate of the industry."

The Director

Like the gamble that production companies make for talent, directors also occasionally forego portions, or their entire standard ten percent fee, to put more of their creative vision onto the screen. Directors generally recognize that by throwing a bit more money at the video on the front end of their careers, they sometimes can make a video visually stronger, which can later lead to bigger and better videos—with bigger and better budgets.

"I have been involved in projects where the director threw in part of his or her ten percent fee," reveals Catherine Finkenstaedt. "When I submit a budget on a job, it's done in collaboration with a producer and director, and we all agree on the parameters from a treatment-bidding process. Sometimes, once preproduction is well under way, there's an enormous creative impact on a location, or something else where something unseen happens, and putting more money into a job is reasonable. In a situation like this, I'll often split the cost with the directors, meaning that they take part of the payment from their fee, and the company will take part from our fee. However, I do expect directors to take responsibility for their own decisions. For instance, I always have directors sign off on budgets before submitting them to the label. If a director agrees to 8,000 feet of film, once we're over that, due to choices the director has made, I expect the director to help pay for the additional film. If the director personally amends his or her treatment, and it has a negative economic impact, we discuss sharing the responsibility with him or her. Music video is a director-run medium. Thus, they should learn to be financially responsible as well. Plus, it helps them down the line, because they will be held responsible in all other film mediums, such as feature films."

The Producer

Traditionally, the producer earns five percent of the below-the-line expenses of the budget. However, due to the drop in video budgets, the basis for the producer's fee has shifted as well. In other words, producers nowadays do the same amount of work for less money. Since producers don't reap the same kind of prestige from creating a music video that the director might, they have much less incentive to throw in part of their fees to increase the production value, meaning that production companies and directors—who might put in all, or part, of their profit from the video venture—don't expect it. It is becoming more common for the producer's rate to be based on a commercial scale day rate, similar to a member of the crew, rather than a percentage of the budget. Jay Wakefield says Oil Factory Inc. still pays the producer the five percent fee that traditionally covers preproduction through postproduction. Catherine Finkenstaedt, on the other hand, prefers to do a mix of both day rate for preproduction, shoot days, and wrap—she finds a day rate more palatable for lower budget projects—and a flat fee for postproduction supervising. This way, if the producer cannot stick around for post, there is a specific, built-in fee to hire a postproduction supervisor.

Pension and Welfare (P&W)

While the pension and welfare payment must appear as a line in the budget, the payroll company handles the actual dispersal of money to the P&W funds when they process the paperwork for the crew's payroll. Depending on the project, 27 to 34 percent of each crew member's remuneration goes to the P&W plan, which includes paying the payroll company per timecard. Before putting together a budget, a producer should speak with the production company's executive producer to confirm their standard percentage of P&W to include.

"P&W can vary greatly, depending on if the crew is union; whether they are working in an IATSE position or a teamsters position; where the job is shooting, Los Angeles, New York, etc.; and what tier level the budget is working in," explains head of production Jay Wakefield. "P&W percentages range from twenty-seven percent in

Los Angeles to thirty-four percent in New York," says Catherine Finkenstaedt.

Insurance

Insurance typically accounts for 3.5 to 6 percent of a video's overall budget, depending on the production company. As previously explained, the percentages are based on only certain aspects of the budget, namely line items A through K, not the entire budget. Established production companies have annual insurance policies. The fees for the specific policy are based on projections of their gross income, the number of claims they've had, and other factors, depending upon the individual insurer and company being insured. At the end of each year, the insurer audits the production company to learn its gross income. They use that figure as the basis for the next year's insurance fee. The annual income variation is the cause of the percentage of insurance charged per project—the 3.5 to 6 percent, which accounts for what they'll pay for their insurance policy—to fluctuate from company to company.

About fifty percent of the time, the production company uses its own insurance policy for productions. The other fifty percent of the time, the record label has the production company use their insurance policy for the specific video project.

"Atlantic Records," independent music commissioner Jill Kaplan explains, "maintains an insurance policy which covers video shoots." As labels have merged and become larger over the past several years, this has become more common. Should the record label agree to insure the project, all of the insurance certificates issued for the specific shoot (as explained on page 161 in Chapter Eight) will come directly from the record label's insurer on the label's policy. These certificates show all of the vendors as additionally insured including the production company. Since the production company is not using their own insurance, they don't need to report it to their insurer, and, consequently, it eliminates the need to bill 3.5 to 6 percent for the cost of insurance in the budget. The producer simply leaves the cost of insurance in the budget at zero.

"The production companies in the past did this for me if it was cost effective," adds Nicole Ehrlich from Geffen Records, "but now we cover the insurance for the project, because as a big corporation we get exceptional rates, and I rather have the extra money saved go on the screen."

CREATIVE COSTS

The costs of the creative elements of a budget depend on what the treatment calls for, as well as the demands of the artist and the label. These costs are much harder to pin down than the standard expenses based on percentages. Consequently, the producer must carefully research the costs of the materials that will go into realizing the creative concept of the video. This involves calling potential vendors and crew; determining the needs of the director, the commissioner, and the artist's management; and clearing everything through the executive producer. To put together a realistic budget, the producer must be fully aware of every element and challenge involved, and must be able to answer any questions about particular costs as they arise.

"After a certain point, producers get good at knowing how much stuff costs: how much trucks cost to rent, how much cameras cost, how much lunch and breakfast cost," says producer Caleb Dewart. "It's important to really understand how things are going to be executed, or else you can get into serious trouble—especially financially."

Treatment Realization

As previously noted, the producer uses the treatment as the main guide when developing a budget. To ensure that a budget encompasses the treatment's full vision and won't be depleted, the producer must understand what it takes to commit all aspects of the treatment to the screen and assign realistic dollar amounts to the various elements. The treatment is a map, defining what the final product will be. For example, if the video treatment calls for a "slick, glistening city street," the producer will want to ask the director if a street will need to be wet down. If so, the costs of wetting down a city street must be incorporated into the budget. If the treatment calls for a rainy night, it is imperative that money be allotted in the budget for renting the equipment to make rain, such as a water truck and crane—as well as lighting and lifts or cranes for the lights. Additionally, it's feasible that more grip trucks will have to be rented to deliver the extra lights to set, and money will have to be budgeted for this cost. Every detail of the treatment must be taken into consideration and translated into its cost.

Another key element that must be kept in mind when translating a treatment into dollars and cents is that a video treatment is subjective. A treatment that calls for "several hot women" is wide open for interpretation. "Several hot women" means one thing in a rap video, but may mean something completely different in a heavy metal video. In light of this, it's extremely important that the producer and the director completely understand each other in order to budget the video correctly. Just how many women does the director mean by "several"? What does "hot" mean to him or her? What should the women look like? Can the director use his or her female friends and thus reduce the budget by hiring some friends that may work for a free lunch, a few hundred dollars, and the kick of seeing themselves in a music video? Or does the director envision Ford models, which will add over a thousand dollars (per woman) to the budget in talent charges alone—not to mention all of the amenities that an A-list model might demand in her contract (private honeywagon, her own hair and make-up team)? We will look more closely at such examples in Casting Talent on page 103.

The main categories in the budget assigned a cost based solely on the interpretation and translation of the specific treatment (as opposed to being a standard percentage cost) include:

- Crew: How many people does the shoot require?
- Casting: Who, if anyone, other than the artist(s) will appear in the video?
- Art Department: Sets and props.
- Wardrobe & Glam Squad: Hair stylist, make-up artist, wardrobe stylist.
- Equipment: Lighting and grip, camera, playback.
- Film Costs: Type and amount of film stock.
- Location & Travel Expenses.
- Time/Scheduling: Including determination of pre-light, build, wrap days, etc.
- Specialty Items: Stunts, pyrotechnics, animals, etc.
- Postproduction: Processing film, telecine, editing, and special effects (if applicable).

The Director's Team

The stature of a director correlates to the caliber of his or her crew, as well as the expectations of the vendors and equipment. It's a simple equation: the more established and well-paid the director is, the more he or she will require a more established and well-paid crew and equipment.

For example, A-list music video director Brett Ratner only works with A-list cinematographers. Thus, when producing one of Brett's videos, the budget must include enough money to hire an A-list cinematographer. An A-list cinematographer will only work with an A-list crew, so the budget must accommodate an A-list crew, too.

The same equation also applies to a B-list director. However, a producer can usually get away with hiring a B-list cinematographer and crew for a bit below the A-list rate. The B-list directors, cinematographers, and crews aspire to increase their credentials and reputation to rise to the A-list. A truism of music videos is that an A-list team almost never needs to cut their rates.

What makes a great music video?

"A great video is an extension of the song."
—Joseph Uliano, Executive Producer

"Ultimately, it's like going to the movies. Like when the lights come on and you go, 'Was that good or wasn't it?' A quick answer. There has to be an immediate, visceral kind of reaction. A really great video works on both an emotional and a mental point of view. It kind of lingers with you and haunts you. The videos that drive me are idea-based. I really enjoy an interesting twist on an idea. I enjoy visual eye candy, too. A great video is the perfect synchronization of the emotional impact of the song with the imagery. It just gives you a chill."

—Noble Jones, Director

Client Relations

There are two parts to the client relations cost: (1) artist specific costs, and (2) client consideration. The artist specific costs are part of doing business. The producer, out of both courtesy for the client and control over the budget, discusses specific aspects of the budget with the video commissioner that directly concern the artist, such as travel, wardrobe, and glam. The artist's needs and expectations directly translate into dollars. The commissioner can help the producer assess the necessary monetary amounts to include.

The client considerations, on the other hand, are not so cut-and-dry. They include catering to the record label commissioner and artist in ways that are above and beyond the shooting requirements in order to keep the clients happy. For example, if it is known that the record label commissioner is environmentally conscience, it pays to make sure that the caterer uses paper cups rather than Styrofoam cups. Another huge morale booster is to find out, in advance, what the artist prefers for both lunch and craft service, and then make sure that his or her favorite foods are available. These small considerations can go a long way toward the overall spirit of the day, especially if the shoot itself turns out to be a difficult one.

"I expect the budget to take care of my artist," says Nicole Ehrlich. "If the artist is happy, the day goes smoothly; if the artist isn't happy, it's just another hurdle we have to deal with. I expect the producer to be creative and make things work ahead of time and on set if my artist needs something reasonable."

During the bidding phase, a good producer will ask the commissioner about certain budget items from the outset to avoid problems and potential overages that may occur down the line. "Sometimes the basic stuff is not in the budget, such as wardrobe, security, and motor home," explains director of video production at Sony BMG Sabrina Rivera, "I'm like, 'What do you mean you don't have a motor home for my artist?' Security, actually, became a major issue for me on one job, and that's something that I pay attention to now very closely. What I would say to producers regarding the budgeting process is the devil is in the details. You just forget the smallest thing, and it could be a big problem. For my videos, which are primarily urban, you really have to think in terms of glam, which is going to cost you an arm and a leg. So I would suggest budgeting a lot more money than you think you need there, because they always end up going over, and it pisses me off. I always end up going over on my glam situations, because they always want more—especially with friggin' caliber artists, too, which always becomes a problem." Consulting with the commissioner about the details in the beginning allows a producer to be proactive rather than reactive.

Sometimes the label or artist will pay for the artist's wardrobe and glam squad out of their own pockets. For instance, if the commissioner says that the producer must include the wardrobe budget in the production company's bid, the producer needs to find out from the label commissioner how much money to assign to all the details of the wardrobe budget, which include how much money to designate to clothing and accessories and how much to allot for the wardrobe stylist's fee for the prep day(s), shoot day(s), and return day(s). A wise producer will do his or her best to get these details in writing. This way, if a problem arises later, the producer has already consulted with the label, has already been told what monies to allocate to the specific line item, and has a paper trail to prove it.

It is becoming increasingly more common for the actual music video budget to include all of the aforementioned items. The most updated version of the Point Zero bid breaks out these items with a separate page (the talent related costs section of the budget). In the past, the basic production budget either included these costs as below the line expenses, or completely removed them if the record label paid. Being below the line expenses, these artist-driven costs were part of the monies that the fee percentages were based upon. Today, however, the budget addresses these expenses as a separate, above the line category in the main shooting budget. They are no longer included in the fee structure, yet they are still considered the producer's responsibility. This means that the fee percentage for the production company, director, and producer will exclude the artist's costs.

The entertainment industry relies on relationships. How people form and maintain these relationships can make or break careers. Therefore, it pays to ask the label for specific requests at the beginning. When a producer regularly works with specific labels or artists, he or she begins to learn their likes and dislikes. Catering to the clients is one of the smartest and, in the long-term, most cost-effective strategies every producer should employ.

SCHEDULING: TIME EQUALS MONEY

The treatment and budget can be thought of as two road maps for a music video. Time is the third major consideration. In order to budget properly, the producer has to have some idea of how long it will take to shoot the various elements of the treatment. Considerations include:

- How many hours and/or days will it take to shoot the entire video?
- Is it a day or night shoot, or both?
- Does it need a location, or does the art department need to build a set in a studio?

- How much time will the grips and electricians need to light the location?
- What can be prepared in advance?
- What needs to happen at the shoot?
- Is a pre-light day required, meaning, does the shoot require a day in advance just to set up the lights?

The producer must avoid, at all costs, getting into a situation where the director expects something that the producer hasn't budgeted. The list of questions about time and scheduling goes on and on, but the abovementioned seven are paramount to putting together a budget.

While the assistant director will eventually put together the final schedule, the producer needs to have a strong sense of how much time everything should take to properly budget the money needed. And since the assistant director doesn't get hired until the treatment and budget are in place, the producer must know from the beginning what a good crew can, and cannot, accomplish within the parameters of the time and money allotted to make the video.

CREATING THE BUDGET

Whoever says that accounting is not a creative activity has certainly never put together a music video budget. A seasoned producer needs to account for every possible scenario in the budget so that money problems don't arise during the shoot. This includes knowing how much padding to add, and where to add it.

"The best thing any producer can do when it comes to budgets is to communicate with the EP and the director about where you stand in the budget," says former executive producer Helen Cavallo. "The process is ever evolving, and things come up when you're on set. It's important to know what you, as the director and the production company, have promised to the client and be aware of any add-ons that have come about by the client or artist."

The main categories in a budget include:

• Crew
• Location
• Travel
• Equipment
• Film
• Casting and Talent
• Art Department
• Specialty Items
• Postproduction
• Miscellaneous Expenses and Items
• Overages

All producers and executive producers have their own strategies for creating a budget. "In terms of things to add to the budget: overtime and pad the art department," producer William Green advises. "Art departments always go over budget, and you never make your day. If you can pad other areas, such as locations, to cover yourself, then I would do that as well." Executive producer Larry Perel's budgeting strategy is a bit more open ended. "Give yourself the ability to move money around," he says, "and don't add things that are extraneous."

THE CREW

All union crew positions have a standard day rate they must receive for a union shoot, and all music videos with a gross budget of more than $50,000 fall under the jurisdiction of The International Alliance of Theatrical Stage Employees, Moving Picture Technicians, Artists and Allied Crafts of the United States, its Territories and Canada (IATSE.) IATSE is the labor union representing technicians, artisans,

and craftspersons in the entertainment industry, including live theater, motion picture and television production, and trade shows. However, some elements of their payment are negotiable, especially the ratio of money promised for time worked. For instance, a ten- or twelve-hour workday can be negotiated at a specific rate, as can the point of where overtime turns into time and a half, and then again when double time comes in. For the most part, though, crew rates are based on the IATSE union guidelines sliding scale. The IATSE-MVPA AGREEMENT, found in Appendix C on page 218, contains the information needed for negotiating a crew budget. This agreement was negotiated between the union—IATSE—and the trade association—Music Video Producer's Association (MVPA), which is a nonprofit trade organization representing music video production companies, providing a forum for discussions among production companies, record labels, crews, and vendors and educating its members to the latest developments in the ever-changing world of music video production.

Crew Rates

At the time of writing, the general rates for a mid-budget music video for a ten- or twelve-hour shoot day are as follows:

PRODUCTION TEAM
• Producer: $500–$1,000 (If a day rate has been agreed upon as opposed to 5 percent of the below the line budgetary expenses.)
• Production Supervisor (also called the Production Manager): $450–$550
• Assistant Production Supervisor (also called the Production Coordinator): $300–$400
• Office Production Assistant (PA): $200

CAMERA CREW

- Director of Photography (DP): $2,500–$5,000
- Camera Operator: $900–$1,300
- Assistant Camera (AC): $500–$550
- Second AC: $475–$525
- Loader: $350–$500
- Steadicam: $1,250–$1,800

ELECTRIC CREW

- Gaffer: $500–$550
- Best Boy Electrician: $475–$525
- 3rd Electrician: $450–$500
- 4th Electrician: $450–$500

GRIP CREW

- Key Grip: $500–$550
- Best Boy Grip: $475–$525
- 3rd Grip: $450–$500
- 4th Grip: $450–$500

ASSISTANT DIRECTOR TEAM

- Assistant Director (AD): $500–$1,200 (average is $900)
- 2nd AD: $450
- 2nd 2nd AD: $350–$400

SOUND DEPARTMENT

- Playback: $500
- Boom: $250–$300

VTR DEPARTMENT

- VTR Operator: $500

ART DEPARTMENT

- Production Designer: $750–$1,200
- Art Director: $500–$750
- Scenic: $350–$500
- Set Decorator: $350–$450
- Inside Prop: $400–$450
- Outside Prop: $400–$450
- Carpenters: $300–$450
- Swings: $275–$350
- Prop Assistant: $200–$300

CASTING TEAM

- Casting Director: $650–$950

STORYBOARD TEAM

- Storyboard Artist: $500–$800

GLAM SQUAD

- Wardrobe Stylist: $950–$3,000
- Wardrobe Assistant: $250–$400
- Makeup Artist: $650–$3,000
- Makeup Assistant: $250–$400
- Hair Stylist: $650–$3,000
- Hair Assistant: $250–$400

DRIVERS AND OPERATORS

- Grip Truck Driver: $450 for 8 hours, but must add lots of overtime
- Generator Driver/Operator: $450 for 8 hours, but must add lots of overtime. (On a lower budget job, many production companies have a generator dropped off which the grips handle. However, on a higher budget tier, the union will insist on a generator operator.)

FIRE SAFETY OFFICERS

- Fire Safety Officers: $450 for 8 hours, but must add lots of overtime

CRAFT SERVICE

- Craft Service: $200–$250

PRODUCTION ASSISTANTS

Production Assistants: $150–$200

These fees should be used as a basic guideline in conjunction with the IATSE-MVPA Agreement rules, since they will change with time. Keep in mind that a producer has more leeway and negotiating power on the lower budget jobs than on the higher budget jobs. As explained earlier in this chapter, the A-list crews don't have the same need to negotiate as do the B- and C-list crews, and the union specifications are more rigid on higher budget jobs.

Paying The Crew

Members of the crew receive their money via a payroll company time card. Even "indirect hires," such as the grip truck driver and the generator operator—who come with the equipment—fill out these cards. The production company pays for these hires.

The production team and the assistant director keep track of each day's timing, including when crew members arrive (per their call time) and when the production wraps at the end of the day. The production coordinator collects the time cards at the end of the shoot. During the full wrap of the production over the next few days—when the production team makes sure they return all of the equipment, postproduction is well under way, and the budget is actualized—either the production manager or the production coordinator checks all cards to ensure that each crew member filled them out properly. (See page 204 in Chapter Ten for more information about payroll time cards.)

Although members of both the crew and the production team may see themselves as freelancers or independent contractors, the law categorizes them as part-time employees of the production company. As such, the production company must pay all the taxes in accordance with each crew member's tax status. The payroll company takes care of this, and is covered in the budget through the cost of P&W. The only time a production company would want to have a crew member bill them directly and not go through a payroll company is when the crew member earns less than $600 from the production company in any given year. In that case, the production company doesn't have to submit tax paperwork on the crew member.

Since anything that can go wrong will, a seasoned producer always adds some overtime (OT) into the budget as many shoots run behind, sending the crew into time-and-a-half extra innings. It's better to predict this up front and have the finances to cover it than to panic when it happens.

CREWS REQUIRED FOR A SHOOT

While so far we have talked about "the crew" as a single entity, a music video can require several separate crews. The AICP bid format has one page for the preproduction crew, which includes the crew necessary for prepping the shoot, such as location scouting, determining necessary equipment, and fitting wardrobe; the wrap crew, which is the crew brought in at the end of the shoot to breakdown and put away the equipment; and a separate page for the shooting crew

Preproduction Crew

For the budget page entitled PREPRODUTION/WRAP CREW, the following positions must be considered for the preproduction section and most of them, if not all, will be included:

PRODUCTION TEAM

Members of the production team—the producer, production manager, production coordinator and office PA(s)—need anywhere from a few days to a week or more of preproduction fees built into the budget. Others who may need additional preproduction time and fees built into the budget are as follows:

DIRECTOR OF PHOTOGRAPHY

The director of photography, or DP, needs at least one day of prep to work with the director and producer to place the camera, lighting, and grip department orders. Sometimes the DP can do it all on the scout day, but sometimes it requires additional time.

LOCATION SCOUT/MANAGER

The details of the particular video project, specifically how quickly they can find the location described in the treatment and make a deal with the owner of the location, determines the location scout and/or manager's preproduction time frame.

ASSISTANT CAMERA

The assistant camera, or AC, checks the camera out the day before the shoot. This person charges either a whole day rate or a half-day rate, depending upon the negotiated rate.

ART DEPARTMENT

If the treatment demands a set, the art department may have to come in early to build and dress it.

ASSISTANT DIRECTOR

The assistant director, or AD, needs at least one day of prep to work with the director and producer, putting a schedule together for the shoot day(s). Sometimes they can get this together on the scout day, but sometimes it takes more time.

WARDROBE

The wardrobe stylist and assistant generally need at least one day, usually more, to do the shopping, sewing, and fittings for the video.

HAIR STYLIST

If the artists have complex hairstyles, the stylists need to know the day before the shoot, so as not to waste time on the shoot day. On some occasions the stylist may have to begin working on an artist's hair the day before the shoot, such as when hair extensions are necessary.

PRODUCTION ASSISTANTS

The day before the shoot, the production company hires two production assistants, or PAs, to drive a truck to all of the rental houses and pick up the equipment that has been pre-ordered by the production manager and coordinator after scouting the shoot location.

The producer needs to organize one or more days of scouting out the location, depending on the size of the production. The scout brings the department heads together with the director and the producer to discuss, in detail, what the director plans to accomplish, as well as to establish a finalized schedule, including getting to and from locations— which the assistant director will put together. The details of the scouting expedition depend on what the treatment calls for, and will determine the budget for the scout day. Factors needing consideration include:

- Which crew members need to come on the scout?
- Which crew members are needed for a full day or half-day?
- How much do the crew members charge for a day's work?
- How will the crew members get to the location for the scout?
- Do the crew members need to be reimbursed for their travel expenses?

The people who should be on the scout include the director, producer, director of photography, production manager, assistant director, gaffer, key grip, production designer, location manager/scout. (For a low budget video, often the producer, production manager, or production coordinator assumes this role.) Generally, the people who go on the scout get their day rate. Sometimes, depending on the budget and the crew members involved, the producer and/or production manager can convince the individuals attending the scout to do it for half their day rate, especially if the scout goes to one location that's not far away. If scouting the location takes longer than a few hours, a meal break is required. During the day the producer should provide craft service, such as drinks and small snacks.

Shooting Crew

While it only takes some of the crew to prep and wrap out the production, most of the manpower is necessary on the shoot day(s). For the budget page entitled SHOOTING CREW, everyone necessary on the actual day of the shoot must be included. (See Crew Rates on pages 94–95 to determine how much to budget per person. Also see Chapter Seven starting on page 119 for job descriptions to help determine whom to hire for shooting the video.)

Wrap Out Crew

For the budget page entitled PREPRODUCTION/WRAP CREW, the following positions must be considered for the wrap section:

PRODUCTION TEAM

Members of the production team—the producer, production manager, production coordinator and office PA(s)—need anywhere from a day to a week, or more, of wrap out fees built into the budget to get all of the paperwork in order and take care of any outstanding problems or issues, as well as getting crew time cards to the payroll company. The production team also makes sure the postproduction process has begun and continues to run smoothly. Others who may need additional wrap time and fees built into the budget are as follows:

ART DEPARTMENT

• If the art department builds an elaborate set, they may need an additional day or more to strike it.

PRODUCTION ASSISTANTS

• The day after the shoot, two PAs, hopefully the same two PAs that did equipment pick-ups, drive a truck to all of the rental houses returning the equipment.

GRIPS AND ELECTRICS

• In certain circumstances, a producer may want to hire grips and electrics specifically for the wrap, also called the "load out." When hired for this specialty position, they are then considered the "wrap crew." They will begin working at the end of the shoot. Generally, a wrap crew only gets hired for shoots with extensive lighting, detailed set ups, and a long shooting day. In this case, a producer may not want to continue paying the grips and electricians overtime for simply taking down, or striking, the set. It may be a better idea to send the main crew home after finishing the principal photography and bring in a wrap crew to spend the next few hours taking down all of the equipment, putting it away, and getting it ready to be returned to where it belongs in the morning.

If a crew is brought from out-of-town to the location, they get paid for both travel days. For instance, most of the music video DPs live in Los Angeles, so it's not unusual for production to fly a DP to New York City to shoot a video. A top DP will charge a full day's rate for each travel day, the reason being that when the DP travels, he or she cannot be shooting, and so should receive appropriate compensation. A new DP may only charge a half-day rate, or no charge at all, depending on the circumstances and the negotiation. In addition, on videos with well-known female artists, their glam squad may need to be flown to the shoot.

LOCATION

The cost of shooting on location varies drastically from project to project, and place to place. The more practice producers have in creating budgets, the better their ability to approximate what things will cost. For instance, a producer can use houses in certain neighborhoods as locations for fairly set rates. All it takes is a telephone call to a location scout or the local film commissioner's office with information regarding what kind of location fits the requirements of the video treatment. If a treatment calls for a large mansion in the Hollywood Hills with a pool and a view, a location scout can offer a ballpark estimate of what it will cost.

In New York City, securing a permit to city property (such as public parks) does not cost anything. The necessary information is easily available by calling The City of New York Mayor's Office of Film, Theatre, & Broadcasting. The Special Officers Division, or SOD, is the police unit that services New York City film projects. If the Mayor's Office deems them necessary for a particular project—if the treatment calls for something possibly restrictive due to safety factors, such as a car chase or explosions or shutting down busy streets—then they will be required to be on location. However, they are also free to production. Despite the free location and free police, supplementary items might be necessary to use the location, such as potentially pricey security guards or representatives from the different branches of city agencies, such as the fire department. This is not uncommon, if the treatment calls for something out of the ordinary or if the artist is a celebrity that will draw large crowds. A call to the city can confirm whether these additional location costs will be mandatory, and, as such, need to be included in the budget. These details should be researched before submitting a budget to avoid problems later.

Another important aspect of budgeting and scouting locations is balancing the requirements of the treatment with the restrictions presented by the location(s). Shooting in a New York City park might not involve any rental fees, but it presents issues such as bathroom availability and dining facilities. If the treatment has a band of four people and thirty crew members, at least one motor home (also called a trailer or honeywagon), may be needed for the band, and an additional one for production to work from. If the caterer doesn't have a tent, the producer may need to solicit a community recreational room or church nearby as a place to serve lunch to the crew in case of inclement weather.

In addition, music videos rarely have a weather contingency built in, so the producer must anticipate and prepare for every possibility and add it to the budget. Generally, the label will choose to shoot, rain or shine, and refuse to incur any overages due to inclement weather.

TRAVEL

The cost of travel varies from project to project, depending on who's going to where and who's paying for it. The IATSE-MVPA Agreement has specific travel rules. For instance, there is the 45-Mile Zone rule stating that in Los Angeles the 45-mile "Studio Zone" is the circular area outward from the intersection of Beverly Boulevard and La Cienega Boulevard. In New York City, the studio zone starts from Columbus Circle. For other cities, the "Production Zones" are areas within a 45-mile radius of the production centers of the state's city hall. Additionally, the rule specifies that the mileage from Studio Location will be at 0.36 cents per mile outside of the zone, with no mileage allowance within the 45-mile zone. More travel details can be gleaned directly from the agreement, including detailed guidelines in regard to overnight travel rules as well (see Appendix C on page 218).

EQUIPMENT

Although the cost of the equipment varies with each production, certain costs remain fairly consistent in accordance with particular directors and DPs. For example, the cost of a standard 35mm camera package will remain pretty much the same. The price can drastically change when the treatment calls for something other than the standard, such as specialized lenses or filters, for example. One reason some directors choose to work with certain producers on a regular basis is that the producers know the directors' style and tricks of the trade, which translates into how much they need to budget without having to research extensively.

FILM

One of the more consistent expenses in the budget for a music video is the cost of film. This expense may vary from project to project, but often not as much as other items, because most music video projects use fairly standard film stocks. Occasionally, a director writes a treatment that calls for more uncommon stocks, and this may affect the budget. Generally, for a standard four-minute music video, a producer orders about 9,000 feet of 35mm film, or about 4,400 feet of 16mm film. Keep in mind that a roll of 35mm film offers approximately four minutes of shooting time, while a roll of 16mm film gives approximately eight minutes. A good producer researches the history of the director in the budgeting phase to figure out how much film to purchase based on how much film the director usually requires per shoot.

The budget form in the Point Zero spreadsheet program calculates the cost of film to purchase per foot as well as the cost of film to process per foot. A seasoned producer knows the going rate for both. A beginning producer can either ask the executive producer, or head of production at the production company, what film costs to include in the budget, or research the costs directly with the film supplier, such as Kodak, or the lab used to process the film.

Almost all directors prefer using 35mm to 16mm, but the choice may depend on what the budget will tolerate, as 35mm film costs twice as much to purchase, and requires twice as much film for the same amount of time as 16mm. It also costs less to process 16mm film. The film format is included in the contract with the record label, so it needs to be determined up front.

Some directors choose to shoot super 16mm film when on a tighter budget. Still less expensive than 35mm, Super 16mm has a wider film frame than regular 16mm film. In general, the larger the film format, the better the quality of the recorded image. The area of the 16mm frame is only one quarter of that of the 35mm frame and, when projected side-by-side, the 16mm film looks noticeably grainier, less sharp, and usually dimmer. However, technological improvements and advances made in lenses, cameras, filters, and film emulsions allow for the extensive use of 16mm in professional filmmaking. Similarly, many music video productions use 16mm film, in part because immediately after shooting the music video, the film gets color corrected and transferred to tape. Only the people in postproduction actually see the raw 16mm footage. With a good DP, after all of the manipulation, it's frequently hard to tell the difference between 16mm and 35mm.

Super 16mm film uses the maximum image area available on conventional 16mm film by extending the picture-area into the area normally reserved for the soundtrack, giving it a similar look on the screen to the wide-screen cinema format seen in movie theaters. Consequently, it requires very little cropping to convert to this picture format. The greater frame width of Super 16 and the need for less cropping on the top and bottom gives Super 16 an approximately 46 percent increase in image area over standard 16mm film when displayed on the wide-screen. This means better quality pictures from Super 16mm film. Super 16mm doesn't have room for a conventional soundtrack, but when shooting a music video, it doesn't matter.

What does matter is that shooting super 16mm film stock requires a specially modified 16mm camera. When budgeting and ordering equipment, a producer must take into account that shooting Super 16mm film requires the camera body to accommodate the film format. Also, when exposed Super 16 film is sent to the lab, it must be clearly marked to ensure the laboratory develops, prints, and, if applicable, screens the rushes, or dailies, in the correct ratio. Since 16mm and Super 16mm are the same size, without definitive instructions the lab may process it incorrectly.

While still primarily shot on film, as digital cinematography systems improve, more and more people shoot music videos in high definition, or HD, and 24p digital video. Many long-form music video producers already use these formats. Currently, digital filmmaking can be excellent for the up-and-coming directors working on a shoestring budget.

Though definitions vary, the term HD generally refers to a television screen offering at least double the resolution of the highest quality standard definition TV screen such that the on screen image appears in a ratio of 16:9 compared to today's analog signal ratio of 4:3. The image appears sharper due to the increased resolution, with over twice as much information on the screen. To fully reap the benefits of HD, the video project must be shot in the HD format and then viewed on an HD screen. By shooting in high definition, the filmmaker cuts out the need to purchase, develop, and, depending on the project, telecine the film. Digital allows manipulation via computer software rather than film, which, depending upon the treatment, can make the process of creating a music video less expensive. "HD video has no film costs, no processing costs, you can pretty much see what the shot it going to look like on the shoot, and there's quick change between tape," says head of production Jay Wakefield.

Currently, the downside of shooting high definition, which is only used for big budget music videos, is that the savings, if any, are incidental, and there are still some creative limitations. Due to the need to hire an HD engineer, who doubles as a sort of technical second DP for the complicated digital system, and the need for the same amount of lighting as traditional film production, the only savings are in the cost of purchasing and developing film. Thus, in short form productions, where a relatively small amount of film is used to begin with, the savings, if there are any at all, are nominal. In addition, some directors feel that the HD lenses haven't yet caught up to the film lenses. Most agree that digital is the way to go for special effects in postproduction, as well as for wide shots, but close-ups are still questionable. Also, if a telecine is required or desired, there is not as much latitude with an HD telecine as with a film telecine; transferring HD dailies is similar to transferring reversal film dailies. "Sometimes HD doesn't look as good as film and the postproduction cost can be more expensive," says Wakefield.

When faced with a very low budget video, shooting 24p digital video and editing with Final Cut software is an excellent option. Film's innate frame rate is 24 frames per second. 24P refers to the high definition format. The "P"

means "progressive image scanning," which is a method of image scanning that processes image data one line of pixels at a time, creating frames composed of a single field, as opposed to "interlaced scanning," which is a scanning system in which two fields of lines are interlaced as alternating rows of lines. Progressive or non-interlaced scanning is any method for displaying, storing, or transmitting moving images in which the lines of each frame are drawn in sequence. Progressive scan pushes the limits of standard resolution and provides a more film-like image when viewing DVDs on a television. This is in contrast to the interlacing used in traditional, standard television systems.

"24p and Final Cut are easy and accessible," says executive producer Catherine Finkenstaedt. The technology allows up-and-coming filmmakers to realize creative ideas within a limited budget. "The digital non-HD camera is smaller and more mobile," explains Wakefield. "And there is no need to purchase, develop or telecine film." Editing with software like Final Cut can be done on home computer systems. So the entire production process can be accomplished inexpensively and quickly. "There's not much of a downside shooting digital unless you're a film purist," says Finkenstaedt. "Digital is super affordable to do lower budget jobs. A lot of the people shooting 24p are also editors, so they shoot lots and then edit it on Final Cut themselves."

The downside of 24p digital video is that it may not look as good as film or have the creative potency of film. "I love the look of film," says Finkenstaedt, "but it's not always financially feasible for new directors." And the ease of the process, some say, inherently allows for less creativity in the overall music video business. "Technology has opened up the industry, especially with regard to 24p and Final Cut. It's nowhere near as creative now, because there is not as much heart and soul and passion since it doesn't cost anything," reveals Finkenstaedt. "Everyone is a director and it's very difficult to eek out the talent; it's a real needle in a haystack more than ever."

CASTING AND TALENT

Sometimes the treatment calls for people besides the artist to appear in an artist's music video. *Talent* generally refers to the actors hired for the video. *Principle talent* is the lead, or leads, and *extras* are the secondary roles.

Because casting takes time and is a specialized area all of its own, the cost of finding the music video talent must be included in the budget, along with the casting director, and his or her assistant's fee. Sometimes the talent will have an agent or manager who will also insist on getting paid a negotiated percentage of what the talent receives. Casting tools, such as a video camera, tape stock, and a location at which to do the casting, must be budgeted, too.

Additional costs associated with the talent that need to be included in the budget include a honeywagon, or other holding area, where they can hang out when they're not shooting, use the bathroom, eat meals, get into wardrobe, and deal with the glam squad. Other considerations might include additional wardrobe, hair or make-up stylists, food, transportation for the talent, and additional parking.

ART DEPARTMENT

The art department budget changes significantly from project to project. For example, building a set, as opposed to using a location, usually raises the cost of the video. The rule of thumb is to rely on the production designer to submit a realistic budget for the project after reading the final treatment and speaking with the director. If the estimated budget is too high, then it's time to begin working with the production designer, the director, and the producer—and perhaps even the record label—to figure out how to creatively bring the cost down without compromising the integrity of the project.

The art department is usually self-reliant and self-contained. Most often, the producer and production designer negotiate the department's budget. Once they agree on a budget, the art department generally handles all of their own vehicles, pickup and returns, meals—except for the shoot day—and time cards. "I generally budget a lump sum for the art department and let them do their own thing," says executive producer Catherine Finkenstaedt. "It's such a gray area with such high demands."

When negotiating the art department's budget, it is well known that they very often go over budget. A producer may want to anticipate this and build some extra money into the art budget.

SPECIALTY ITEMS

Some video projects call for specialty items, like stunts, pyrotechnics, or animals. These must be taken into account when budgeting. If the treatment calls for rain, the budget needs lines for a water truck and crane. If it calls for fire or explosions, the budget will need to include money for a pyrotechnics specialist and any permits needed. If a treatment calls for stunts, the producer will need to set money aside to hire a stunt person and/or stunt coordinator. If a treatment calls for lions, a lion and handler need to be hired.

A director can achieve some special effects through the union of in-camera special effects and post visual effects. These are often more technically detailed, and, as such, more difficult to accomplish—in which case the producer may need to hire a post effects supervisor to help achieve a specific shot, look, or effect. For instance, green, or blue, screen effects and motion control have detailed rules to follow while shooting so that what's captured on film can be utilized properly in the postproduction process.

POSTPRODUCTION

All aspects of postproduction can cost a fortune. When putting together the initial budget, the producer works with the director, the DP, and the executive producer to decide on the postproduction facility they will use. Most likely, it will be at a postproduction facility where one or all of the above individuals have an existing relationship. The producer then calls the facility's account rep to find out the specific costs. Postproduction is another area of the budget where it's better to place more money than too little. Technical problems easily occur, and can easily push a project over budget.

It also helps to know how the director works during postproduction when drawing up the budget. Questions will need to be answered, such as: How many hours does it usually take to transfer film to tape and correct the color (telecine)? Is working night hours, which costs less, reasonable to expect of the director? How many days does the project need for the various steps in editing?

MISCELLANEOUS ITEMS AND EXPENSES

Miscellaneous items, such as petty cash, special insurance, and air shipping, must also be taken into account. For instance, during the course of preproduction and the shoot, a producer will need petty cash for small items. Special equipment, stunts, or pyrotechnics might require the producer to buy special, or additional, insurance.

Over-nighting tapes or DVDs back and forth gets expensive as well, especially if preproduction is happening in Los Angeles and the clients are in London. The production company can cover itself financially by putting enough money in the air shipping line of the budget. Nowadays, most production companies and postproduction houses have the capability to post different versions of the cut online to avoid shipping tapes to the client. In rare instances, however, the client may want to receive a tape or a DVD instead of viewing the cut online.

PADDING THE BUDGET

Creatively padding the budget is an important aspect of creating a budget. "Always make sure you have a bit of pad somewhere," advises producer Rachel Curl. "Unexpected things always come up, no matter how prepared you are, and sometimes when you least expect it. You need to have something to play with for the unexpected emergencies. On the flip side, do not overdo it with the pad, as you do not want to take advantage of the record company. Do not try to pull the wool over the commissioner's eyes, as they often have quite a bit of production knowledge. Be realistic but have a small cushion/contingency for your protection."

There are various tricks to padding a budget. For instance, specifying the retail price for tape stock in the budget and then purchasing it at a wholesale dealer can save money. Or the P&W percentage can be included as a point higher than needed. It's surprising how much money can be saved with small tricks like these throughout the entire production process. "Producers should always add a buffer in departments that have the tendency to change as the job progresses, such as art department and post," suggests executive producer Kelly Norris Sarno. "Producers should always be prepared for the unexpected. Paddings are important because they go fast."

When working with an experienced record label commissioner, it should be kept in mind that they often know these tricks. Janet Kleinbaum, senior vice president of marketing and video production at Jive Records, recommends not padding the budget because, speaking on behalf of all commissioners, she asserts, "We'll figure it out somehow. That's the other thing, too. Learning how to read a budget is a whole other skill-set. And producers know how to do that. Commissioners learn how to do that as they go along, unless you already have a production background."

OVERAGES

The producer must be able to foresee when additional money may be needed. He or she should never spend more than the amount allotted in the budget. If it is discovered that production does require more money, the producer must inform the proper people—the executive producer and the record label commissioner—in a timely manner so that they can decide if they want to increase the budget. However, the producer should only ask for additional funding—an overage—for appropriate reasons, as he or she cannot give in to every request the director makes. "A new producer should know how to walk the line with a director," director's representative Tommy LaBuda cautions, "and knows when it's ok to say 'no'."

"The budget line items can vary wildly, depending on who the artist is, who the director might be, and even who the commissioner is," executive producer Doug Kluthe warns. "If you are producing a rock video, the hair, make-up, and styling might not be as important as it would be for a diva in an urban video. Try to anticipate what might be potentially problematic issues before they become problems and get back to the client. You do not want your EP to do your clean up, so try to be a problem solver rather than the constant harbinger of bad news."

CHAPTER SIX
CONTRACTS

Like any modern business enterprise, making music videos requires a slew of contracts and forms. The first contract that is issued immediately after the video project is awarded is between the record label and the production company. Afterward, several standard contracts and forms are needed once preproduction begins, which include the following:

- Letters of Commitment and/or Confirmation
- Talent Releases
- Location Releases
- Crew Deal Memos
- Payroll Timecards
- Overage Forms

The details of the contracts and forms must be strictly adhered to. If not, the production company, record label, artist, and director may face legal problems down the road.

THE CONTRACT BETWEEN THE RECORD LABEL AND PRODUCTION COMPANY

Once the video treatment and budget are agreed upon, the record label offers a contract to the production company. Each record label has a standard contract that lists the terms and conditions of the agreement. The contract lays out the details of what responsibilities the record company and the production company have to each other. In addition to identifying the artist(s), the song, and the director, it states the following:

- Delivery specifications
- Dates and time schedule
- Ownership of the video
- Cost of the project and payment structure

DELIVERY SPECIFICATIONS

The contract may state whether the production company is required to deliver just one master video or the original along with a dub, and whether the video should be in DigiBeta (or digital Betacam), which is a half-inch professional videotape cassette that is the most common format for mastering music videos. Sometimes, additional dubs may be asked for as well. The label requires that the production company include a *slate,* which is a synopsis of the pertinent details of the video project that lists the artist, the song title, the director, the record label, the production company, and the date. It is usually placed at the head of the tape, as a title page, and includes specific information about the video clip before the video begins. The copyright notice appears at the end of the clip.

DATES AND TIME SCHEDULE

The contract for the music video locks in the shoot date(s) and the final delivery date, which is generally determined by the artist's availability and touring schedule. The preproduction and postproduction schedules are then determined around the shoot date(s).

OWNERSHIP OF THE VIDEO

A representative of the record company, the production company—usually the executive producer—the director, and sometimes the freelance producer sign the contract. The agreement defines the video as a work-for-hire by the director and the production company, which means that the record label owns the video and its copyright. This allows the label to make any changes or edits as they see fit without having an obligation to consult the director or the production company. The work for hire also covers any outtakes, making them the property of the label. Additionally, since the director is a work-for-hire, he or she receives a straight salary for his or her work on the video, rather than a percentage of the music or video sales.

"The directors do not own the video. It is a work-for-hire. They [the directors] can put it on their reels, though," explains senior director, video commissioner Lorin Finkelstein. The contract generally limits the rights of the production company and the director to using the video for self-promotional purposes (on a promotional reel), as long as the reel does not get used for public broadcasting purposes without permission from the record label. Often, this provision does not get written into the contract, as both parties regard it as an industry standard. "The director certainly can put the video on their reel that they physically send out to solicit other jobs. I do not think they can put their reel on the Internet," says independent video commissioner Jeff Panzer. "The general public remains unable to download it for free. They can use it in any other way with that exception."

What do you love about music videos?

"What I love most about having a career in music videos is that I'm a fan. I was a fan of MTV when they started; I watched it at my friends' house because my family didn't even have cable. I begged my parents for years to get cable so we could get MTV. I love that there are artists that I've worked with that are historical; they're really artists for the ages. I feel like I am some kind of part or witness to the visual history of an artist's career."
—Danny Lockwood, Vice President of Video Production; Sony BMG Music Entertainment

"Of course, the wonderful thing about music videos is that all you're doing is adding visuals to music, and music is wonderful. The nature of music is that it's a playful thing. And the best stuff in life is playful."
—Mark Kohr, Director

"What I love about my job is the interaction with the artists and the people, getting things done and making stuff happen. What I hate is our reputation. I really hate how people perceive major labels, because I've been at a major label my entire life, and I don't believe in the evil 'This is what they only care about.' I've never had that experience. My experience has been that when artists were able to state their cases, they got money. We always work together. There was a lot of stuff in the beginning of the music industry that was not cool, and a lot of wrongs that we needed to right. But as a young person in the music industry, I want to see all that stuff change. I want something more equal with the artist. I want artists to look at the record company as a partner that can help them."
—Livia Tortolla, Senior Vice President of Marketing and Artist Development; Atlantic Records

The contract usually states that the production company and director's services are "unique and extraordinary." In addition, the agreement stipulates that the director's inability to complete the project "cannot be adequately compensated in damages," which means it cannot be transferred or "subbed out" to another director or production company. Per the standard contract, the production company also "warrants and represents" that it will obtain prior licenses and permissions, such as talent releases or location releases, required to ensure that the entire production stays within the law.

COST OF THE PROJECT AND PAYMENT STRUCTURE

As explained on page 28 in Chapter One, the record label gives the director's rep a monetary figure up front to use as a benchmark as the director comes up with the idea for the video and writes his or her treatment. The cost of the project, as explained in Chapter Five starting on page 80, is put into a standard budgeting format using the director's treatment and the label's monetary figure as guidelines. The cost is negotiated and determined at this point, prior to advancing to the contractual stage. The video treatment and budget are tweaked simultaneously in the earliest stages, and both the label and the production company make accommodations for each other so that the treatment and budget can be agreed upon. Once agreed, the treatment and the budget are included in the contract. The total budget amount is written into the contract in a lump-sum figure with a corresponding payment schedule.

The record label agrees to give specified amounts of the entire budget to the production company at various points in the production process. The standard payment structures are as follows:

- Fifty percent of the budget when the label awards the video, comes to an agreement with the production company, and the contract is signed
- Twenty-five percent when the production company delivers the rough cut
- Twenty-five percent when the production company delivers the final, approved video

Jeff Panzer explains Universal's payment approach as, "We give the first half of the total production budget up front, which gives the production company start-up money to move forward. Then, with the next twenty-five percent, I want to see what the footage looks like. And the final twenty-five percent payment is issued upon the delivery of masters, elements, edit list—everything to do with that job." RCA's approach is similar. "We give the production company fifty percent up front to start the job," explains Lorin Finkelstein. "Then we give them twenty-five percent to pay the bills. And the last twenty-five percent is given at the very end so that if there is an extreme problem, we have some leverage left to finish the clip."

Of course, not every record label follows the same payment structure. For example, Atlantic Records pays as follows:

- Fifty percent of the budget when the label awards the video, comes to an agreement with the production company, and the contract is signed
- Twenty-five percent when the production company delivers the rough cut
- Fifteen percent when the production company delivers the final, approved video
- Ten percent when the production company delivers a full copy of the wrap book

Warner Brothers occasionally employs the 50-25-15-10 payment structure as well. "If it's a long back end—long postproduction, for example—it's just a courtesy to get the production company money in the meantime to pay off their vendors," says Devin Sarno, vice president of visual content at Warner Brothers Records.

As previously explained, the wrap book includes all of the paperwork generated by the production company during the course of a music video project. Some of the labels ask for a copy of the wrap book at the end of the shoot for two reasons: first, they want to make sure that the production company used the money properly, and second, they may want to have all of the receipts from the specific project in case the government, or an artist, ever audits them. For certain labels, such as Atlantic Records, asking for the wrap book is standard. Other labels, such as Universal Records, only ask for the paperwork if there is a problem with the shoot.

"I've only asked for the actualized wrap books two or three times in my whole career," says Jeff Panzer, "and only when a project went awry. I once did a video with a guest artist who pushed the budget over about $80,000. At that point, I asked for the book to see a breakdown of how that happened. Generally, if the video is great, and it comes in on budget, I don't get into it because there's no reason to." Devin Sarno concurs, saying "If it's a troubled production or there were questions or concerns about how certain things were handled, asking for the wrap book is a way for us to be able to double check that the accounting was on the 'up and up,' as it were."

The artist usually pays for fifty percent or more of the video out of royalties, and consequently, may question where that money was spent. A provision in every artist's contract allows him or her to have an accountant to go through the record company's books to ensure that they receive everything they earn. If the label has the wrap book from specific projects, it simplifies the process for the music video department.

LETTERS OF COMMITMENT AND/OR CONFIRMATION

Once the record company awards the music video to the production company, the pace of committing it to film would put NASCAR to shame. But, as the old saying goes, the wheels of the law grind slow and fine; the legal department at the labels often cannot keep up with the rapidity of production. "So many of these things are last minute and down to the wire—you've got to

---

Snapshots from the Set

"I did a music video for New Order. I love their music and I love the song, but I knew they were kind of a tricky band to work with because they really don't give a shit about their marketing or their image, or anything—especially Bernard, the lead singer who runs the show. I was talking with him about the [video's] idea over the phone. The conversation went fine, but the next day, I got a message from the record company that said, 'Um, we need you to call again, because, actually, when you called, Bernard was drunk and doesn't remember the conversation.'"

—Peter Care, Director

"I did a video in New York where the artist took eight hours to put on a pair of jeans and T-shirt and have her hair and make-up done; she was twenty-four."

—William Green, Producer

quit or commit," says Jeff Panzer. "And a lot of times the business administration of a label needs an abundance of information. But if you're Universal Records and you have several subsidiary labels, the details are not automatic. If you commit to a director and treatment and you have the people at the label saying 'go for it,' you do the video. Sometimes, I even shoot without a contract." However, if preproduction begins and the production company spends money before receiving the contract, and then the record label decides not to do the video after all, the record label legally does not have to pay out-of-pocket expenses to the production company, as the contract has not yet been executed. To avoid this problem, the production company gets a signed letter of commitment and/or confirmation from the record label commissioner.

If the label cannot offer a contract to the production company quickly enough for preproduction to begin, the whole schedule can fall apart. In order to ensure proper prep time for the video and to allow the production company to cover its initial expenditure, the production company generates a letter of commitment or confirmation stating that the label agrees to pay certain costs even if the label or artist cancels the video. The production company often requires the commissioner to sign off on it. This ensures that the production company gets reimbursed for any out-of-pocket money they spend in their good faith effort to get the video done on time, even if it gets cancelled before the actual contract is signed.

Jeff Panzer says that he has excellent relationships with the main production companies. His word is generally good enough to begin a production. Nonetheless, he will sign a letter of commitment if the production company is adamant. Devin Sarno, on the other hand, says he will not sign this sort of agreement, so his word is, in effect, of the utmost importance. Lorin Finkelstein will sign a letter of commitment "as long as RCA's chief financial officer, general manager, and business administrative people are okay with it."

The production company and its representatives should, in theory, never spend money on a music video project before receiving the agreement or, at the very least, getting a signed letter of commitment or confirmation from the label commissioner. Imagine this scenario: the commissioner awards the video, but the contract has yet to work its way through the record company's legal department. The executive producer has a producer and production manager on hold and wants to hire them right away in order to get rolling on preproduction. The executive producer, meanwhile, has an excellent DP on first hold, but the DP's agent says that he or she either has to book or release the DP from the hold, as another production company has cash in hand to pay for the DP's services. In this case, the executive producer must determine the total cost of the three salaries—the producer, production manager, and DP—and get written permission from the record label to spend this money. The written permission takes the form of a letter of commitment or confirmation. Of course, if the job doesn't get cancelled—and most don't—once the contract is signed, it overrides the letter of commitment.

If a commissioner refuses to sign a letter of commitment, the production company must weigh all of the pros and cons to determine if the risk, inherent in the music video industry, is worth taking. Since it's a small industry with a limited number of commissioners, it quickly becomes apparent which label can be trusted when they give their word. Like everything in the music video business, many details are dependent on personal relationships.

ADDITIONAL CONTRACTS AND RELEASES

It takes many people to create a music video, and several of them require some sort of a legally binding document, such as a contract, a letter of agreement, a deal memo, or some other piece of official paperwork. Like most legal documents, the binding document must set specific terms and ensure that all the parties adhere to certain laws, rules, and practices. If two or more parties cannot quickly resolve any disagreement, documents such as a talent release, a location release, a deal memo, or a payroll timecard can be used as a defense should the issue go to court.

TALENT RELEASE

As previously mentioned, when an individual agrees to appear on film, the agreement usually takes the form of a talent release, which basically states that the person agrees to allow his or her image and likeness to be used for the video. Using someone's image in a music video without permission is illegal. Talent releases protect the artist, record label, production company, and director in the event that people claim they didn't know they were being filmed and do not want their image to be used in the video.

Even using a famous person's name can be problematic if permission is not obtained beforehand. In 1999, Rosa Parks, revered as the mother of the modern civil rights movement because of her refusal to give up her bus seat to a white passenger in 1955, filed a lawsuit against the group Outkast. Parks alleged defamation and trademark infringement because the duo used her name without permission in their song "Rosa Parks," the most successful radio single from OutKast's 1998 album *Aquemini*. Parks also named director Gregory Dark, a former pornographer, and producer Braddon Mendelson as part of the lawsuit, alleging a willful defamation of her name. This First Amendment lawsuit was carried until April 2005, when Outkast, the record label, and the producers paid Parks a cash settlement to end the case.

To avoid running afoul of the law, the production team must make sure that every person appearing in a video signs a talent release. The only exception is the artist or band for whom the video is being made. The record company usually provides a standard talent releases as an attachment to the contract.

In the event that the video calls for large crowd shots, getting signed talent releases from everyone in the crowd and maintaining a shooting schedule can prove impossible. In this case, it is generally acceptable for the production company to obtain a mass consent by posting large signs around the set stating all of the information in the talent release. These signs inform those in the crowd that by remaining in the vicinity of the shoot, they are agreeing to have their image used in the video. The producer must make sure to film the sign(s) at the beginning of any scene featuring the crowd of extras to prove they were informed.

"A group talent release is good enough in a crowd scene," says Jeff Panzer, "because in a concert video or club scene, you can't expect to get a release from everyone. So, the group release protects you. Most times we also shoot a release sign on the film as double protection." Devin Sarno says that the group talent release is fine to use "as long as no one is featured, or singled out in a group shot, and as long as the shot is general and wide." RCA's legal department, however, is more rigid. Lorin Finkelstein says that it is not okay to do a general group release for his label, explaining, "these days, with all videos being

Do you need a great song to make a great video?

"No. You don't have to have a great song to have a great video. But again, that's probably the stand-alone thing, where you have a song that you don't particularly like and then you make a video for it that elevates the song. It might not work as a song by itself, but together with the visual, it just seems to click."
—Little X, Director

"You can have a great video that has a shitty song, or vice versa—a really good song with a shitty video. And that's the worst. Imagine having a hit song, with a really shitty video, and it playing fifty times a day. I can name ten right now. But I won't. You can easily have a really bad song and a really good video. But when it lines up perfectly, when the artist is represented the right way, it works. And that's the best."
—Lorin Finkelstein, Senior Director, Video Commissioner; RCA Records

"Ninety percent of making a good music video is having a good song. If it's a good song that you can hear over and over, that's half the battle. If you have a song that's difficult or doesn't work, you're fucked—no matter how clever your visuals are."
—John Landis, Director

sold, we need everyone to sign exhibit B, the talent release included in our contract issued to the production company."

When filming children or young adults, additional rules must be followed. "Anyone under the age of 18 needs a parent or guardian signature on the release form," says Sarno. Additionally, Panzer says, "a child can only be used for a certain amount of time per day and must have a schoolteacher on the set. Also, there have to be breaks at certain times throughout the day, even if the child isn't tired."

LOCATION RELEASE

Similar to a talent release, a location release indicates that the owner, or the legal representative of a location, has given his or her approval in writing for its use in the music video. In most cases, the location release outlines details of the agreement such as as:

• Time limitations
• Fees and payments for the use of the location
• What the production company may and may not do on the premises (particularly pertinent in regard to noise and art department issues)

The location manager, or location scout working on the project, makes sure the proper people sign the release. If the video doesn't have a location manager, usually the production manager or production coordinator handles this duty.

DEAL MEMO

The deal memo outlines all terms of employment, including dates, times, fees, payment schedule, and travel, including such details as:

• Base Fees and Overtime
• Payment Due Dates
• Flight

• Grade of Hotel
• Ground Transportation
• Daily Expenses (also called per diem)
• Cancellation Policy

The director of photography and the glam squad frequently have agency representation. These top crew members, who are generally recognized by law as independent contractors, often request deal memos, usually via agents negotiating on their behalf. Sometimes the production designer and the offline editor do, too. More often than not, the director of photography, the glam squad, the production designer, and the offline editor are the only individuals with an agent on a music video shoot. The agent negotiates on behalf of his or her client, often insisting a signed deal memo offering provisions befitting of the clients' high caliber.

The rest of the crew rarely request or require deal memos, since music videos have a much quicker turn around than longer film projects such as feature films, for example.

PAYROLL TIMECARD

"Unagented" members of the crew that are not recognized by the law as independent contractors need to fill out a *payroll time card*, which is a specific form used by the payroll company that the worker must fill out to record his or her starting and quitting times each work day, as well as any additional and pertinent payment information. The production company—the producer, production manager, or production coordinator—negotiates the terms with each employee. The law regards these crew members as part time employees of the production company. As such, the production company must withhold and pay taxes from their paychecks.

To avoid getting bogged down in a pile of complicated bookkeeping after every shoot, a production company will hire a payroll company. This company takes on the legal responsibility of acting as the crew members' employer. At the end of the shoot, each member of the crew fills out the payroll timecard supplied to the production company by the payroll company. Included are how many days the crew person worked, how many hours per day, their negotiated fee, and any overtime incurred, as well as a kit rental fee, if applicable. A worker's kit is comprised of tools purchased and maintained by the worker that are specific to his or her job, such as tape and gels for a gaffer or a laptop computer and office supplies for a production manager. The worker may charge a rental fee for the use of the kit (see page 142 in Chapter Seven for more details). The crew person is required to sign the timecard and supply the payroll company with a W-4 Form, the federal government's Employee's Withholding Allowance Certificate; an I-9, the Employment Eligibility Verification form that is required by the Department of Homeland Security, United States Citizenship, and Immigration Services to document eligibility for employment in the United States; and additional documentation, such as a valid passport, driver's license, or social security card. The payroll company keeps the information on file so that once the crew supplies these items to a payroll company, they won't be asked for it again, at least for some time.

The production coordinator collects the payroll timecards at the end of the last shoot day and reviews them during the production's wrap to make sure they are all filled out correctly. The producer then signs off on all timecards. Once they are all in order, the production company sends the timecards to the payroll company, which calculates all of the necessary costs, such

What makes a great music video?

"A great video has the component of repeat watchability. When you watch a movie, you see it once or maybe twice, and a great classic you can watch over and over again. Movies are made to be watched singularly, for the most part. But videos are a rare art form—commercials are like this, too—such that hopefully, when your video hits MTV, it's successful and gets played a lot."
—Roman Coppola, Director

"A great video is something that complements the song, that complements the artist, and that takes that artist to a different level."
—Retta Harvey Hatfield, Vice President of Video Production; Universal Music Group Nashville

as P&W and taxes, adds it all up, and charges a percentage of the entire cost as their fee. They break down the costs and calculations into a detailed payroll report and forward the report to the production company. The production company, in turn, cuts one lump sum check to the payroll company, which sends checks to the crew members and pays the crew member's pension, welfare, and taxes on the check.

OVERAGE FORMS

While a skilled EP and producer can usually come up with a reasonably accurate budget, unforeseen things can happen to cause *overages*, or costs that are not included in the initial budget. Overages can happen at any point in the production process. Throughout the making of the video, the producer moves money around and finds creative solutions to budgetary restraints. However, occasionally, the director or artist make a request or a problem comes up that the budget cannot cover. At this point, the producer must speak with the executive producer or the label commissioner about the possibility of receiving additional money.

"I hate overages, but they do happen," Panzer says. "I try to be Judge Judy and assess who is responsible for what and why this overage happened. Was the crew slow? Was my artist late getting there? Did they not have the outfit ready or did glam take too long? There are certain aspects that the label is responsible for, but there are also crews that are too slow, and that's the production company's responsibility."

An overage can occur for many reasons, such as the director wanting to add something to improve the video, the artist hating the set and wanting it torn down and rebuilt, or the group deciding to show up at noon for a 7:30 A.M. shoot. If, for instance, the director decides that a Steadicam will drastically enhance the overall video, he or she may ask the producer to hire one, even though the initial budget didn't include a line for a Steadicam operator and rig. If the producer cannot find money for the overage and the director is adamant about having it, the producer must speak to the executive producer. Depending upon the circumstances, the executive producer might:

- Authorize paying out of the production mark-up (the production company's fifteen percent fee).
- Call the commissioner (or have the producer call the commissioner) and ask for more money from the label to cover the cost.
- Reject the cause of the overage (in which case the director will have to either pay for it out of his or her director's fee or forego the Steadicam).

"I do a 'Letter of Panzer,' which is similar to the production company's letter of confirmation," explains Panzer. "It incorporates the same concept as purchasing a home, stating that once we settle on the dollar figure at the very beginning of the project, you can't all of a sudden ask for more money. However, once preproduction is well under way and there's a valid reason to ask for more money, then it's cool. For example, a venue may change from the one originally budgeted, and the new one may be more expensive but give us more shooting options. However, on the day of the shoot, I'm in a creative mode, so don't talk to me about money. Unless the artist is late, don't approach me. The production company is being hired to do everything and anything to make this video happen for a specific, agreed upon amount of money."

Artists' requests and demands, as well as their tardiness, often cause overages. If an artist insists on having a more expensive wardrobe or a specialty item, like a Lear jet, these additions can lead to considerable overages. If the artist or the artist's manager makes an expensive request of production that is not in the initial treatment or budget, the producer must first speak with the director to see if they are in agreement with the addition or opposed to it. If the director agrees to it, the producer tries to make it work by fitting it into the budget. If that's impossible, the producer informs the executive producer of what's going on and then calls the video commissioner. The producer must explain the request; how the director feels about it; who made it; and how it affects the treatment, the shooting schedule, and the budget, while also letting the commissioner know the cost of the additional request with respect to the base fee—as well as any potential overtime or other unforeseen costs. If the commissioner agrees to pay for the additional item requested by the artist, the producer must submit an overage form to the commissioner to sign.

"The way I handle requests for more money really depends," says Finkelstein. "If it is an artist request that is not in the budget then I'll sign it." Generally, no producer will take on the added expense until the commissioner signs off on an overage form that binds the record label to pay for it. Without a signed overage, when final bills are submitted to the record label, the producer has no way to prove that the commissioner agreed to the extra costs, and, therefore, the label has no legal obligation to pay.

The *overage form* includes the name of the artist, the video, shoot date(s), record label, video commissioner, production company, director and producer. It also succinctly states what the additional item is, how much it costs, and if there are any potential overtime or surplus costs that may be incurred.

A common cause of music videos going over budget is the artist arriving to the set late. As we saw in Chapter Five, time is money, and time becomes part of the budget negotiation between the record label and the production company. If the production company budgets a shoot for a twelve-hour day, and an artist shows up two hours late, the producer must add two hours to the shooting schedule in order to keep the treatment intact and executed as planned. This will cause the producer to call the commissioner about that extra two hours of overtime. Because the artist has created the need for this additional expense, the label may be willing to accept responsibility, thus agreeing to pay for the additional two hours and what it entails. "If the artist is late and causes production to be behind, then we figure out how far behind and pay the overtime or meal penalty," says Lorin Finkelstein. Devin Sarno comments, "I am okay with an over-age, if it's band-related in nature. If production has been responsible and made efforts to keep things on track, but things just got out of control, as happens from time to time, I will be okay splitting overages with them in an effort to keep things moving—but only if it's evident to me that they were not slacking."

When the record label does not agree to an overage, the director and producer are left in the position of having to figure out how to complete the treatment in less time than initially scheduled. "You have to be ready to trim the concept and think rock n' roll," says Jeff Panzer. "You're always fighting time—time is your worst enemy on a music video shoot. You never have enough of it, so you have to be prepared to think on your feet and not count on overages to save you."

Although there are occasional threats to shut down a shoot in the middle due to money problems, this never really happens. "Pulling the plug is like playing chicken. The director and the producer threaten, but this is the time to get resourceful," says Panzer. "This is when expertise comes into play. What do you have, what do you still need, and you go from there to get it."

The people who work on music videos are excellent problem solvers, and inevitably figure out how to deal with time and money crunches. Any producer worthy of the title constantly works and reworks the budget, finding creative ways to address problems, as well as predict additional expenditures before they happen. They do their best not to spend one extra dime until either someone agrees to give more money by way of an overage or by absorbing the added cost in an existing fee, or the problem is solved by creative means.

The producer usually submits the paperwork for the overages at the very end of the job.

The record label may include the overage with their final payment, or they sometimes pay for it separately. They never pay overages before they have a finished and accepted video in hand.

Of course, video commissioners do not like overages. Nonetheless, there are plenty of occasions when they are unavoidable. Commissioners can be helpful in resolving problems and escaping overages because their responsibility, ultimately, is to the artist and the label. "If it gets to a stressful point by the lunch break, I will get the director, producer, and assistant director together to assess where we are," says Panzer. "Sometimes I may have to tell the artist, as I do with Nelly, that 'we got it,' even if he wants to shoot more. 'Dude, you got your video already. It's in the can. All the rest is gravy you don't need. Ultimately, it's your money. If you don't need it, why burn the money?' That's what I tell the artist fairly often. Ultimately, Nelly knows that I'm looking out for his best interest. The last thing you want to do is screw up the artists' money. By the same token, the company has gotten more corporate about it—they need a good explanation to spend more money, or they need an amazing video. I'm the gatekeeper of the label's money because I'm responsible for the video production department's bottom line, so you have to give me a damn good reason to spend more money than initially budgeted."

PART TWO
PRODUCING THE MUSIC VIDEO

CHAPTER SEVEN
HIRING THE CREW

Once the record company awards the music video to a director and production company, preparation for making the video begins. At this point in the process, the core players—the director, producer, and executive producer—hire their crews, contact their vendors, prepare the artist, and get the postproduction team on hold and ready to begin as soon as the shoot has been completed.

Hiring the crew is a huge part of preproduction. *Crewing up*, or hiring the crew members for the video shoot, and preproduction happen simultaneously, usually in a frenzy. For the sake of organization, this chapter focuses specifically on crewing up.

In music videos, the term "crew" is versatile. Music video professionals use crew in both the singular and plural form and as both a noun and a verb. Also, "crew" and "crew members" are used interchangeably. There are several different crews, such as the lighting crew, the grip crew, the camera crew, that, when combined, form a single crew hired to make a music video. Traditionally, the entire crew is composed of:

- Camera Crew: assistance camera techs that help the director of photography
- Electric Crew: gaffer and electrics
- Grip Crew: key grip and grips
- Art Department: production designer, art director, and others, depending on the size and scope of the video project
- Sound Department: playback tech and, if recording sound, a boom person
- Drivers: grip truck driver, generator driver/operator, and others
- Specialty Item Operators: crane operator, motion control operator, and others
- Production Assistants: general helpers
- Glam Squad: wardrobe stylist, hair-stylist, and make-up artist
- Casting Team: casting director, casting assistant(s)

The last two crews may not be considered part of the crew in certain contexts. For example, if the AD reviews a meal break with the producer, he or she may ask if the crew or artist has eaten. The crew, in this context, means the technical crew who are on the set—the electrics, grips, camera department, sound department, drivers, and any other departments whose full attention is needed while the shoot is taking place. The AD would most likely differentiate the glam squad and casting team in this situation. These individuals are usually afforded the opportunity to break for a meal at other times, perhaps more in line with the artist's schedule, so there is not nearly the urgency of a specified and timed meal break for them. However, when the producer asks the AD at the end of the shooting day if the entire crew has been wrapped, he or she is generally referring to everyone working on the video, making the term crew completely inclusive. The meaning of crew is situation specific, and only through hands-on experience and practice can one know exactly who is being included when it's used.

Some people consider crew members as those "below the line," meaning any worker hired on the project who is hired on a day rate, not on a percentage basis. According to this definition, in music videos, everyone is part of the crew except the director and the producer. Generally speaking, the production team, the director, and the director's assistant(s) are not considered part of the crew. In this chapter, we will define each crew needed to make a music video and explain how the various members of the crew interact with one another.

CREWING UP

As explained, once the music video is awarded to a production company, the company hires a producer who, in turn, hires a production manager and production coordinator. The producer then *books,* or hires, the key people on the project, such as the director of photography, the production designer, the wardrobe stylist, and the assistant director. As discussed earlier, to mitigate the rush of a music video production schedule, the production company may contact many key crew members in advance and have them tentatively pencil the project into their schedules. Once the production company has won the job, the producer can then hire them immediately.

The producer also puts the rest of the crew—such as the electrics, grips, and production assistants—on hold, hiring them when the job is awarded and while all of the other logistical necessities are being arranged. (See Holding or Confirming Crew Members on page 140 for additional information regarding the logistics of crewing up.)

There is no official hard-and-fast rule regarding what members of the crew get hired in which order, other than the director, producer, and their teams being hired first, followed by the heads of each department. Once the producer or production manager tell each department head how many spots to fill and the amount production can pay for each spot, based on the budget, the department heads hire the rest of their teams and simply give the names of those hired to the production team.

As often happens, a job can change shape as the production gets under way, or the producer quickly realizes that the production company underbid the project. Remember, underbidding a project means that the production company knowingly submitted a lower budget to secure a video project. For instance, a crew of two electrics and two grips might have been unrealistically budgeted for a shoot that entails a big lighting setup. In such a case, a department head may insist on additional help. If he or she has a valid request, the producer must figure out a way to cover the additional expense within the budget, or be willing to submit an overage.

Until fairly recently, job responsibilities on a music video tended to be vague compared to other forms of film and video production. As the music video industry has become unionized, job responsibilities have become more codified. Still, there are plenty of overlapping roles and expectations that change from a project-to-project basis. As a result, the following job definitions should be recognized as basic guiding principles and responsibilities of each team and crew.

THE DIRECTOR'S TEAM

As has been discussed, the director is the creative force behind the music video. As such, he or she drives the entire production. Because it's a demanding role that requires considerable organization and delegation of responsibilities, the scheduling and logistical help of the assistant director(s) is crucial.

The Assistant Director

The AD takes charge of the set, keeps everyone on schedule, makes sure everything runs smoothly, and sees that the director commits all the necessary shots to film. The AD supervises the talent, staff, and crew, as well as responding to any demands from the director.

The assistant director also works closely with the producer and the production manager to create a shooting schedule after the team finds a location that satisfies the project's creative guidelines and budgetary constraints. The shooting schedule includes:

• Crew Call Times
• Equipment Call Times
• Meal Times
• Company Move Times

The schedule also contains all the logistical details of the shoot, such as where the vehicles are to be parked. For example, the equipment and generator trucks and honeywagons must be positioned in specific locations near the set, and

it falls to the assistant director to ensure proper parking placement. In addition, the AD ensures everyone's safety on the set.

Typically, the assistant director works on a music video shoot for two to four days. He or she is usually hired for one combined tech scout and prep day, as well as for all of the shoot days. The *tech scout* is when the producer and director take the heads of each department to the chosen location to discuss in detail what the director plans to accomplish. Everyone works together to determine what equipment and planning will be necessary to make it happen (see Chapter Eight starting on page 144 for more details). The ADs *prep day* is when he or she prepares for the shoot by taking all of the information disseminated from the department heads on the tech scout and working with the director and producer to finalize plans and devise a realistic schedule for the shoot. If the budget allows, the assistant director might be hired for two days prior to the actual shoot—one day of scouting and one day of prepping—rather than rushing all of it in one day.

The 2nd Assistant Director

The 2nd AD works with the assistant director, making sure that the artist, talent, and extras are ready when needed on set, seeing them through make-up and wardrobe. The "second," as he or she is sometimes referred to, relieves the "first," or AD, from the responsibility of managing the backstage of the video shoot. The 2nd AD is usually hired only for the shoot day(s).

The 2nd 2nd Assistant Director

If a video's production is very large and has many extras, as well as lots of wardrobe, make-up, and other backstage excitement, an additional experienced 2nd assistant, or "second, second" director may be hired to pick up the slack.

THE PRODUCTION TEAM

While the director has complete charge of the creative aspects of the music video, the producer takes complete responsibility for the business aspects of the video project from the moment the record label awards the job to the moment the completed video lands on the commissioner's desk and the wrap book lands on the head of production's desk. The producer works with the upper management of the project—the director, executive producer, and the label's video commissioner—in addition to the key hires—the production designer, director of photography, editor, and assistant director—to prepare the budget and production schedule. The producer supervises the production on a daily basis to make sure that the production goals are being met and oversees the following:

- Hiring of the Crew
- Gathering of Equipment
- Signing of Necessary Contracts
- Acquisition of Required Permits

The producer hires his or her production team and deals with the logistics of the project, working in tandem with the director to find the best way to bring the vision in the treatment to the screen. To do this properly, the producer must count on his or her team, delegating chores to the production manager and production coordinator, secure in the knowledge that they will accomplish what production needs.

The Production Manager

The producer's right-hand person, the production manager, also called the PM or production supervisor, negotiates equipment and crew rates and adheres to budgetary guidelines per the producer's instructions. The PM is usually in charge of petty cash, doling it out as necessary to workers on the production crew, and collecting the change and receipts at the end of the shoot. The PM works on the project from pre-production through wrap, supervising the production coordinator (see below) throughout the process.

Producer William Green says that he and his production manager have a checks and balances system. His PM covers Green when he makes a mistake, and remembers things when he forgets. Producer Caleb Dewart expects his production manager "to be smart and understand the big picture of what we're trying to do. Bad production managers and coordinators get bogged down in details and don't see the global view. Attention to detail is really important, but understanding why we're doing what we're doing is just as important."

Producer Oualid Mouaness begins building his crew with the heads of the various departments involved in producing the video. He then turns over the rest of the crew negotiations to his PM to complete.

"My production manager is my backbone," says producer Rachel Curl. "Her job is to track every penny and keep constant management of the budget. She and I go through the working budget constantly to make sure we know where we stand. She essentially 'manages' the job, negotiating crew and equipment rates, handling the nitty-gritty details of the job."

The Production Coordinator

The production coordinator, also called the PC or assistant production supervisor, coordinates the mountain of paperwork that accrues during the course of a video project. The production coordinator has complete control over the wrap book, keeping track of all purchase orders and crew information—as well as accounting for every dollar of petty cash dispensed and collected from the production manager. The coordinator works directly with the PM from preproduction through wrap.

"The production coordinator," says producer Rachel Curl, "creates the preproduction book, the call sheet, daily schedules, oversees travel, unless it's a big travel job—in which case I hire a travel coordinator."

"I usually expect the production coordinator to keep the project very organized and support the production manager," Mouaness adds. "The PM relates vendor and crew info to the coordinator, who, in turn, puts it together in a presentable manner and creates the contact and call sheets."

THE CINEMATOGRAPHY TEAM

Headed by the director of photography, the cinematography team includes the entire camera crew, whose size varies from project to project. In music videos, the director of photography usually works as the cinematographer as well, and he or she has at least one, or more, assistants. Depending on the size, scope, concept, and budget of a project, the video may require several cameras. Each camera necessitates, at minimum, one camera assistant. The more cameras required on a project, the more camera assistants the production needs to hire. All of the team members fall under the supervision of the DP.

The Director of Photography

The director of photography knows what it takes to get the image onto film—how to light the scene, what equipment to use, and, in the case of a music video, how to work the main camera. Also called the cameraman or cinematographer, the DP answers to the director. Working with the

director, the DP determines the look of the video and designs specific shots.

The director of photography translates the written words of the treatment onto the screen, supervising the operation of the lighting equipment and the camera crews. The DP participates in the scout, usually spends one or more prep days, and works on the shoot. When possible, the DP also tries to go to the transfer and color correction day during postproduction. This is when the look of the film is manipulated, or corrected, while it is being transferred from the film to digital videotape (see page 189 in Chapter Ten for more information). The DP likes to go to this session to help set the look of the video; however, few video budgets have enough money to pay the DP for the time. Thus, he or she often handles the task as a point of pride to make sure the film comes out looking as good on screen as it did in the camera. The DP usually makes him or herself available via telephone for several days before the shoot, independent of the prep/scout day.

"I design and execute the lighting, and I work with the director to design and execute the shots. I also run the camera crew and lighting crews," says director of photography Joaquin Baca-Asay (Jay-Z's "99 Problems," directed by Mark Romanek and Mansun's "Legacy," directed by Mike Mills). "My goal is to bring the director's vision forward." Baca-Asay also says that he tries to attend the telecine for every music video he shoots. However, "since DPs aren't paid to go the telecine for music videos, we often end up on other projects. So I'd say that I end up going about twenty percent of the time. A lot of the time I take stills on set and send the dailies of the shoot to the colorist with instructions on setting the look. I view it as my responsibility to be there, if I can, and, at the very least, to set the look. In an ideal world, I'd always be at the telecine."

The Camera Operator

The camera operator works the film or video camera per the director of photography's instruction. In music videos, the production has to hire an additional operator for each additional camera the treatment requires. Their skills include framing shots, selecting appropriate photographic lenses, and using equipment such as dollies and cranes to achieve the desired look at the behest of the DP.

The Steadicam Operator

Some treatments call for a Steadicam, rig, and operator. A Steadicam uses a patented gyroscopic device that allows a hand-held camera to move without shaking, which used to plague filmmakers before its invention. Worn on a harness by the operator, a Steadicam does not require a dolly or other wheeled device. A well-operated Steadicam shot looks like it is floating through space. To properly shoot with a Steadicam, the operator must have a great deal of training, often becoming a specialist. Usually hired just for the day of the shoot, the Steadicam operator works closely with the DP. Normally, the Steadicam operator supplies the Steadicam rig, charging a day rate for the service and a kit rental fee for the equipment.

The 1st Assistant Camera

The 1st camera assistant, also called the 1st AC or the focus puller, is in charge of the technical aspects of the camera. Pulling focus, the AC's responsibility, is the act of keeping the camera in focus as it is shooting, and is one of the most important—and difficult—jobs on a music video set. During the setup of a shot, the AC marks out the distances between the camera and the main object of the shoot. Then, during the shot, the numbers on the outside of the lens tell the 1st AC how many feet will be in focus. By reading these numbers and following the series of marks, the 1st AC can focus the lens accordingly.

The 1st AC is also responsible for maintaining the camera; keeping the lens and film gate clean during filming; applying or removing any necessary or unnecessary accessories, such as filters, video assist devices, etc.; loading the film into the magazines, also called mags, which are the containers that hold and transport the film past the lens; and inserting the mags into the camera. If there isn't enough money in the budget to hire a 2nd AC or a loader, the 1st AC must take on this responsibility. The 1st AC oversees the 2nd assistant camera operator in addition to any other member of the camera assist team, such as loaders and camera production assistants.

The day before the shoot, also dubbed the "pick up day," the 1st AC goes to the camera rental house and makes sure that the camera works and that the camera package includes all of the lenses, filters, and any additional items requested by the DP. The camera checkout process usually takes about half a day, which the 1st AC is paid for. The producer usually adds a full- or half-day rate into the budget, depending upon the negotiated deal, for the 1st AC.

The 2nd Assistant Camera

The 2nd assistant camera, also called the 2nd AC, assists the 1st AC on the shoot day. He or she operates the slate, also called the clapper, at the beginning of each take, and loads the film stock into the camera mags between takes, if a loader wasn't hired. The 2nd AC keeps detailed records of how much film was received, when it was received, and how it was used. The 2nd AC also keeps camera reports, which contain information on each roll of film that was shot: the type of film (color, black and white, 16mm,

35mm, etc.); the roll number; the scene number; the take number; and special processing instructions, if applicable. The 2nd AC brings the unexposed film magazines from the loader to the set, and then runs the exposed film back to the loader.

The Loader

The loader inserts unexposed film into the magazines, takes the exposed film out of the magazines, prepares it for the trip to the lab for developing, and then refills the magazine with unexposed film. The loader works with both the 1st and 2nd ACs on the shoot day.

THE ELECTRIC TEAM

Everything having to do with electricity on the shoot is within the domain of the "electrics," or the electric department. The electric department is headed by the gaffer, who works with the DP to create the lighting scheme for each shot.

The number of electrics depends on the specific project. The second electric, who works directly under the gaffer, is called the best boy electric, or best boy, for short. After the best boy electric, each team member's place in the hierarchy is designated by a number. Thus, the 3rd electric works below the best boy, the 4th electric works below the 3rd electric, and so on. The electrics' duties include the following:

- Unloading the lighting equipment from the truck
- Making sure the lights are powered up
- Running cables from the power source to the lights
- Putting gel filters on the lights to obtain the desired effect
- Breaking down the lights at the end of a shoot
- Packing all lighting equipment

The Gaffer

The gaffer is the chief lighting technician. He or she is in charge of all the lights, managing the lighting crew, and working with the DP to ensure that the lighting realizes the director's vision. Prior to the shoot, the gaffer accompanies the DP on the scout to assess which electrical equipment and power are needed on location. On the shoot day(s), the gaffer instructs the electrics on which lights to use, where to place them, and other relevant information.

The Best Boy Electric

The best boy electric is the second position in the electrics team. Female best boys are common, although they are still called "best boy." The best boy assists the gaffer, carries out the gaffer's instructions, and gives instructions to the rest of the electrics team. In addition, the best boy electric runs and positions all of the power cables necessary to run the lights for each shot. Once the lights are placed and powered up, electrics adjust them according to the gaffer's instruction.

THE GRIP TEAM

The grips work very closely with the electrics, assisting them in the task of shifting the lights to new places, setting up scaffolding or rigs for the lights, and helping the art department to erect the set(s). The electrics handle all electrical aspects of the lights, while the grips help with positioning. The grips team must be resourceful, because they are often called to fix broken parts or mount equipment in unconventional places.

The number of grips depends on the specific job. Mirroring the structure of the electric department, the second grip, who works directly under the key grip, is called the best boy grip or best boy. After the best boy grip, the grips also have a hierarchy, with the 3rd grip working below the best boy grip, the 4th grip working below the 3rd grip, etc. The grips' responsibilities in regards to lighting may include the following:

• Helping to hang the lighting (assisting the electrics)
• Creating shadow effects for a shot
• Supervising the placement of platforms or supporting structures for the camera
• Operating camera cranes and/or dollies
• Assisting the camera operator, if necessary

The grips' responsibilities in regard to the art department may include:
• Erecting, assembling, and adjusting sets before and after principal photography (the shoot)
• Building scaffolding above the perimeter of the sets to hang lights
• Constructing stationary and rolling platforms to hold sets, lights, and cameras
• Installing backdrops or large painted backgrounds
• Dismantling the backings, sets, and scaffolding, along with the art department, upon completion of the shoot

The Key Grip

The key grip leads the grip team. Working with the DP and the gaffer, the key grip determines which lights, sets, and props need adjusting to best realize the director's vision. The key grip also accompanies the DP in scouting locations to assess the needs of grip equipment and manpower.

The Best Boy Grip

Similar to the best boy electric, the best boy grip, the second position of the grips team, assists the key grip, carrying out his or her instructions and delegating information to the rest of the grips.

The Dolly Grip

The dolly grip is in charge of operating the camera dolly. He or she places, levels, and moves the dolly track during shots.

The Crane Grip

If the shoot calls for a crane, it is operated by the crane grip, who sets up the crane, makes sure it is in proper working order, and follows all safety procedures. The crane grip operates the crane to get the best shot possible as instructed by the DP, director, and assistant director. In cases where the rental company sends a crane operator with the crane, a crane grip is not needed.

THE LOCATION TEAM

If the treatment calls for real locations, as opposed to building sets on a sound stage, the producer may need to hire a location team. On low budget shoots, there may not be a line included in the budget for a location scout, which means that the production team has to handle the location details and secure the proper permits. This is especially common when the treatment calls for a pre-determined location, such as the Brooklyn Promenade Park in Brooklyn, NY, and requires simply securing permits not scouting or negotiating fees.

Alternatively, if unspecified locations must be secured, such as a huge, modern house with a pool, a scout or location service—which is discussed in greater detail in Chapter Eight starting on page 144—is hired. On lower budget productions, the location manager may also serve as the scout. On bigger, more complicated videos, which call for several locations, the location manager may hire one or more scouts.

The Location Manager

The location manager is in charge of negotiating the deal with the owner of a location, whether a private owner, city, state, or federal government. The location manager secures all permits and location releases, is in charge of safety issues on location, and usually has contacts at various locations regularly used by film crews, as well as relationships within a city's film office. The location manager informs the production team how they need to pay for the location and how they have to protect it. For instance, in some locations, the grips and electrics need to cover the walls and floor during the load in and load out to protect them from scuffing or scratches.

The Location Scout

The location scout hunts for suitable locations as required by the treatment, taking photos of each one to show the producer and director. If the treatment calls for a trendy club, the location scout spends a day or more going to clubs and taking photos. The photos are brought back to the producer to review with the director. When a club is selected, either the location manager or someone on the production team negotiates the details.

THE ART DEPARTMENT

The art department team takes care of the art requirements for the music video, such as the sets, props, and backdrops. The art department is often treated as a self-contained unit within the budget. The art department specifies in the budget what they will need to accomplish the director's vision. Out of the budget, the production designer pays for the art crew salaries, which still go through the regular payroll channels; building materials; props; preproduction; and wrap meals. The production designer and art coordinator usually create their own line items as they see fit.

The size of the art department depends on the treatment and the budget. A minimal art department may be needed when a location shoot, for example, requires only props. Other times, the video calls for a huge art department, such as when the treatment calls for the construction of elaborate sets.

"In the music video art department, you have to have all-around experience," says production designer Teri Whittaker (Ludacris's "#1 Spot," directed by Fat Cats/Chaka Zulu and Bjork's "It's Oh So Quiet," directed by Spike Jonze). "Most of the crew has the know-how to do several jobs. The lead man can also be a carpenter, scenic, and PA all on the same job. We all have learned all the aspects as a necessity. You have to be able to hang a picture, paint a wall, or know where to get fabric. I have driven five-ton trucks to scenicing [painting] walls to sewing curtains. The more you are able to do, the better. Most of the music videos do not have the budgets to support a large list of crew. Only the big budget videos have that level of crew, and they are few and far between."

The Production Designer

The production designer heads the art department. He or she conceives the look of the set and creates the blueprints for its construction, using the director's instruction and the treatment as a map. On the conceptual side, the production designer works closely with the director and often the DP to develop a visual and thematic approach to the video. To get the vision executed involves working closely with the art director or art coordinator.

"The production designer works to make the director happy with the creative, the producer happy with the budget, the AD happy with being one step ahead, and the cinematographer happy by having something great to shoot," explains production designer Teri Whitaker. Accordingly, a production designer must be diplomatic and excellent at multitasking.

"I think of my job as an organizer," Whittaker says. "I need to be able to interpret the director's vision and make it happen. Sometimes it can be difficult to understand exactly what they [directors] may want. It's like seeing an accident: everyone sees it differently. It's very important to be able to ask the right questions and show pictures and drawings of ideas to insure you're on the right track. After the initial meeting, I start to formulate designs, what items we need, and personnel—all, of course, working within a budget. This all happens very quickly. You can have three days to two weeks—very rare and only with very large videos—with the average being five days before you are on stage, if it's a build, or you start shooting, if it's a location. Once on set, my job is to make sure all the elements are ready for shooting and on schedule, with all the necessary pieces of the puzzle put together. I am also responsible for any special effects and picture vehicles—basically, everything in front of the camera except talent, wardrobe (although I can have input and have designed special costumes), and makeup. I am there for the director, a second set of eyes to make sure it all looks great. We all work as a team. I need to communicate with not only the director, but the cinematographer, gaffer, and grips. Creatively, we all get thrown in together and have to work as a well-oiled machine."

The Art Director

The art director, when the budget allows for one—which is a rarity for music videos— implements the production designer's plans while keeping an eye on the art department's budget. He or she creates and maintains the visual consistency of the art elements, including the design, construction, and color of the sets and props according to the production designer's scheme. The art director works closely with each department head within the art department to make sure that set construction and set dressing are in line, both in terms of the creative needs of the video and the budget. "Production designers do work closely with an art director, but it is a luxury in the world of music videos," Whittaker adds. "Instead, you hire a coordinator."

The Art Department Coordinator

On most music videos, the art department coordinator assumes the responsibilities of the art director. In addition, he or she handles the budgeting for the entire department, working closely with the production designer. This is more of an administrative position, rather than a creative one. The art department coordinator keeps accurate records; tracks the ordering, inventory, and use of material; schedules the work; keeps abreast of safety issues; and supervises the entire art department crew.

The Carpenters

The carpenters build the set(s). The lead carpenter is the foreman of the carpentry crew, making sure the woodworking meets the specifications of the production designer and art director.

The Scenics

The scenics paint the set(s), as well as backdrops. They are responsible for the surface treatments of the set(s), which can include special paint treatments such as aging and gliding; simulating the appearance of wood, stone, brick, metal, or stained glass; and anything else needed by the production designer. Using the sketches and ideas of the production designer and art director, the scenics bring the sets to life with color and texture. The lead scenic, or key scenic artist, supervises the crew of painters and is often a master craftsperson.

The Set Decorator

The set decorator's responsibilities include all the aspects of the set's appearance, such as providing furnishings and other objects that are seen in the video. He or she is responsible for both the look of the physical structure of the set as well as how it is dressed (decorated). Once the carpenters finish the construction of the physical walls of the set—or the location scouts and producer agree on a location—the set decorator's crew brings in the furniture, rugs, lighting fixtures, and props, called set dressing.

Set decorators are only hired on high-budget music videos, so they are rarely seen on video projects. "As far as my experience on music videos has been, I have never had a set decorator handle the physical structure of the set or be responsible to the colors, textures, and prop size. This has always been set by the production designer," says Whittaker. "A set decorator is a luxury. A lot of times, it's myself and a shopper/dresser doing it."

The Lead Person

The lead person assists the set decorator, taking responsibility for the logistics and personnel involved in dressing the set. This person is the foreman of the on-set crews, responsible for coordinating the transport of props and materials to and from the set. The lead person works directly with the set decorator or art director/coordinator to schedule and coordinate all activities involving the set.

The Set Dressers

The set dressers on a music video furnish, and subsequently remove, those items that dress or cover the set. The set is constructed by the carpenters, painted by the scenics, and then dressed by the set dressers. They are responsible for the placement of items such as furniture, drapery, carpets, doorknobs, and wall sockets. Most of the work of the set dressers occurs prior to, and after, the actual shooting, but, generally, one set dresser, known as the on-set dresser, remains with the shooting crew. The set dressers work under the supervision of the set decorator or art director/coordinator.

The Property Master

The prop master designs, identifies, locates, selects, acquires, positions, maintains, and disposes of all movable props under the supervision of the set decorator or art director/coordinator. He or she is responsible for preparing the prop breakdown and budget. These props include all set furniture dressings, set furniture, set dressings, trim, hand props, personal props, and plants.

The Assistant Property Master and Property Assistants

Depending on the scale of the shoot and the size of the art department, the art department team may require an assistant prop master(s) and prop assistant(s). On a massive scale video, there can

also be an inside assistant property master, with assistants and a similar team on the outside. The outside team selects and purchases the props. The inside team receives, unloads, inventories, and unpacks those props, subsequently placing them on the sets with the prop master's guidance. Usually on music videos, the property master does all of this by him or herself.

The Art Production Assistants

Art PAs do essentially the same job as general production assistants—assisting the crew with menial jobs—except they are under the direction of the art department. Art PAs are all-purpose, entry-level assistants who perform varied functions, including office clerical work, going on runs for meals and coffee, answering phones, and assisting in any way necessary. The production designer or art director hires them as needed.

THE SOUND DEPARTMENT

The only audio requirement for most music videos is reproducing the video's song. Because while shooting the video, the artist lip-syncs to the song, the artist must hear the track in order to lip-sync effectively. The playback operator works the playback equipment. In the rare case that the video requires dialogue or ambient sound, a boom operator is hired as well.

The Playback Operator

The playback operator works the playback equipment, which normally consists of a DAT machine—which is the device that plays the digital audio tape (DAT) recording of the song—headphones for the playback operator; a slate that syncs the cameras with the DAT machine;

and either a speaker for the playback music or a wireless headset so that the artist can hear the playback music. The production team supplies the playback operator with a DAT tape of the song with an audio time code burnt in, as well as a lyric sheet with the time in the song noted. This allows the playback operator to easily find specific points in the song without having to continually hunt for particular cues before each take. The digital slate syncs up with the play-back system, generating the audio time code so that the camera can roll on the numbers at the beginning of every shot, eventually allowing the audio track and the visual image to be married in postproduction. The playback operator spe-cializes in the on-set technicalities that facilitate this process.

The Boom Operator

If the treatment calls for recording sound, such as spoken parts, ambient noise from the location, crowd noises, or the like, the production team hires a boom operator. The sound boom is a long arm, called a fishpole, with a microphone at the end. The boom operator holds the fishpole, get-ting the boom microphone as close to the speak-er's mouth as possible to pick up the dialogue, or as close as possible to where the ambient sound is coming from, while at the same time holding it out of frame so that the camera doesn't catch it on film. The sound is incorporated into the video during postproduction.

THE GLAM SQUAD

The glamour squad, or glam squad, for short, con-sists of the wardrobe, hair, and make-up crew. An artist's appearance in a video is extremely impor-tant, since it is a major component in establishing the artist's image. Since wardrobe, hair, and make-up are vital tools for storytelling and image making, the individuals who specialize in these fields can be extremely important to the video making process.

Music videos have had an enormous effect on the fashion world, and vice-versa. Artists like Madonna have set trends through the medium since the onset of MTV, creating styles and incorporating fashions of the day and affecting the overall look of popular culture through widespread distribution of their music videos. Wardrobe stylists, hair stylists, and make-up artists help make trendsetters out of the artists they dress.

Seasoned artists have their own wardrobe stylist, hair stylist, and make-up artist. In the case of a new artist, the record label sometimes hires specific individuals for these roles, or they defer to the choices of the director and producer. Shoots often require at least one assistant for each position to work with additional talent or extras in the video, especially if it is a major artist making a big budget video with intricate costumes, elaborate cosmetics, and/or prosthetic applications.

The Wardrobe Stylist

The wardrobe stylist researches and designs the clothing and accessories for the artist, similar to what a costume designer does on a feature film. The stylist oversees the acquisition of all wardrobe including clothing and accessory purchases or rentals and/or the purchase of fabric to be made into an outfit for the artist. He or she supervises all wardrobe fittings and, at the end of the shoot, the disposal of all wardrobe items. The wardrobe stylist works directly with the director, video commissioner, and artist to create the desired look and image for the video. Sometimes the stylist purchases all of the clothing, some-times they are borrowed from a designer, and at times the wardrobe may even be custom made, depending on the treatment and budget.

Whatever the video's budget, the wardrobe stylist must be both creative and well versed in the fashion industry, knowing what's "in," what's affordable, what looks good on the artist, and what color scheme and style works with the treatment and the artist's image. Fashion is a big part of an artist's image, so the wardrobe stylist plays an extremely important role in the video-making process. Although the wardrobe worn by an artist is assembled based on the artist's own personal style and image as projected in the video, depending on the treatment and the budget, a director may come up with a concept in which the wardrobe is reliant on the art department. For instance, one of Missy Elliot's costumes in her "Sock It 2 Me" video directed by Hype Williams was an outrageous sci-fi outfit that matched the scene's art department. The wardrobe was more of an art piece than a wardrobe item. Her dancers wore similar costumes so that the entire choreographed dance completely matched the backdrop, creating a consistent, composed, and finished look.

The wardrobe stylist is the head of the wardrobe department. At times, the wardrobe department consists only of the stylist and an assistant. On bigger budget projects, the stylist can be in charge of dressing several extras, as well as the artist—in which case the stylist will hire more assistants and have more preproduction time built into the schedule.

The wardrobe stylist keeps track of all costs and expenditures. This bookkeeping information is turned into the production coordinator at the end of the project, along with a list of the clothing and what became of it. For instance, was the clothing borrowed from the stylist's kit? Was it purchased and subsequently given to the artist to keep? Was it borrowed or rented from a designer or costume house? This information, along with the cost, is well documented by the wardrobe stylist for the production team and the wrap book.

The Wardrobe Assistant

The wardrobe assistant works directly for the wardrobe stylist and is responsible for the selection, acquisition, rental, and care of all wardrobe items. He or she may also prepare a breakdown of the wardrobe involved in the shoot, detailing what is to be worn during each scene. It is usually the assistant's job to make sure that the clothing is clean and pressed for the shoot, as well as cleaned after the shoot, if it is going to be returned to a vendor or designer.

The wardrobe assistant is often hired for one or more days prior to the shoot to pick up clothing and is kept on for a day or two after the shoot to return unused or rented items. On most music videos, the budget can only support a wardrobe stylist and one or two assistants, so the stylist manages the wardrobe budget. However, on more expensive productions, the wardrobe assistant may assume this responsibility.

The Tailor/Seamstress

If the budget allows, the wardrobe stylist may employ a tailor or seamstress on set to adjust the wardrobe and sew last-minute alterations. The tailor's responsibility is to be well versed in sewing specialty items, altering, hemming, mending, repairing, and replacing parts of garments and reconstructing garments, if necessary. The tailor may also be called on to remove stains, or press and/or steam the wardrobe.

The Hair Stylist

The hair stylist designs the artist's hairstyle for the shoot, working closely with the director, the video commissioner, and the artist to create the artist's look. If the artist's hairstyle for the video will be particularly intricate, the hair stylist needs to begin the process of creating the hairstyle a day or two before the shoot. The stylist may also be required to cut, color, and/or wash the artist's hair or design a wig for the artist.

Throughout the shoot, the hair stylist stays by the monitor and watches as each take is filmed, making sure that the artist's hair continues to look good. (It's very easy for the performer's hair to get in his or her face, or for a loose curl or bit of hair to bounce in an unflattering way.) When shooting a dance sequence, where there is a lot of movement, or shooting in a location that is wet or hot, the hair stylist is briefed prior to the shoot and may even consult with the artist, director, and video commissioner beforehand to address potential issues before they arise.

Hair stylists build and maintain files of their clients' hair in a portfolio, which should include different ethnicities, historical periods, and interesting, unusual looks. The hair stylist's portfolio serves as an audition. It's a means to demonstrate his or her skill, similar to a resume.

Successful hair stylists keep up with the latest hair trends and innovative technologies. They must have excellent color vision, as well as creativity, imagination, and refined interpersonal and communication skills. Most hair stylists are self-confident and outgoing, working well with all sorts of personalities, and are adept at accepting suggestions and criticism. Hair stylists must be flexible and be able to work long hours. Many hair stylists are also make-up artists. However, only on very low budget projects, or projects that do not require detailed hair and make-up attention—such as all male rock bands—will the same person do both hair and make-up.

The Hair Assistant

The hair assistant works directly for the hair stylist. The assistant is called to do various jobs, such as shopping for hair supplies or wigs, prepping the artist's hair either the day before the shoot, if necessary, or on the day of the shoot. This may mean washing his or her hair or simply brushing it or preparing it for special color or bleaching treatments. The assistant may help the hair stylist by holding supplies, such as brushes, curlers, or scissors while the stylist is using them on the artist. The assistant's role may also include styling the extras' hair while the main hair stylist works on the artist(s).

The Make-up Artist

The make-up artist applies cosmetics to enhance the artist's natural beauty, or pats down the artist's face and applies powder to combat perspiration, which causes the artist to appear shiny on film. If the treatment calls for a dramatic or costumed look, the make-up artist creates a specific look in consultation with the director, applying theatrical make-up to achieve it. Generally, the goal is to make the artist look as appealing as possible. The make-up artist applies the cosmetics for the shoot; prepares a make-up schedule, if necessary; and supervises and coordinates other members of the make-up team, including assistants and special effects make-up artists—for prosthetics or other effects—as necessary. Applying the make-up can be as basic as powdering down a male rocker between takes or as intricate as developing a futuristic look. In rare cases, the application of a prosthetic mask for a complete transformation may be required.

To create designs, the make-up artist considers what the treatment calls for, the budget, and the artist's image. If the treatment is a period piece, which portrays a period of time, either in the past or future—the make-up artist must take that into account. Many factors play into the make-up design, including the age of the artist, the location(s) of each scene, the lighting, the time of day, and the overall mood of the treatment.

As with the hair stylist, once the initial application is finished, the make-up artist spends the shoot day by the monitor and watches each take, making sure that the artist's make-up continues to look good and consistent. The artist's make-up must be perfect in every shot. Caring for it can include everything from touching up elaborate cosmetics, so the dance diva looks the same in every shot, to keeping male heavy metal rockers powdered down, so their faces don't shine under the lights.

Make-up artists must keep on top of the technology and trends of cosmetics, as well as understand the basics of lighting and the photographic process, especially as it pertains to colors, skin tones, and the impact of both basic make-up on skin and basic special effects. They need to know how to minimize or eradicate any blemishes on the artist's skin and prevent any unpleasant side effects from the use of specialized make-up techniques.

Occasionally, music videos employ special make-up effects or prosthetics, the most famous example being Michael Jackson's "Thriller" video, directed by John Landis, in which Michael turns into a werewolf. Award-winning make-up artist Rick Baker created this metamorphosis. A special effects make-up artist familiar with casting facial and body molds sculpted from latex foam, known as prosthetics, must be employed when doing this type of detailed make-up.

The Make-up Assistant

The make-up assistant works directly for the make-up artist. The assistant helps the make-up artist on the shoot day, carrying the make-up kit, holding and passing brushes and equipment to the make-up artist, while he or she works on the music artist(s), and chores of this nature. The assistant's role may also call for applying cosmetics to the extras while the main make-up artist works on the music artist(s).

THE CASTING TEAM

If the treatment calls for more performers than just the artist to appear in the video, the producer hires a casting director, and, sometimes—when the shoot requires a large group of extras—a casting assistant. The casting team oversees auditioning and hiring talent and extras. They may also have to gather together the talent and extras on set, acting as their link to the production team and making sure their basic needs are met on the shoot day(s), such as assuring an easily accessible bathroom and craft (food) service. The role of the casting point person usually falls to the casting assistant, who makes sure that the talent and extras do what they were hired to do in a timely manner for the sake of the production schedule.

The Casting Director

When the treatment calls for specific casting requirements, the producer gives the casting breakdown to a casting director who has professional relationships with talent agents. Generally, the casting director auditions models, actors, and dancers, and tapes the audition, checking scheduling conflicts and the union status of the talent. He or she then shows the videotape and headshots to the director, advising on casting choices. Since casting is such a critical element in the value of the production, the final casting decision is made by the director or occasionally the artist, often in consultation with the video commissioner. Once the director makes final choices, the casting director offers the cast the going rate, which, on a low budget video, is called a flat fee—meaning overtime is not built in. On a bigger budget project, the casting director negotiates the fee either with the talent or with that person's agent.

The Casting Assistant

During the auditioning process, the casting director may require the help of an assistant to organize headshots; call models, actors, dancers, or agents to schedule audition times; run the video camera; act as the reader with the auditioning talent; or the like. During the shoot, the casting director often sends the assistant to the set to make sure that the producer treats the talent and extras appropriately and takes care of their needs, as well as ensuring that the talent and extras behave and work in a professional manner. The casting assistant also makes sure the talent and extras fill out the proper talent releases. This position may overlap with that of the 2nd AD, depending on the scope of the project.

ADDITIONAL CREW POSITIONS

The following positions are other crew positions that are usually part of the music video production team but do not fall under any of the specific departments discussed above.

- VTR Operator
- Grip Truck Driver
- Generator Operator
- Crane Operator
- Fire Safety Officers
- Craft Services
- Storyboard Artist
- Production Assistants

The Video Tape Recording Operator

The video tape recording operator records everything shot by the camera(s) on the VTR machine. A VTR machine archives video dailies in real time so that the director, video commissioner, artist, or anyone on set can review footage that was recently shot. If there is a question such as how the artist looked in a shot or if a visual effect was pulled off properly, the VTR allows the team to review the footage and make an informed decision. The video tape recording operator starts and stops the recording equipment, monitors video and audio levels, and verifies the actual recording on the VTR. The operator also labels tapes and tape cases in order to avoid confusion.

The Grip Truck Driver

The grip truck driver drives the truck, supplying the equipment from the lighting and grip rental business to the location of the shoot. He or she stays with the truck all day. If it is a two-day shoot, the driver takes the equipment back to the rental house when the first day wraps, and either the same driver or another one returns with the equipment on the next shoot day.

The company supplying the lighting and grip equipment usually hires the driver, in addition to supplying the truck to transport the equipment to the location of the shoot. However, the production company normally pays the driver out of their budget—as opposed to the rental house paying for the driver.

The Generator Operator

The generator operator, also known as the genny operator, drives the generator truck to the location of the production. He or she stays with the generator, or genny, which is attached to the truck, all day, taking it from location to location as necessary. The generator operator also helps the electrics connect the power cords to the generator—also known as "tying in"—to provide power to the lights and troubleshoots if there is an electrical problem having to do with the generator. On a two-day shoot, the genny driver takes the generator back to the rental house when the first day wraps.

The company supplying the generator may hire a generator truck driver to bring the generator to the set and run it, depending upon the size and budget of the production and how much power is needed. Once again, it falls to the production company's budget to pay the driver. However, it is not uncommon for the producer or production manager to order a free-standing genny to be dropped off at the location and have one of the electrics work it.

The Crane Operator

In certain specialized treatments, a crane operator may be hired to operate a specialty crane, such as a technocrane. This apparatus is a telescopic remote camera crane that moves up and down, extends forward, and retracts backward to create a flowing visual effect.

Fire Safety Officers

Certain states or municipalities require the presence of fire safety officers in certain situations. For instance, the Los Angeles County Fire Department has various rules and regulations about hiring fire safety officers who are retired Los Angeles County Fire Department personnel specially trained to recognize and resolve fire and safety hazards associated with the film industry. In Los Angeles, the production staff calls the project in to the film commission, which determines if they are shooting in a high-risk fire area and need a fire safety officer on location. In New York, there is no such position.

The Craft Service Person

The craft service person shops for food snacks and serves them on the shoot day(s). This person makes sure that the crew and the cast are always able to find well-prepared food and hot and cold beverages during the shoot.

The Storyboard Artist

Some directors and producers hire a storyboard artist to draw key scenes of the treatment so that the director can visually express the shots and sequences for the record label, artist, and crew. Some directors, like Marcus Nispel, prefer to draw the storyboards themselves. "I do shooting boards, so I get as many possible visuals in one video," Marcus says. "I think the style of my videos is that there are a lot of images in it. I've started to board more to allow myself to get into set-ups where I can get as many possible situations. I am aware that some music video directors don't use boards. I don't know how they can do without them."

The hiring of a storyboard artist depends on the budget. If hired, this individual creates storyboards at the very beginning of pre-production to use as a visual reference throughout the prep and the shoot.

The Production Assistants

Production assistants, or PAs, are utilitarian, entry-level assistants who perform various functions, including office clerical work, running errands, answering phones, and assisting in any way necessary. As we've noted, many teams have production assistants, including:

• Office PAs, who assist the production team
• Set PAs, who work for the AD team
• Camera PAs, who work for the camera team
• Art Department PAs, who work for the art department team
• Parking PAs, who are hired to hold parking spaces throughout the night before a shoot, if necessary

• Pick up and return PAs, who pick-up various equipment the day before the shoot and return it the day after the shoot.

LESS COMMON CREW POSITIONS

Some videos require non-standard crew positions. Although there are many types of crew positions hired on an "as needed" basis, the most common are:

• Security Staff
• Wrap Crew
• Teamsters

Security Staff

The production may need security staff to protect a film set and the people on it, depending on the artist, the location, the number of extras, and the time of day. For example, at night, a location may be less safe than during the day or a location may be busier at rush hour and require additional security.

The Wrap Crew

The wrap crew begins working at the end of the shoot, breaking down all of the equipment and putting it away. While this task usually falls to the grips and electrics, who set up the equipment, certain circumstances—especially if there are extensive lighting setups and the schedule calls for a long shoot day—require that the production hires a wrap crew at a regular pay rate to help avoid racking up huge overtime expenses. Additionally, a tired crew works more slowly, and a prudent producer does not want to work a crew to the point of exhaustion.

The Teamsters

The International Brotherhood of Teamsters, commonly known as the Teamsters, is one of the largest labor unions in the United States. Teamsters Local 399 in Los Angeles and Teamsters Local 817 in New York provide animal trainers, auto service personnel, casting directors, chef drivers (the person who drives the catering truck for location catering services), couriers, dispatchers, drivers, location managers, mechanics, warehousemen, and wranglers to the motion picture and television industry. Depending on the budget tier of the music video, and if the production company is a signatory of the union, the Teamsters may demand that productions use their members. For any production with a budget under $50,000, the Teamster agreement does not apply. For budgets above $50,000, a production company that has an agreement with the Teamsters must follow strict union rules.

SPECIALTY CREW POSITIONS

Some treatments require special crew positions on an "as needed" basis per the requirements of the treatment. Examples of some of these positions include:

• Stunt Coordinators and Stunt People
• Pyrotechnic Specialists
• Lighting Designers
• Animal Handlers
• Helicopter Pilots
• Motion Control Operators
• Water Truck Operators

The Stunt Coordinator

If the treatment calls for stunts, the producer has to hire a stunt coordinator. This individual, in conjunction with the production team, takes charge of hiring stunt people and dealing with the logistics of the stunts in the video. The stunt coordinator choreographs the action sequences so that they are performed safely yet look real to the viewer. He or she hires the stunt people for each sequence and acts as the department head, assembling the stunt people, negotiating rates, ordering stunt equipment in tandem with the production team, and overseeing rehearsals and the stunts.

Stunt People

Stunt people specialize in creating death-defying acts for film. They are specially trained to handle a variety of stunts, from diving through a glass window to jumping off buildings, from wrestling and boxing to car crashes and running through fire.

The Pyrotechnic Specialist

The pyrotechnic specialist has detailed knowledge, experience, and training in creating fire effects. The pyrotechnic gives advice, plans, and supervises the safe execution of a fire effect to give the director the look he or she needs. He or she specifies and procures all explosives and other material based on the look the director has described; ensures all materials are fit; makes sure the equipment gets transported and stored safely; and identifies potential emergency measures, such as fire fighting and first aid. The pyrotechnic also guides the production team through the process of obtaining proper permits and informing necessary city, state, or federal agencies and individuals in the allotted amount of time.

The Lighting Designer

A lighting designer, or LD, is hired when the video calls for rock and roll lighting, which is akin to live concert lighting. He or she works with the director, DP, and set designer to help create an overall look and tone for the video. The LD works with the gaffer and electrics for much of the hands-on technical work, such as hanging and focusing the lights, and is in charge of programming and operating the light board.

The Animal Handler

A treatment calling for the use of animals necessitates hiring an animal handler, who finds special animals trained for specific shots or who trains the animal specially, depending on the scenario and the time frame. An animal handler is hired for everything from a tiger pacing in a cage to a dog that is trained to fetch items to bees swarming. He or she helps plan and coordinate the shot in order to achieve the desired animal stunt, using humane standards of care for the animal.

The Helicopter Pilot

If the treatment calls for aerial shots, the production hires a helicopter pilot who is familiar with the area being photographed from above and who knows how to rig the camera system to the helicopter with specialized, gyro-stabilized mounts that are supplied by the aerial photography company.

What makes a great music video?

"[A great video is] when you've added to the song and if you can elicit an emotional connection in three minutes."
—Kate Miller, Senior Vice President of Film and Video; Capitol Records

"A great video respects the artist and relates to the music in some capacity. It sort of captures something inside of you. It doesn't have to have a meaning directly, but it just does something to you inside."
—Peter Care, Director

The Motion Control Operator

Some videos call for a rig that allows the camera to move finely and smoothly past a model of any size. The images this camera records is used in postproduction to create convincing cinematic illusions. To create these effects, a motion control rig is needed. This is a computer-controlled camera crane that allows the camera to maneuver in ways that would be difficult or impossible to control manually. Using this equipment requires hiring a motion control operator and a technician specially trained to shoot these effects. (See page 157 in Chapter Eight for more information on the motion control device.)

The Water Truck Operator

If a treatment calls for rain or a large-scale ground wet-down, the production must bring in a water truck and someone who knows how to use it properly. The water truck operator brings the water truck to the location and monitors the amount of water used with a water meter. He or she is cued by the AD to release the water and shut it off.

HOLDING OR CONFIRMING CREW MEMBERS

While the record company draws up the contract and all the technical and logistical details for the music video get sorted out, the production company most often puts the crew on hold. This avoids cancellation fees that may occur when a production books crew members and the project falls through. IATSE-MVPA rules dictate a minimal grace period for cancellation. If the worker is cancelled by 3:00 P.M. the prior non-workday, or by the end of the prior workday, or by 6:00 P.M.

the prior day for weather reasons, the production company does not have to pay the penalty. However, though legal according to the union, waiting that long often annoys the crew member, who may think twice about taking another job with the production company.

On the other hand, top positions, such as the DP or a high-end wardrobe stylist, often require *play or pay* deal memos, which state that the individual hired gets paid even if the job never happens. For example, highly sought-after DPs usually have agents. It is common practice for a producer to put a DP on hold for a possible shoot date as soon as it looks like the job is going to book, meaning the record company awards the shoot to a specific director. If another producer calls the agent afterward, the agent puts the DP on a first hold for the producer who called first and a second hold for the producer who called second—first come, first served.

If the company with the second hold is ready to book before the company with the first hold, the agent calls the producer with the first hold and gives him or her the option of booking the DP immediately or passing. Normally, the first hold producer asks the agent for as much time as possible in order to consult with the label's video commissioner. The agent may agree to wait until the end of the day, which is hopefully enough time to get instructions. The commissioner tells the producer either to book the DP or to pass. If told to book the DP, the producer asks that the commissioner immediately send over the contract for the video or asks for a signed letter of confirmation or commitment so that the label will pay for the cost of the DP (see Letters of Commitment and/or Confirmation on page 109 in Chapter Six). If instructed to pass, there's a good chance of losing the DP to the second hold producer. More and more often, production companies insist on the right to cancel the play or pay deal if the DP's agent finds him or her other work for the same time period.

In general, the crew members most likely to have agents are the DP, the glam squad, the production designer, and the offline editor. Because they are represented by agents, their deals are more difficult to negotiate, and, in turn, are stricter when it comes to the cancellation policy. This makes it much more desirable to keep these individuals on hold as long as possible before booking them.

DETERMINING CREW MEMBER STATUS AS INDEPENDENT CONTRACTOR OR EMPLOYEE

Although members of the crew and the production team consider themselves independent contractors, or freelancers, when the production company books them for a shoot they become part-time employees of the production company according to the definition by the United States government. There are various legal technicalities involved in being an independent contractor. These laws can impact both the contractor as well as the company hiring the contractor.

The Internal Revenue Service—the federal agency responsible for administering and enforcing the United States Treasury Department's revenue laws by collecting taxes, making the rules for pension plans, and related activities—has set guidelines of twenty factors to determine where an employer-employee relationship exists and a situation where a company can consider a worker an independent contractor. Additionally, each state also has its own rules regarding the status of workers.

The main factors when determining the difference between an independent contractor and an employee include:

• Behavioral Control
• Financial Control
• Relationship of the Employer/Employee Parties

Other factors include whether the person works during specific hours, or is provided with any training; whether the worker incurs and pays for his or her own business expenses; and whether the worker is free to work for others during the same time period. Each factor specified in the IRS list of 20 Common Law Factors (or more for some individual states) assists in determining who controls or has the right to control the details and terms of employment. If the worker controls those terms, the tax code classifies that individual as an independent contractor. If the employer controls them, the person is classified as an employee, even if only part time. Since video production demands that crew members show up at a specific time and place for a specific amount of time, the employer has to play it safe, and as a result, production companies treat most workers as part time employees.

All of these definitions and guidelines boil down primarily to one thing: taxes. Employers withhold taxes from their employees' earnings but not from independent contractors' earnings. Independent contractors pay their own taxes. The same is true for unemployment benefits. If a company employs a worker, that worker can, if he or she meets the other guidelines, collect unemployment benefits from that company. An independent contractor cannot collect unemployment benefits.

A production company can save a lot of money in taxes by hiring independent contractors. However, the Internal Revenue Code imposes substantial penalties on employers for calling actual employees independent contractors for the purpose of avoiding the payment of taxes.

A production company can save a considerable amount of money—the twenty-seven to thirty-four percent P&W costs—by having a crew member invoice the company and get paid directly, completely avoiding the payroll company. However, this is illegal because very few workers on a film production fit the government's definition of independent contractor. Consequently, the government can come after the production company for back taxes and penalties. In the end, this can cost the company far more than it saved by not withholding and paying the taxes in the first place.

Because an employee's status is a gray area, most production companies choose to use a payroll company for all the workers on the set. In addition to acting as the employer for each worker, the payroll company supplies worker's compensation insurance, an integral aspect of production (see page 47 in Chapter Three for insurance details). The payroll company becomes the official employer of each worker hired by the production company.

What if someone on set—the producer, for argument sake—has her own company and prefers that her paycheck be written out to her company rather than to her as an individual? She can do this and still be paid through the payroll company, which is the cautious way to handle the situation. This is called using a *loan out company*, the production company hiring another company to do a job. In other words, the production company hires the producer's company as the producer on the job—as opposed to simply hiring the producer outright. Rather than paying the producer and also withholding taxes through the payroll company, the producer fills out a specific *loan out timecard* supplied by the payroll company. Some payroll companies don't have a separate timecard for this, but they do require specific information for the regular timecard, such as the loan out company's federal identification number instead of the individual's social security number. The payroll company then takes out only the appropriate taxes, if any, and the producer's production company pays the taxes on the income from that specific project.

Government rules and regulations allow a company to pay six hundred dollars to an individual over the course of one year without taxing that income. As a result, the production company should only pay a worker directly for his or her services when the total cost of the payment is six hundred dollars or less for an entire year. Otherwise, the production company should insist on having all of its workers paid through the payroll company.

Part of what creates and perpetuates the gray area between the concept of independent contractor and employee in music videos is the use of personal *kits*—tools purchased and maintained by a particular worker that is specific to that person's job—and the common practice of *kit rentals*. Along with hiring the person's services, the production company can rent the person's kit as needed, on a project-by-project basis. For instance, the production team—producer, production manager, and production coordinator—each have their own laptop computer as well as their own kit—supplies and items that are flexible enough to fit into any company's system that are as generic as pens and pencils, and as detailed as standard location releases. The production manager or the production coordinator should have the most detailed kit of the production team.

There are plenty of occasions when the production team is working out of a space that's not a fully stocked office, such as a motor home on location. In these situations, the production team must bring pens, pencils, tape, a printer, and any other supplies and paperwork they might need. This is all part of the kit, which can also be added on to by the production office. On most productions, depending on the budget, the production manager and/or coordinator then charge a kit rental fee, above and beyond their day rates. The time cards have a separate space to include a kit rental fee.

One IRS guideline as to independent versus employee status has to do with whether the individual has supplied his or her own equipment to do the job, or whether the employer supplied the equipment. Because several workers on a film production have their own kits, this adds to the confusion over their employment status. However, there is a space on the payroll timecard for the worker to add his or her kit rental fee, which is treated as a reimbursable expense by the payroll company and therefore not taxed by the government. It is always better to be cautious in these circumstances.

Other departments that often have kits and require kit rentals are the art department, either the production designer or the art director, and the DP or gaffer. The production designer or art director generally own tools and rent them to the production for the length of the prep, shoot, and wrap. The DP or gaffer often own "expendables"—tools and items that get used once and then thrown away—that they'll charge production for on a per use basis.

Concurrently with hiring the crew, all other aspects of preproduction are also underway and the music video production quickly takes on a life of its own.

CHAPTER EIGHT
PREPRODUCTION

At the same time the production company staff starts hiring its crew to work on the video, a flurry of other activity begins as well:

- Scouting and Securing Locations
- Renting Equipment and Hiring Vendors
- Determining the Shooting Schedule
- Standard Business Necessities and Details

Once the project is commissioned, the race begins. As important a commodity as money, time never seems to be on the side of the producer or director. Although everyone knows what he or she needs to do to prepare for the shoot, getting it done before the clock runs out is always a challenge.

SCOUTING AND SECURING LOCATIONS

Because it's generally less expensive than building a set, music videos are often shot on location. Once the project is awarded, the production team determines where it will be shot. Sometimes the location stated in the treatment is so specific that the team can secure it without the help of a scout. If, for example, a treatment calls for a backdrop of the Bethesda Fountain in New York's Central Park, the production manager or coordinator can simply go to the New York City Mayor's Office of Film, Theatre and Broadcasting and acquire the necessary permit. A more obscure or general location—such as a gravel pit or a location open to interpretation, such as a trendy nightclub—would most likely necessitate hiring a scout to find the location, handle the permission request, and obtain the permit.

To save money, the producer may use a *location service* prior to hiring a scout. These services keep photos on file of many locations, although they don't go out and search for new ones. If the director and producer find an appropriate location in the files, they will not need to hire a scout.

THE TECHNICAL SCOUT

Once the location scout or location service finds the right spot, the producer and director scout it out to make sure the location will work. If it meets their needs, the producer instructs the scout or service to *book* the location, meaning negotiate a fee for its use, and execute a contract regarding the agreed upon rules, regulations, and time frame, and obtain a permit, if applicable—if it's a private residence, there's a good chance that a permit will not be required.

Key members of the crew then go on a *technical (tech) scout*. The point of the tech scout is to bring the department heads together on location with the director and the producer to discuss in detail what the director plans to accomplish. They physically walk through the space where they intend to shoot and figure out what technicalities they need to deal with as well as what equipment they need to order to bring the director's vision to life.

The tech scout takes place prior to the shoot. The *turnaround* time on music videos—colloquially meaning their commencement, manifestation, and completion—occurs quickly. Because of this, the scout inevitably takes place two to three days before the actual shoot. The members of the team attending the tech scout are the:

- Director
- Producer
- Director of Photography
- Production Manager
- Assistant Director
- Gaffer
- Key Grip
- Production Designer
- Location Manager/Scout

If the treatment calls for stunts or pyrotechnics, the stunt coordinator or pyrotechnics technician may also join the scout to assess the situation. In some instances, additional crew or city officials may need to come along, as determined by the details of the treatment, the location, and city rules and ordinances. For instance:

(1) If a treatment calls for pyrotechnics of any nature in most large metropolitan areas, a city fire official and the pyrotechnics technician must attend to give permit approval.

(2) If a treatment calls for shooting in a subway system, a transit official needs to come to sign off on the plan of action.

(3) If the treatment calls for filming in a forest, the governing laws may require that the production have a forest ranger on the scout.

(4) If the treatment calls for closing down an active roadway, local police will insist on joining the scout to make sure the desired shot is safe before agreeing to close down the street.

The tech scout is important for a host of reasons. It better enables key workers, such as department heads, to go into the shoot on the same page, ensuring tighter organization on the shoot day(s). After hearing the director's ideas and doing a walk-through of the location, each department can then put together an order of what equipment they'll need for the shoot. The production manager gathers these orders and submits them to the appropriate equipment rental houses.

The tech scout allows the gaffer to check out the location's power supply. This is particularly important for a location shoot, as opposed to one taking place on a sound stage. By thoroughly examining the power supply, if any, the gaffer determines if it's both possible and safe to tie into the existing power source or whether the shoot will require a generator.

Once they finish the tech scout, the assistant director can schedule the shoot day with the producer, determining what time the crew needs to arrive to the set, and when each set up and *company move*—when the entire production wraps one location and goes to another location for additional shooting—will occur. The director then adjusts the specific shot list accordingly. All of this preparation makes for a far smoother shoot.

Depending on the location, the production team may need to supply a production van for crew transport to the scout and, subsequently, the shoot. In this case, the production will hire a PA to drive. The IATSE-MVPA Agreement outlines a set of travel rules that includes when transportation must be made available for the crew and when they have to get to the location on their own.

Frequently, the production team obtains a permit for the scout from the local film office. This allows for special parking privileges for the vehicle(s) during a specific time period. Lack of access to special parking can cause a major problem, especially in cities such as New York or Los Angeles.

THE HOLDING AND STAGING AREAS

If the treatment calls for extras, during the scout the producer and AD must decide where to set up the *holding area*, an area for the talent and extras to stay when they're not being filmed, and the equipment *staging area*, a place to house the items taken off the equipment trucks in preparation for their use. They also need to locate an out of the way area to set up the craft service table and, when it's time, set up catering, tables, and chairs for crew meals.

Other considerations include whether the location offers amenities like bathrooms or, for an outdoor location, what to do in case of rain. The tech scout allows the production team to address these logistical details. If there are no easily accessible bathrooms, as in a large park or a forest, the production team hires either a motor home for crew facilities, or portable toilets. The ideal solution is to hire a motor home to double as crew toilets and the production office, but if there is a large crew, more than one bathroom may be required, in which case portable toilets are the best options.

A rain contingency plan is important, especially since music videos rarely, if ever, carry weather insurance. For the most part, they shoot "rain or shine." If the shoot is taking place somewhere completely exposed to the elements, such as a mountain top or wide open field, the production team should consider hiring a tent with the capacity for enclosed sides to keep people and equipment from exposure to the elements.

PERMITS

Permit requirements change from location to location and are based on federal, state, and city laws as well as local jurisdictions. The production must have proper permits to film at public places, such as parks or libraries, and federal, state, or city property. The local film office, usually in the government area of the Yellow Pages, can help with obtaining these permits. Sometimes obtaining a permit involves the payment of a fee, as in most areas in Los Angeles. Sometimes location permits are free, as in New York City, which even supplies police from the Special Officer's Division (SOD) at no charge if the powers that be at the Mayor's Office of Film, Theatre and Broadcasting feel it is important for the safety of all involved on the shoot. If the treatment necessitates closing down active roadways or if a high profile artist is involved, which could potentially create a crowd control problem, the Mayor's Office may insist that the production company hire additional police or traffic officers.

Generally, filming on private property does not require a permit, although local ordinances may govern certain aspects of the shoot. For instance, some townships have laws dictating sound levels. Although it may be legal to shoot at a private home all night, the municipality might consider blasting *playback*—the song played through the sound package so the artist can lip-synch to it—past a certain hour a disturbance of the peace. When filming in a city, shooting in a privately owned apartment might not require a permit, but running the cables from a generator parked in the street next to the apartment may, because the sidewalk is city property.

Filming in a city, especially one as crowded and tight to maneuver in as New York, usually requires parking permits issued by the city's office of film and television. The production team can obtain a parking permit for the scout to save time and avoid the hassle of trying to find parking spots. Parking permits allow the production to reserve parking near the location and, at times, to park in usually forbidden spots. In the case that a vehicle under the jurisdiction of the film permit is mistakenly given a parking ticket, the film office that issued the permit will reverse it, provided the production team submits the ticket according to the film office guidelines and in a timely fashion.

If a shoot has special requirements, especially those that can be dangerous—such as pyrotechnics, stunts, or shutting down an active roadway for filming—the governing body issuing the permit often insists on approving the action in advance. This will be noted on the permit. Generally, the permit details the action to be filmed, where it will be taking place, and at what time, sometimes stating whether the shoot requires any city officials—such as police or fire safety officers on site for the specific action.

If the location is in a high traffic area, the production may need to hold parking spots overnight to ensure that the equipment trucks have a place to park near set. It's not uncommon to hire parking PAs to hold parking spots through the night, especially in a city like New York, where parking is at a premium.

RENTING EQUIPMENT AND HIRING VENDORS

Every production company uses standard equipment such as a camera, grip, and electrical supplies. While some of the equipment used depends on the crew and the results of the technical scout, the contract will call for a shooting format, for example, so that the production staff can immediately put either a 35mm or 16mm film camera body—or, in rare occasions, a digital camera body—and a basic lens package on hold with a camera rental house. Once the tech scout has been completed, the DP can order the specific and special equipment for the camera. The same holds true for the basic grip/electric package, as

What do you love about music videos?

"I love being on sets and seeing how people work. That whole dynamic is a lot of fun. I actually really do love the post process too. I always have."
—Devin Sarno, Vice President, Visual Content; Warner Brothers Records

"I love two things. One is that it helped me get to where I'm at, in terms of my career and my feeling that I've done some kind of good work. I wouldn't be here, physically in America, and I don't think I would have been a filmmaker if I had to rely on making feature films in England or becoming a DP at BBC or something. I just wouldn't have been able to get to a place where I'm expressing myself with film. So that's very important. Second, in terms of the overall picture, just being more objective and just thinking what's good for cinema and art and culture. I'm proud to have been part of music videos. It did change things, and it did give people a different way of looking at things. There was a lot of intelligence behind the good work, and it increased peoples' awareness of film as an art form."
—Peter Care, Director

"I love videos. You don't need continuity in music videos. That's one of the charms of it all. It's one of the few places that says, 'Here's a canvas; go paint.'"
—Jeffrey A. Panzer, Independent Video Commissioner; Formerly Emperor of All Videos/Music Executive at Universal Music Group

well as other items. Once the tech scout is completed, the department heads put in their orders, and the production team begins ordering the equipment requested. Basic equipment and supply orders generally include the following items:

- The Camera Package
- The Sound Package
- The Audio Package
- The Grip/Electric Package
- The Generator
- Cranes and Lifts
- The Dolly
- The Video Tape Recorder (VTR)
- Walkie-talkies
- Production Trailers/Motor Homes
- Vehicles
- Production Supplies
- Expendables
- Film Stock
- Caterers
- Specialty Needs

THE CAMERA PACKAGE

Vendors that rent film camera packages to film production companies generally carry both 16mm and 35mm cameras. They also have the capability to adjust their 16mm cameras to accommodate the Super 16mm format. The camera rental houses carry all of the equipment the DP will order, such as lenses, filters, matte boxes, magazines, tripods, and the like, in addition to the basic package. Some companies rent digital cameras with all of their accoutrements (lenses, filters, etc.) as well, especially bigger, well-known outfits.

For music videos, a *crystal sync* camera must be used. This is a camera that has a crystal in it that moderates the timing of the frames to synch with the *audio playback*, the music track for the video that the artist lip-synchs to. The speed of the camera is locked to exactly 24fps, the normal frame rate at which the film goes through the camera—or whatever speed the operator sets it to—by a controlling circuit that has a crystal oscillator as a reference. An MOS (motion omit sound) camera does not have this. The film must run at exactly the same speed, or frame rate, as the DAT (digital audiotape) in order for the sound and image to match up in postproduction.

The camera houses also rent a *video tap,* alternately known as a *video assist,* which is a video system that taps into the camera—hence the name—to give an immediate video image of what the camera gets on film. Cameras with video taps divert some light from a reflex viewfinder to a video recorder or monitor. On music videos, it's standard practice to order a video tap with two, or more, monitors: one for the director to look through while filming, and one, placed further away, for the video commissioner to view.

THE SOUND PACKAGE

A basic sound package normally consists of a DAT machine, speakers, headphones for the playback person, a *digital slate,* alternatively called a *clapboard* or *clapper,* and either a speaker for playback or a wireless headset for the artist to hear the playback music. The slate connects to the DAT machine, and is able to electronically read the audio timecode. Those numbers are transmitted on a light-emitting diode (LED) screen on the slate, and they run in tandem with the song playing. The AC writes on another part of the slate, in erasable ink, the identification of the scene, and the *take number*—the first take is the first time the scene is shot, the second take is the second time the scene is shot, and so on. At the head of each take, the camera immediately rolls on the slate. This records the audio timecode for synchronizing (synching) the sound to the image, the scene identification, and the take number. The slate usually marks the beginning of a scene, though sometimes the director uses a *tail slate* to note the end of a scene.

As mentioned in The Camera Package on page 148, the film and the DAT must run at the same speed in order for proper synchronization to occur between the images and the music. Normal frame rate and playback rate is 24fps. The film records the time code from the slate, which are numbers being generated by the DAT machine, allowing the two to be married later in postproduction.

Playing the music loud for the artist to lip-synch to on the set is the preferred way to use the playback. It increases the energy and removes the possibility of the headset showing up in the film. At certain locations this is not feasible, such as exterior public locations in New York City where blasting playback is not allowed. In these cases, the artist must listen to the playback music through a wireless headset.

It is rare to record sound on a music video shoot, but sometimes the treatment calls for it, in which case the sound package will require recording capabilities. Audio vendors who supply equipment to film shoots have playback sound packages for rental as well.

THE AUDIO PACKAGE

The *audio package* contains the song—the track—for the music video on different formats to be used at specific points of the production process with various types of equipment. Simply put, it's the track that's played back on the sound package and the track that's played back in postproduction.

A digital audiotape (DAT) of the track for the music video, supplied by the record company, goes to the producer. In turn, the production team ships the DAT to an audio facility, which puts together an audio package based on the producer's specifications. A standard audio package for playback on a music video shoot consists of:

- A DAT for playback on set
- A DAT for playback/audio in telecine (see page 189 in Chapter Ten)
- A Digibeta, Beta SP, DV Cam tape, or another format with both audio and visual capabilities, for the offline edit, as specified by the offline editor, depending upon the system being used and its configuration (see page 193 in Chapter Ten)
- A Digibeta (with audio and visual), the master tape for the online edit (see page 198 in Chapter Ten)

The audio facility generates matching SMPTE audio time code on all of these items. (SMPTE stands for the Society of Motion Picture and Television Engineers, which is the organization that sets standards in the motion picture and digital cinema industries.) All of the tapes—audio (DAT) and visual (Digibeta, Beta SP, DV Cam)—will have a SMPTE audio time code, which is an internal, un-erasable, locked time code, burnt in. This allows the tape to be read by the DAT machine on the set, the DAT machine in the telecine bay, and the computers in the offline and online edits, respectively. With the flip of a specific switch on a tape deck, a box appears on the screen showing the audio time code for the DAT and/or videocassettes. The audio time code on the audio tape can then be matched with the audio time code seen on the slate when the film initially rolls at the beginning of every take, thus allowing the synchronization of audio (song) and visual (artist lip-synching).

Slow Motion Lip-synch with Real Time Music

If the treatment specifies slow motion visuals (lip-synching) set to real time music, the production team must order special items as part of the audio package. To see the images, lip-synching and all, in slow motion, and to hear the artist singing in real time, the playback DAT runs faster than real time—such as double time (fast)—and the artist lip-synchs along with it. When ordering the audio package, the need for the playback DAT to be double time must be specified. The camera, on the other hand, runs at half time (slow). During telecine, the audio is played back at normal speed (slowed down) and then synched up with the visuals so that the images are seen in slow motion, moving at half time, as well as the visual lip-synching, while the audio sounds completely normal.

High Speed Lip-synch with Real Time Music

The same principal applies, in reverse, to speeding up the image. The DAT runs at a ratio much slower than real time (such as half time) and the artist lip-synchs along at half time (slow). When ordering the audio package, the need for the playback DAT to be half time must be specified. The camera, on the flip side, runs at double time (fast). Later, in telecine, the audio is played back at normal speed (sped up) and synched with the visuals, so that in the final product the images play in fast motion, moving at double time, as well as the lip-synching, but the audio sounds completely normal. It's harder to do this on off-speeds (quarter time, third time), although it can be done with more detailed mathematical calculations.

It's always a good policy to confer with the postproduction facility that will be doing the telecine and edit, as well as audio facility that will put together the audio package, before finalizing the order for the audio package to ensure that the production team orders the correct items for what the director wants to achieve. Sound synching problems can be horrible! Although matching digital sound to analogue film is common, accidents happen, and, for a music video, it's important that the synching be done correctly. If there are any concerns, the producer should check all of the specs with the audio facility making the audio package, the post facility doing the telecine, the on-set camera department, and the on-set playback engineer. Bad lip-synch kills a great video.

THE GRIP/ELECTRIC PACKAGE

All of the lighting equipment and the grip equipment used to mount the lighting, such as stands, clamps, flags, and the like, come from a vendor that rents lighting and grip equipment for film and video productions. For a small production, the production manager may rent a truck and have the PAs pick up the equipment. The vendor usually sends its own truck to accommodate a larger lighting package. The director and DP determine the basic light, grip, and electrical package on the scout. The basic packages usually come in one-ton, three-ton, five-ton, or ten-ton grip packages, with the five-ton package used most frequently.

THE GENERATOR

Lights for movie making use a great deal of electricity, so during the scout the gaffer and electric department needs to make sure they will have enough juice to get them through the shoot without blowing fuses or causing a fire. The number of amps required by a given light, and all of the lights used together, must be determined to avoid overloading circuits and blowing fuses.

When a location doesn't have enough power to supply the lights or when there is an outdoor shoot with no available power, the production team must hire a generator to power the lights.

When in a bind and on small productions, sets of car batteries can be used for power. They can run regular tungsten lights at normal *color temperature*, which is the method for measuring the overall color and degree of warmth or coolness of a light source, expressed in degrees Kelvin (deg. K). The higher the degree K, the more blue, or cooler, the lamp appears. The lower the degree K, the more red, or warmer, the lamp appears. Daylight is approximately 5500 deg. K, and professional tungsten studio lamps (movie lighting) are 3200 deg. K.

CRANES AND LIFTS

The treatment for a music video can require the use of cranes and lifts to position people, lights, or equipment up high, or for certain visual effects. The various types of cranes and lifts can be rented from different vendors. They come from camera houses, grip/electric houses, or independent vendors. A few of the most commonly used cranes and lifts for music video sets are:

Jib Arm

The jib arm allows for a more fluid movement of the camera in all directions (raised, lowered, diagonal) for a desired effect. A camera remote head, also called a *hothead*, a remote control camera device that is much lighter than the full camera body, is often attached to the end of the jib arm. Camera rental companies often supply jib arms.

Straight Shooter

The straight shooter is a unique job arm. It has a third axis that allows the camera to move in and out by means of a linear bearing at the end of the arm. It's a rigid one-piece arm with a reach of up to six and a half feet. The camera mounts in an under slung position with a maximum camera weight of 100 pounds. It provides a floating camera with a smooth, horizontal roll.

Condor

A condor crane, a type of cherry picker crane, moves on wheels and has a long arm with a bucket on the end used to lift people and/or equipment above the ground to varying heights. On film sets, it's generally used to put lights up high or to lift water/rain machines for rain shots.

Scissor Lift

A scissor lift is an aerial platform that goes straight up, above its base, on a scissor system of hinged beams. It's used to lift people and/or lights up high, but not as high as a condor crane.

Technocrane

Common to higher budget music video sets, the technocrane is a camera crane on which the boom can be extended or retracted without physical attachments or dismantling, creating a flowing visual effect. The crane comes with its own hothead, so the camera rental facility need not supply one.

Phoenix Crane

If a video production is unable to obtain a technocrane, the second choice is often a Phoenix crane, which can support one or two camera operators.

Slide and Glide

A camera platform that slides and fully rotates, the slide and glide adds up to six more feet of camera movement to a given shot. It has a smooth linear bearing movement, full clockwise and counterclockwise rotation, and is quick and easy to setup. It's frequently attached to the dolly with several mounting options.

THE DOLLY

The dolly is a camera mount with smooth rolling wheels that allows the camera to be moved along the ground to create the distinct cinematic effect of the camera floating through space. Although most dollies are large, there are fold-up versions that fit in a van. A dolly is generally rented from the grip and electric rental house.

THE VIDEO TAPE RECORDER

The video tape recorder (VTR) has stop, rewind, and playback functions for the immediate viewing of the video tape without having to wait for the film to be processed and seen in the telecine,

should the director or client want to see the footage. In the past, the VTR was primarily used on commercial sets, and has only recently become a mainstay for music videos.

WALKIE-TALKIES

Walkie-talkies are handheld, battery-powered radio devices that send and receive communications between two or more people, using dedicated frequencies over short distances. They are always on and activated instantly by pressing a button and talking. Every department head on a film set, as well as all of the production crew and on set PAs, should have a walkie-talkie for the duration of the film shoot. It is essential for instant communication, especially on locations that are spread out.

PRODUCTION TRAILERS/MOTOR HOMES

When filming at an outdoor location with no facilities close by, or at a venue so small that it lacks appropriate areas for the artist's dressing room and/or offices for the production, the company will have to rent at least one motor home, also called a honeywagon or a winny (derived from Winnebago, a brand name of a specific type of motor home). The artist needs a dressing room, bathroom, and place to hang out between shots. Motor homes also take care of necessities like bathrooms for the crew and/or talent/extras. A variety of companies rent motor homes solely for film productions.

VEHICLES

Depending on location and crew specifications, the production company will have to hire vehicles and drivers to transport equipment and people. The number and type of vehicles differ for each project, but almost every music video calls for at least one truck to transport equipment.

Even when shooting on a sound stage, the production requires at least one cube truck to pick up the camera from the camera rental house, and whatever other equipment doesn't come with the sound stage (sound package, inexpensive expendables, etc.). When renting this equipment truck, the production manager should make sure that it has an automatic lift gate for ease of loading heavy equipment.

When a support vehicle is required, it is usually either a fifteen-passenger van or a minivan. This vehicle is used to take the crew to the location scout, to drive the director to the set, or to run errands on the shoot day(s). The need for other vehicles (cargo vans, cube truck, etc.) depends on the treatment, the location, and the budget.

PRODUCTION SUPPLIES

A production might also require miscellaneous items, such as the following, which can be rented from supply houses:

- Tables and Chairs
- Rolling Wardrobe Racks
- Coffee Makers
- Wind Machines
- Portable Heaters
- Large Coolers
- Traffic Cones
- Trash Cans
- Dollies
- Small Generators
- Ladders

EXPENDABLES

On a film or video set, disposable supplies are called *expendable*s, which are items that the crew uses and discards during the course of the shoot. Depending on the project and the gaffer, the production company may purchase some of the following items on an "as used" basis as part of the gaffer's kit rental fee, or the production company may purchase these products from an expendables supply house:

- Tape (masking tape, gaffers tape (cloth), glow tape, board tape, duct tape, paper tape, camera tape, etc.)
- Gels, or gelatins, which are sheets of dyed plastic for use with the camera or lights. They are the least expensive filters. Gels are made in a dull clear form to soften the look of the light. They can be used behind the camera lens or mounted in a frame and placed in a matte box. Gels also come in large sheets and rolls, and can be mounted in front of the lights to add a certain effect.
- Diffusions, which are translucent sheets made of lace or silk. They are used in front of a light to cut down the shadows.
- Visqueen, which is a type of plastic sheeting used to add certain effects.
- Sash cord, which is large string, or small rope of various thicknesses, used for many purposes, but most commonly to secure items so they won't shift while in a truck.
- Foamcore board, which is polystyrene sandwiched between paper that is often used to make flags. Flags are used to protect the camera from stray light or for creating a gradual transition from light to dark to avoid hard shadow lines. They can also be used to help separate and control light spillage in the scene. Some foamcore has an aluminum side that can be used to bounce light of off as a lighting technique. It is stable and easily cut.
- Show card, which is a white artists' cardboard used as a reflector or for various other purposes. It is somewhat flimsy, and, as such, easily cut and formed.

- Duvetyne, which is a heavy black fabric treated with fireproofing material used to completely blacken light out of windows and hide cables.
- Black wrap, which is black aluminum foil used for wrapping lights, controlling light spill, making small flags, and for various other purposes.
- Lens cleaner, which is a special fluid for cleaning camera lenses, and lens tissue, which is a special tissue used to apply and wipe off the lens cleaner from the camera lens itself.

FILM STOCK

As previously mentioned, music videos are usually shot on 35mm, 16mm, or Super 16mm film stock, also called *raw stock,* meaning that the film is raw before it's exposed, depending on the budget. 35mm is the most expensive film, followed by Super 16mm, and then 16mm. The budget generally dictates the film format to be used, which is an important detail included in the contract between the label and the production company.

After the director and the director of photography discuss the specs of the shoot, the DP determines what film stock to use. Each stock has a unique formula—a unique chemical emulsion that reacts differently to light exposure—and therefore has a distinctive look.

One aspect of the decision as to what stock to use is its speed, which deals with light sensitivity. The film manufacturer recommends an exposure index for each stock that is usually given in the form of an ASA number (American Standards Association Institute).

Most video productions prefer to use Kodak film. Although rare, some prefer Fuji or other brands. The choice depends on the director and DP's preferences, the look they are hoping to achieve, and the cost. Buying film from a reseller such as Raw Stock in New York City, which buys unused whole magazines of film back from productions that purchased more than they used, can save money in the budget.

Using *recans*—an unused part of a spool of film that is recanned for use at another time—on a professional shoot should be avoided. If the AC loads four hundred feet of film into the magazine, but the DP only shoots one hundred feet, the AC will "recan" the additional, unexposed three hundred feet by putting it back in its original canister and securing it. These recans can be sold to a dealer, who in turn sells the film at a very low price to another production team. Although recans are very inexpensive, on a professional project it's not worth the savings compared to the risk of having a problem with the film.

Film is extremely sensitive to light exposure and scratches; thus, the more the unexposed film is handled, the greater the risk of it being damaged. Therefore, it is best to use film stock that is new and which has never had the occasion to acquire defects.

Knowing the basics of ordering film is essential, because the production team orders from the manufacturer using the catalogue number and stock name. For example, Kodak Color 5245 and 7245 are low-speed color negatives that are great for shooting daylight. Kodak Color 5293 and 7293 are medium to high-speed color negatives that can be used in a wider range of shooting conditions. This stock is good in low light conditions, such as nighttime or a dimly lit indoor location. In Kodak's stock system, 52 stands for 35mm film, and 72 stands for 16mm film.

"One artist made a request that instead of having our caterer make her food, she wanted to cook it herself. She gave us a list of ingredients, including the spices and the type of grill she had to cook on. We were in a very remote area, so it was quite a fiasco to get everything, but in about six hours we got it all, including the grill she wanted. Once we had everything set up, she changed her mind and asked our caterer to cook for her."

—Rachel Curl, Producer

"As a very green producer, I was thrown with [director] Francis Lawrence for a very ambitious shoot for the Long Beach Dub Allstars. It involved shooting in and around Long Beach for three days—tons of locations, tons of company moves. We were unable to obtain the proper location permits to shoot on Seal Beach due to time constraints. After much hand wringing, we decided to shoot without a permit. We were shooting one of our unpermitted locations, and just as we're about to get the first shot, a motorcycle cop pulls up to our set. I'm standing with the head of production and the video commissioner and I'm sweating bullets. We'd made a decision not to tell the client about our situation. My heart is pounding. Our location scout dashes up to the cop to run interference, because I'm too nervous to deal with the situation. There's some gesturing and some lengthy conversation. The location scout runs back to his car and gets some papers to give to the cop, and my heart is in my throat. Finally, the cop and scout shake hands, and the cop drives off. The scout comes back with a big grin on his face. It turns out the cop is a big fan of the band and actually grew up with them. He wanted a map to the afternoon location so he could bring his son by the set once his shift ended."

—Caleb Dewart, Producer

"Lisa Loeb once spent over eight hours with her personal hair stylist. She made the crew wait. I just sat on an apple box with a calculator, adding up how much money she was wasting. When she finally came out she asked me what I thought, of course I said she looked great because I wanted to shoot—even though her hair was in a little bun and made her head look like an egg. The video turned out great in the end, but during the shoot I imagined myself driving away with the sound stage in my rear view mirror. I imagined the panic of my producer when he couldn't find his director and yelled, 'Phil Harder to set, Phil Harder to set. Has anyone seen the director?'"

—Phil Harder, Director

CATERERS

Union rules demand that the crew is provided with a hot, catered lunch, so the production needs to hire a caterer to provide this meal, at the very least. Some production companies provide a hot breakfast, as well, if the budget can sustain the cost. Sometimes a hot dinner is provided, if the day runs long. Companies specializing in service to film productions understand the intricacies and quirks of catering to movie crews. Before the shoot, the production coordinator or production manager gives the caterer a head count as to how many people will be eating, which—in addition to the call time and location—determines the final cost. Some caterers set up a buffet with hot plates on a table, and serve buffet style. Others cook and serve from a catering truck that has a kitchen set up inside, preparing food to order. The second choice is more desirable, and, as such, is more expensive.

SPECIALTY NEEDS

Every project has its own unique requirements. Before finalizing the treatment and figuring out how to get the finalized treatment on film, the production company cannot anticipate all of the equipment the shoot will require. A company may need camera car platforms; crane cars; front-car or sidecar camera mounting trays; pyrotechnics; stunts; projectors; animals and animal handlers; specialty cars; effects and prosthetic make-up artists; specialty cameras; specialty cranes; aerial shots; underwater shots; stock footage; wet-downs; dance sequences; shutting down busy streets; or effects generated by green screen or motion control—just to name a few.

Most production needs can be found in either the LA411 or the NYPG (New York Production Guide), which are excellent resources for researching how to perform certain tasks and achieve specific looks. Although many cities have their own production guides, since the largest film communities in the United States are in Los Angeles and New York City, their guides offer the most information. In the world of filmmaking, it's possible to do almost anything, although it may require substantial research. Common specialty items include the following:

Choreographed Dance Sequences

For choreographed dance sequences, the record label often hires the artist's choreographer, who in turn usually hires the dancers. The producer needs to find out:

• Who pays the choreographer and the dancers?
• How many days of rehearsal they require?

• Whether the production needs to rent a dance studio for the rehearsal?
• What other pertinent details will be needed relating to the dance sequence?

Wet Down

A lot of outdoor exterior music videos, especially on city streets, call for a wet-down. The glistening appearance of a wet street can add to the look of the video, and can be achieved in one of two ways: (1) The production team can obtain the city's permission to open a fire hydrant near the location. In New York City, this entails leaving a deposit with the fire department to rent a special wrench that opens the hydrant and a meter that gauges the amount of water used, or (2) the team can hire a water truck and meter the truck for water consumption. Most producers prefer hiring a private water truck, because employing a professional to supply the water is more reliable than expecting someone from the production team or the art department team to know how to use the special wrench on the hydrant—not to mention the uncertainty of the hydrant even working.

Shutting Down Streets

If the shoot involves shutting down an active roadway, most locations require the production to hire parking PAs "to hold the street" beginning the night before the shoot. Although a city permit generally allows the production team to hang signs saying that anyone who parks on the particular street will be towed during the dates specified, people often park in the spots anyway. Consequently, it's a lot easier and more effective to have a few PAs hold the parking spots overnight to ensure that no one will park there rather than hire a tow truck the morning of the shoot. Towing cars away can hold up the shooting schedule, and time is one of the most important and precious assets in the whirlwind world of music video production.

Special Effects

Special effects are defined as effects created in-camera during filming, such as explosions or rain. While common to music videos, they can be complicated and entail a lot of planning and detailed supervision. These differ from visual effects, which are defined as effects created with computers during postproduction (see page 199 in Chapter Ten for more details). Often special and visual effects overlap.

Executing special effects properly takes cooperation between the DP, who employs specific techniques while shooting the film for an effect, and the editor, who completes the process of creating the effect by taking the original footage and treating it in postproduction. A lot of care goes into these shots to ensure the process comes out right. Often, due to the intricate nature of these shots, an effect's supervisor is brought on at the very beginning of the production to make sure that what's being shot corresponds to what the editor needs to complete the effects.

Motion Control

The technique of motion control is an example of how filmmakers can create convincing cinematic illusions by jointly employing in-camera special effects and postproduction visual effects. By using the motion control rig, which is a computer controlled camera setup that records the motion of a camera during a shot so that visual effects can easily synchronize with the filmed scene, the camera can move finely and smoothly past a model of any size, recording images for use in postproduction. The rig allows the exact same camera movement to occur over and over again while moving through a space of any size, allow-

ing the shot to look interactive and three dimensional as well as realistic.

In music videos, motion control is often used for cloning effects. For example, in George Michael's video "As," featuring Mary J. Blige and directed by Big TV!, two motion control rigs were used to build nine sequences, each one containing more than fifty passes of cloned George Michaels and Mary J. Bliges. Once a take was chosen, the same movement was repeated again and again, placing George or Mary in different positions for their performances within the scene. Frame-accurate VTR systems were used to allow the live image to be mixed with previously shot footage, all with proper lip-synch. The directors could assess the action, relative to previous action, on the spot, and decide if it was a usable take. Various effects passes were also shot, including clean backgrounds, lens flares, and lighting beams. In the final video, the viewer sees a crowded club filled with many Michaels and Marys. The same technology was used for Outkast's "Hey Ya!" video directed by Bryan Barber. The moving shots of several clones of Andre 3000, all as different members of the band, were achieved with a motion control rig.

DETERMINING THE SHOOTING SCHEDULING

As explained, there are several layers to scheduling a music video shoot. At the earliest stage of the project, the major factors include the artist's schedule and the release date the record label has set for the single. Once the label narrows down the time frame for the shoot, they ask directors to write treatments and hire the one they feel best fits the job. The label and production company then determine the shoot date and basic information regarding the location, such as where the shoot will take place. Although this seems self-evident, determining the location based on a popular artist's touring schedule can be difficult. For example, if the Dave Matthews Band is touring internationally and the treatment for their video calls for a jungle location, figuring out when the band has time in their schedule to meet up with the director and the rest of the crew at a jungle that has just the right look per the treatment description is not such an easy feat. Once determined, these details are written into the initial contract for the video between the label and the production company. With the addition of the treatment and the budget, and later, the information assessed at the technical scout, the AD can put together the nitty-gritty details necessary for scheduling purposes.

TREATMENT AND BUDGETARY FACTORS

As previously discussed, the producer must have a basic sense of the schedule during the budgeting process based predominantly on the treatment. The treatment, the budget, and the schedule all tie together and affect one another. In order to put together the initial budget, the producer must know the number of shooting days the video will require, as well as how each shoot day is going to be set up and what the scout and wrap will entail.

One factor involved in creating the initial budget is assessing the general location. If the treatment calls for a summer beach location, it needs to be factored into the initial scheduling process. If it's January and the artist and director are in New York, the budget must reflect the cost of getting to a beach location. If the production determines that Florida would be the least expensive beach location to get to, as well as the most production-friendly place to shoot, the producer clears this choice with the director, executive pro-

ducer, and video commissioner. Once agreed on by all, the producer bases the budget on shooting in Florida in January, breaking out all travel costs involved while creating the Point Zero bid. Once the budget is in place and the job has been awarded, the producer hires an assistant director who takes over the details of scheduling.

THE RESPONSIBILITY FOR GENERATING THE SHOOTING SCHEDULE

As previously mentioned, the assistant director generates the final shooting schedule, which is the basic outline of what will be shot, when,

Advice for Aspiring Directors

"Always look for beauty. Never ask anyone to do something you wouldn't do yourself."
—W.I.Z., Director

"Just get out there and get it done. No one's going to help you. You have to have the passion to overcome the odds. Every director will have stories of incredible hardship and difficulty. We shot my first video for three thousand dollars. We had no permits for the locations; we got chased by the cops; we climbed fences; and just shot film on the run. I couldn't afford to get the film out of the lab, and I had to borrow money from my friends. I couldn't pay the crew, so I had to pay them in installments. But, I just had such a passion to direct and such a clear vision of how I wanted the film to turn out, that I just did it. You have to do it. Because it's not like there's somebody who's going to be walking down the street and give you a handout. That very rarely happens."
—Mc G, Director

where, and in what order. In addition, the AD must also know who and what equipment will be needed during each part of the day and the logistics of all the moves. Generally, both the AD and the production team compile the *call sheet,* which lists the time that the crew and equipment need to arrive on set and outlines each department's instructions.

"The major responsibility of the assistant director is logistics," says 1st AD Joe Osborne (Eminem's "The Real Slim Shady," directed by Phillip Atwell and Beyonce's "Crazy In Love," directed by Jake Nava). "Directors are creative; ADs are logistical. Scheduling and keeping to that schedule, running the set—all information flows through the AD. There are so many parts that have to come together to make a video happen: art, styling, make-up, hair, lighting, camera movement, sound, photography, keeping it all together and keeping everyone informed, and set safety. As I say, 'My job is to finish close to on time and get everyone home safe.'"

Assistant director Michael Estrella has worked with various well-known directors and artists, such as director Sanaa Hamri, shooting Lenny Kravitz and Prince, and director Chris Robinson, shooting Joss Stone. "I'm the lubricant, the coach, logistics, and the time management guy," he explains. "The crew provides all of the necessary gears to run the machine [video], and I keep the operation running smoothly—kind of like oil. I make sure that the team [crew] stays focused and has a clear plan to executing the director's vision. In short, I'm the director's right hand man who sets up, schedules, and mediates across the entire crew."

CREATING THE SHOOTING SCHEDULE

As we've previously learning, once the video commissioner awards the job, the number of days of shooting has already been agreed upon, but there are still many other questions that the AD must address in order to create the shooting schedule, such as:

- Is a company move required during the shoot day?
- If so, how much time will it take to wrap out of one location and load into the next location?
- If it's a day exterior shoot, do certain shots require a certain time of day, such as sunrise or sunset shots?

On the tech scout, the assistant director must learn as much as possible about what the director intends on shooting and how. The AD also needs to know the various requirements of all the department heads regarding the load in and set up, the shoot, and the wrap, and all the rules and regulations governing the filming.

An important part of this process involves outlining all of the logistics involved, not just what's going to be happening on set. For instance, where the equipment trucks and the generator truck are going to be parked will, ultimately, be determined by the AD. The proximity of the set to the generator determines how much cable the electrics will have to run to get power to the lights. The AD has to take this into account, because it factors into the budget, since more cable equals more money—as well as set up time—and more cable means more time to lay the cable. On a shoot where there are several vehicles, the AD has to make sure that his or her team knows exactly where everything is supposed to be parked so that seemingly simple elements don't end up sucking time out of the day.

The AD then faces more technical questions, such as whether certain shots should not be scheduled for specific times of day. For instance, shooting outdoors when the sun is directly overhead is not opportune and should be avoided. Knowing this, the AD will likely try to schedule the daylight exterior shots at either the beginning or the end of the day. Additionally, if the treatment calls for a lot of talent and extras, the producer may ask the AD to try to schedule them so that they're only working for six hours, thus avoiding having to provide a meal for them. This saves both money and time. The AD asks the director, producer, and department heads many questions, working very closely with all of them, and then uses the answers as guidelines to build the schedule.

"A good schedule requires a lot of experience shooting," says assistant director Michael Kahn, who has assisted on well over 250 music videos and has worked with such directors as Jake Nava on Lindsay Lohan's "Rumours" and Billie Woodruff on Britney Spears' "Do Somethin." "The intricacies in doing this are impossible to explain, except to say that when I do a schedule I take into account such minute details as time required for bathroom breaks."

Shot List

Most directors compile a shot list—a list of all of the specific images that the director would like to capture—prior to the shoot day. Once filmed, these individual shots will then be edited to create the whole, final video. The AD uses the shot list as one part of the guideline in creating the shooting schedule for the day.

Directors use all different techniques to create their shot list. Some time the song with a stopwatch and write the shot list with the length of the chorus, verse, and bridge in mind. Others structure their shot list according to capturing a wide, establishing shot of each set up, and then moving in for medium and close-up shots, ordering them based on importance. Some directors can picture the final video in their heads even before they write it up as a treatment, so the shot list puts on paper what they already see in their minds' eye. Other directors leave the process a bit more open-ended, creating a shot list that has more coverage so that they have more footage to work with in the edit.

Pre-light and Wrap Day

After the scout, the AD can determine how ambitious the treatment is, as well as how realistic the director is. Based on these factors, the AD may ask the producer for a pre-light and/or build day, or a wrap day. A *pre-light* is when there is a large lighting set up, which means there isn't enough time to set up the lights and shoot on the same day, so the day before the shoot must be used to set up all the lights. A pre-light often goes hand in hand with building a large set, which may require one or more *build days*—days that are needed to build the set. Due to budgetary constraints, if these days are not established at the beginning of the project, it's usually not realistic to expect that they can be added later. But like everything in music videos, it all depends upon the specific video project. It's always better for the AD to go into each project with a realistic approach and then either add days, if possible, or pare down expectations, which is more likely, if necessary.

A wrap day on the back end may be needed for the same reasons. There may not be enough time in the day to film the video and break down the lights and the set. In this case, a day, or more, would be added after the shoot to wrap the lights and/or break down the set.

Once the director and the producer approve the schedule, the producer generally reviews it with the video commissioner for a

Wardrobe racks.
VIDEO: Beenie Man, featuring Akon's "Girls"
DIRECTOR: Little X
PHOTOGRAPHER: Lara M. Schwartz

The VTR operator sets up the VTR equipment.
VIDEO: Beenie Man, featuring Akon's "Girls"
DIRECTOR: Little X
PHOTOGRAPHER: Lara M. Schwartz

The slate is shown being filmed in the monitor.
VIDEO: Beenie Man, featuring Akon's "Girls"
DIRECTOR: Little X
PHOTOGRAPHER: Lara M. Schwartz

The DP shoots Adam Lazzara, the lead signer, as he performs.
VIDEO: Taking Back Sunday's "Twenty-Twenty Surgery"
DIRECTOR: Jay Martin

A model getting made up.
VIDEO: Beenie Man, featuring Akon's "Girls"
DIRECTOR: Little X
PHOTOGRAPHER: Lara M. Schwartz

The glam squad at work.
VIDEO: Beenie Man, featuring Akon's "Girls"
DIRECTOR: Little X
PHOTOGRAPHER: Lara M. Schwartz

An electric adjusts the lights.
VIDEO: Angels and Airwaves' "Do It for Me Now"
DIRECTOR: Shilo

A group talent release posted on the front door of the studio.
VIDEO: Beenie Man, featuring Akon's "Girls"
DIRECTOR: Little X
PHOTOGRAPHER: Lara M. Schwartz

Shooting bass player Ryan Sinn from a straight shoot'r jib arm.
VIDEO: Angels and Airwaves' "Do It for Me Now"
DIRECTOR: Shilo

The art department spraying foam to create rocks and the rock floor for a moonscape scene.
VIDEO: Angels and Airwaves' "Do It for Me Now"
DIRECTOR: Shilo

Eddie Reyes, founder and guitarist of the band, in makeup.
VIDEO: Taking Back Sunday's "Twenty-Twenty Surgery"
DIRECTOR: Jay Martin

Shooting the lead singer, Tom DeLonge,
with soft light bouncing off the B-board.
VIDEO: Angels and Airwaves'
"Do It for Me Now"
DIRECTOR: Shilo

The camera rolling on Lil'Wayne.
VIDEO: Lil'Wayne, featuring Robin
Thicke's "Shooter"
DIRECTOR: Benny Boom

One of the workers on the art department team paints the stage.
VIDEO: Lil'Wayne, featuring Robin Thicke's "Shooter"
DIRECTOR: Benny Boom

Shooting the drummer, Atom Willard, from a straight shoot'r jib arm.
VIDEO: Angels and Airwaves' "Do It for Me Now"
DIRECTOR: Shilo

Director Nigel Dick operates the camera, shooting drummer Cody Hanson's performance.
VIDEO: Hinder's "Lips of an Angel"
DIRECTOR: Nigel Dick

Adam Lazzara, the lead singer, gets his hair done.
VIDEO: Taking Back Sunday's "Twenty-Twenty Surgery"
DIRECTOR: Jay Martin

On location, the production coordinator reviews the purchase orders and inputs information into the purchase order log.
VIDEO: Taking Back Sunday's "Twenty-Twenty Surgery"
DIRECTOR: Jay Martin

The slate is filmed at the top of the shot.
VIDEO: Taking Back Sunday's "Twenty-Twenty Surgery"
DIRECTOR: Jay Martin

The AC preps the camera and adjusts the lens.
VIDEO: Angels and Airwaves' "Do It for Me Now"
DIRECTOR: Shilo

Beenie Man waits patiently for the
camera and shot to be prepped.
VIDEO: Beenie Man, featuring
Akon's "Girls"
DIRECTOR: Little X
PHOTOGRAPHER: Lara M.
Schwartz

Grip and electric equipment.
VIDEO: Taking Back Sunday's "Twenty-Twenty Surgery"
DIRECTOR: Jay Martin

The camera is placed on top of a dolly.
VIDEO: Beenie Man, featuring Akon's "Girls"
DIRECTOR: Little X
PHOTOGRAPHER: Lara M. Schwartz

In the darkness of the changing bag, the AC takes film out of the canister and loads it into the magazine.
VIDEO: Lil'Wayne, featuring Robin Thicke's "Shooter"
DIRECTOR: Benny Boom

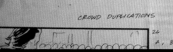

CROWD DUPLICATIONS

The 2nd unit DP shoots glamour scenes.
VIDEO: Beenie Man, featuring Akon's "Girls"
DIRECTOR: Little X
PHOTOGRAPHER: Lara M. Schwartz

Jeff Panzer, Emperor of All Videos, converses with Nelly.
VIDEO: Nelly's "Air Force Ones"
DIRECTOR: David Palmer

Storyboards.
VIDEO: Taking Back Sunday's "Twenty-Twenty Surgery"
DIRECTOR Jay Martin

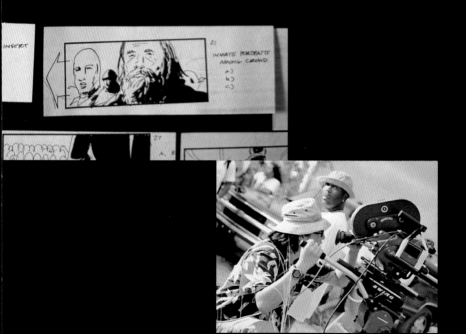

A craft service spread.
VIDEO: Angels and Airwaves' "Do It for Me Now"
DIRECTOR: Shilo

The director watches the performance being shot on greenscreen.
VIDEO: Angels and Airwaves' "Do It for Me Now"
DIRECTOR: Shilo

The director and Jeff Panzer, Emperor of All Videos, watch a shot in the monitor.
VIDEO: Hinder's "Lips of an Angel"
DIRECTOR: Nigel Dick

The editor reviews all of the footage that has been loaded into the Avid system.
VIDEO: Taking Back Sunday's "Twenty-Twenty Surgery"
DIRECTOR: Jay Martin

A grip moves the straight shoot'r jib arm.
VIDEO: Angels and Airwaves' "Do It for Me Now"
DIRECTOR: Shilo

An electric setting a light.
VIDEO: Angels and Airwaves'
"Do It for Me Now"
DIRECTOR: Shilo

The DP shows the director how the shot will look.
VIDEO: Beenie Man, featuring Akon's "Girls"
DIRECTOR: Little X
PHOTOGRAPHER: Lara M. Schwartz

The lighting designer inserts a gel in front of a light.
VIDEO: Angels and Airwaves' "Do It for Me Now"
DIRECTOR: Shilo

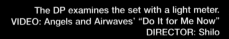

The DP examines the set with a light meter.
VIDEO: Angels and Airwaves' "Do It for Me Now"
DIRECTOR: Shilo

Grips at work.
VIDEO: Angels and Airwaves'
"Do It for Me Now"
DIRECTOR: Shilo

The AC inserts a filter into the mattebox in
front of the camera lens.
VIDEO: Angels and Airwaves' "Do It for Me Now"
DIRECTOR: Shilo

The ACs meter the light and check the measurements for pulling focus.
VIDEO: Lil'Wayne, featuring Robin Thicke's "Shooter"

The playback operator and his equipment.
VIDEO: Beenie Man, featuring Akon's "Girls"
DIRECOR: Little X
PHOTOGRAPHER: Lara M. Schwartz

A model gets her hair done.
VIDEO: Beenie Man, featuring
Akon's "Girls"
DIRECTOR: Little X
PHOTOGRAPHER: Lara M.
Schwartz

Workers on the art department team secure props.
VIDEO: Lil'Wayne, featuring Robin Thicke's "Shooter"
DIRECTOR: Benny Boom

A grip finishes rigging the greenscreen on a scissor lift.
VIDEO: Angels and Airwaves' "Do It for Me Now"
DIRECTOR: Shilo

final approval from the record label. When everyone agrees on the schedule, the AD, the 2nd AD, the production manager, and the production coordinator work together to create the call sheet.

Call Sheet

The call sheet outlines each department's instruction on the shoot day(s), or build or wrap days. It tells them when they are supposed to arrive on location and where they are to go, as well as any other pertinent information of this nature. The call sheet, usually a one-page document, contains everyone's call times—the time that each crew member and all vendor equipment has to be on set, ready to work. Production may use this schedule as an outline to complete the permit, which requires locations, dates, and times, and, sometimes, the specific action that will be occurring—especially if it's out of the ordinary or dangerous, such as pyrotechnics or closing down streets.

STANDARD BUSINESS NECESSITIES AND DETAILS

As discussed in Chapter Three, the production team oversees the complete preproduction process, keeping track of all of the details that ensure the shoot runs as smoothly as possible and that the director has all the tools necessary to realizing his or her vision. Aside from hiring the crew and renting equipment, the team needs to complete many other tasks in preparation for the shoot. This includes making sure everyone has what they require to do their jobs. To achieve this, the team ensures that the proper insurance is in place for every aspect of the production, acquires proper vendor documentation and paperwork, creates a production book, and

Do you need a great song to make a great video?

"No, you don't have to have a great song to have a great video, because you can have simply a great piece of film. It may not be an effective video, because I think the music and the video go hand in hand. I think the video can make the song better, but I think a song can make a video better, too. There have been plenty hit videos that aren't hit records first."
—Janet Kleinbaum, Senior Vice President of Marketing and Video Production; Jive Records

"I'm trying to think of videos that I really admired in which the song's been bad, but I can't think of any. Wow. There are probably some amazing videos done by incredible directors for mediocre music. But I think, and I have to speak purely for myself, that a music video serves the song, and the song has to be great in some way."
—Peter Care, Director

secures record label approvals for various hires and tasks.

ISSUING INSURANCE CERTIFICATES

The production company needs to add every piece of vendor equipment they rent on their insurance policy as *additionally insured* for the project, meaning, for instance, that the company's insurance policy covers the grip/electric vendor's gear for the duration of the shoot. If it's a one-day shoot, the policy covers the contents of the grip/electric truck, as well as the truck itself, for that one day. If it's a two-day shoot, then it covers it all for two days.

The production company's insurer issues specific insurance certificates attesting to the additional insurance. They e-mail these certificates to the production manager, who, in turn, makes sure the paperwork includes the names of the specific vendors. The production manager forwards a copy of this insurance certificate to the vendor, proving that they are included on the production company's insurance policy for the duration of the shoot. The insurance company keeps a copy, and the production company keeps a copy. Most vendors will not rent their equipment to a production company unless the company supplies one of these insurance certificates. It's too big of a risk for such costly equipment.

If the record label's insurance company is insuring the project, then that company will issue the insurance certificates directly to the vendor under the instruction of the production team (see page 89 in Chapter Five for information regarding record label supplied insurance policies).

EQUIPMENT/VENDOR DOCUMENTATION AND PAPERWORK

Each production company has different rules and guidelines pertaining to its standard operation procedures, such as purchase orders, check requests, petty cash, and the like. The production staff must be aware of these guidelines as soon as they begin the project.

Purchase Orders

The company must generate a purchase order (PO) for each vendor it uses. The production coordinator makes sure the purchase orders are kept in good working order and that they include all of the necessary information, including:

- The vendor's legal name
- The vendor's address, phone number, and Web site (if applicable)
- A contact person
- The vendor's federal identification number or, if the vendor is an individual in the government's eyes, not a company, his or her social security number
- The payment information, clearly noted, stating whether the rental or purchase was made on account
  - by credit card (indicating whose card with all of the pertinent information)
  - by check issued upfront (indicating the check number and date written with a copy of the check attached)
- Details regarding specific item(s) ordered
- Backup paperwork attached to the specific purchase order

If and when the accounting department reviews the PO after the shoot, there should be no question as to:

- The full negotiation between the production manager and the vendor
- What was ordered
- How much it cost
- How the payment was made
- Any other pertinent details

Check Requests

If a production company has an account with a vendor, the production manager puts the equipment order on the account. If it does not have an account, the production manager or coordinator issues a check request to the proper person at the production company, usually the accountant, the head of production, or the executive producer. It is important to keep in mind that many vendors refuse checks and insist on either getting paid on account or by credit card.

Petty Cash

Generally, the production manager or the production coordinator is the designated bank that submits the check request for petty cash to the head of production. This request is made in writing to leave a paper trail. Petty cash covers cash expenses throughout the production, and must be fully accounted for and properly reconciled at the end.

For example, let's say the PM puts in a petty cash request for $1,000 and, in turn, gets the cash. From this money, a runner PA—the production assistant designated to spend most of the day running errands—signs out $500 in petty cash the day before the shoot, meaning he signs a receipt for the production manager saying that he received $500 cash. At the end of the shoot, that PA has to give back receipts and cash that adds up to $500 to the production manager. And the production manager has to give back receipts and cash that add up to $1,000 to the production company.

Each person receiving petty cash tapes all of his and her receipts onto sheets of paper and must complete a petty cash log or envelope, depending on the procedures of the specific production company. When the production manager or the producer actualizes the budget at the end of the project, each bit of petty cash spent is categorized under the proper line item. These line items are then inserted into the actualized budget to get a clear picture of how all the money was spent—the electronic budget does this automatically. The production coordinator neatly files the petty cash envelopes in the wrap book according to the company's guidelines so that the company has the paper receipts as well as the budgetary calculation of where all of the petty cash was spent.

THE PRODUCTION BOOK

The production coordinator creates a *production book* to keep all pertinent information about a specific production close at hand. The book contains:

- *Cover*: The artist, song title, director, producer, and production company
- *Personnel*: The production company details (address, point people) and the director's representative
- *Calendar*: A calendar listing all pertinent events regarding the shoot, and the day and time when they are schedule to take place
- *Talent*: The artist and/or any additional talent or extras
- *Lyrics*: The song lyrics
- *Locations*: The shooting location (address and contact information) and photos, if applicable
- *Crew*: Names and contact information for the entire crew
- *Vendors*: Names, addresses, and contact information for all of the vendors
- *Postproduction*: Names, addresses, and contact information for all of the postproduction vendors and workers

Prior to the shoot day, the production coordinator e-mails the production book to the commissioner and the artist's manager. On the shoot day, the coordinator brings enough copies of the production book to the set for everyone. This allows all involved to have general information of the shoot, as well as a quick reference guide to everyone associated with the music video.

Sometimes, the production coordinator includes a basic schedule in the production book, although generally not a detailed shooting schedule. Those specifics are usually reserved for the director, the producer, the executive producer, the commissioner, and the assistant director.

RECORD LABEL APPROVALS

Throughout the production process, the producer is aware of everything that must be approved by the record label. The standard approvals include:

- *Director of Photography*: The commissioner may want to see the DP's reel.
- *Casting* (Talent and Extras): The producer should find out if the commissioner wants to attend the casting session or if videotaping it is sufficient.
- *Dancers* (if applicable): This is similar to the casting of the other talent.
- *Artist's Wardrobe*: Clothing for the artist is separate from costumes for the talent/extras. Generally, the label will want final approval on the artist's wardrobe. They will not be nearly as concerned with what the talent and extras wear.
- *Shooting Schedule*: A simple discussion of the plan of the day with the commissioner usually suffices.
- *Offline Editor*: The commissioner may want to see the editor's reel.

THE DAY BEFORE THE SHOOT

It's crucial that certain tasks be completed at least a day before the shoot day. These tasks include:

- Checking out the camera from the camera house
- Picking up the equipment and supplies
- Making sure all crew and vendors have their call times
- Charging all batteries
- Parking the equipment truck

CAMERA CHECKOUT

The AC checks out the camera the morning before the first shoot day. The AC goes to the camera house and makes sure all of the camera equipment ordered by the production manager, per the DP's instructions, is part of the full camera package and that it's all in good, working condition.

PICK UPS

The day before the shoot is the pick-up day. Two PAs drive a rented vehicle, designated as the equipment truck, to pick up all of the necessary equipment that is not delivered by the vendors. The production coordinator gives the PAs a list of all the places they need to go, including the address, contact person, and item(s) to pick up, along with any paperwork they may need, such as purchase orders, checks, or insurance certificates, for each vendor.

After the AC has inspected the camera package, the PAs pick it up. They generally also pick up the sound package, production supplies, and expendables as well as anything else designated by the production team. At times, they may be required to help the wardrobe stylist pick up clothing or to help the art department pick up props. This all depends on the specific production and how it's organized. The vendors usually deliver the rest of the equipment, such as the grip and electric equipment.

PARKING THE EQUIPMENT TRUCK

After the PAs complete all of the pick-ups, they will have a truck full of expensive equipment. Therefore, it's necessary to lock the truck's back gate with a strong padlock and park it in an insured and bonded parking lot overnight. However, prior to parking the truck, the PAs must bring the batteries from any battery-operated equipment to the production office to be charged.

CHARGING BATTERIES

The walkie-talkie batteries, and any other battery-operated equipment that needs charging, must get plugged in at the production office and left to replenish their power overnight. Prior to the shoot, the PAs go to the production office and pick up these items, loading them on the equipment truck and bringing them to the location for their call time.

The camera batteries usually leave the camera house charged. This should always be confirmed. If the shoot is more than one day, the PAs may need to charge the camera batteries overnight between shoot days. The walkie-talkie batteries should always be charged the night before every shoot day.

CALL TIMES

A night or two before the shoot, the AD or 2nd AD or, in some cases, the production coordinator, runs through the call sheet and phones the crew members and vendors who bring their own equipment to let them know their *call time*, the time that each worker is expected to be on set. This is done with as much time before the shoot as possible; however, due to the rushed nature of music videos, the crew and vendors are often given notice of when and where they have to be only a day or so in advance.

All of the details that are addressed in pre-preproduction are integral. They can be the difference between a good production and a bad production. "I can't stress enough the importance of a good prep," says producer Rachel Curl. "In my opinion you can't over-prep a job. Unexpected things always come up, so the more prepared you are, the better you will be able to handle the curveballs." After completing the preparation, it's time to shoot the video and bring the music video treatment to life!

CHAPTER NINE
SHOOTING THE VIDEO

All of the preparation has led to this day—the day of the video shoot. In theory, nothing should go wrong; there should be no surprises. In reality, however, plenty of problems will occur, and everyone on set must be ready to work with whatever may come their way. This is the nature of music video production. Videos require solid preparedness, perceptive foresight, and savvy troubleshooting.

PRODUCING THE SHOOT

The main goal during the shoot is to capture all of the director's shots outlined in his or her shot list in the allotted amount of time. The AD and the producer work in tandem to make this happen. The AD strives to keep the shooting schedule moving without losing shots. The producer—like a parent—keeps tabs on all of the details of the day, pushing the AD to push the crew to work harder and faster, feeding the crew in the proper increments of time, making sure the director is focused, keeping the client and artist happy, providing for the talent and extras, and meeting all the safety and precautionary requirements.

MANAGING THE SHOOTING SCHEDULE

On the shoot day(s), the assistant director runs the set. He or she has all of the necessary information at hand and serves as the director's "go-to" person, passing along the director's instructions and ideas to the crew and artist. The AD must perform the following:

- Make sure everyone knows how, when, where, and why certain shots are to be set up or broken down
- Attempt to capture all of the director's shots
- Keep the producer informed as to whether the production is staying on schedule
- Ensure the day does not go over the allotted time, thus resulting in additional expenses
- Make sure the vision in the treatment is captured on film in a safe and timely manner

"The key thing I constantly do when I work with the producer is to maintain a very open dialogue about the progress of the day and where I project particular events during the day will lead us and leave us," explains assistant director Michael Estrella. "I try to remain loyal to the director's vision and desires while balancing the economical time restrictions that the producer has outlined for me. Keep the producer informed!"

Because music video shoots are considerably less structured than commercials or feature films, the assistant director must understand the fluid nature of the medium and be able to adapt the schedule to accommodate any unexpected change on the set. An AD needs to be able to roll with the punches, and accept the fact that shooting a music video epitomizes Murphy's Law: Anything that can go wrong, will go wrong.

The producer works with the AD to make sure the entire process is moving along as closely as possible to the schedule. The producer serves as the director's gatekeeper as well, preventing him or her from getting distracted by unnecessary visitors on set. Additionally, the producer is the conduit to the director, speaking on behalf of the client—the label and artist's management—making sure that everyone is on the same page and relaying all of the clients' ideas, comments, and concerns to the director in such a way that he or she isn't pulled away from set or given confusing or conflicting feedback on what is being filmed. The producer also troubleshoots to minimize the problems that inevitably come along.

"I work in tandem with the 1st assistant director in an attempt to stay on schedule and get all the shots the director needs," says producer Jil Hardin. "At times this may require going into the makeup, wardrobe, or artist trailers to get whomever out on set; other times it calls for persuading the location or permit office to let us shoot just one or three more hours. And sometimes it's all about the pep talk to keep the crew or the director on track with what we're there to do and how much time we have left to do it in."

The producer ultimately is responsible for anything that goes wrong with the production. Although the record label is responsible for the artist's timeliness and behavior, the producer must stay abreast of the artist's actions and inform the label about anything the artist may do to impact the shooting schedule and budget. For example, if the artist shows up late, the video commissioner needs to know because the production company is justified in asking the record label to pay an overage based on overtime charges incurred by the tardiness of the artist.

Producer William Green succinctly sums up the role of the producer on set. He says "Keep the client happy, work with the AD, keep the director moving, and try to stop the world and his dog coming by just to say 'Hello.'"

The 2nd Unit Crew

For an extremely ambitious shoot, the production team may hire a 2nd unit crew and enough equipment for them to get the footage they need within the allotted period of time. The second unit is a smaller, subordinate crew responsible for filming the less crucial shots, such as inserts or extras. On music videos, a second unit usually consists of a camera operator and an AC. On larger shoots, there may be a second unit director who gets instructions from the main director. More commonly, the main director will give instructions directly to the 2nd unit camera operator, or the AD, who will then tell the 2nd unit crew what to do.

Crew Meals

Good meals can contribute to keeping a shoot on schedule. They can elevate the overall mood of the shoot and even help to cut down on frustration or anxiety—not to mention low blood sugar—on a difficult shoot. Not only are the quality and presentation of the food important, but also the timing.

Union rules dictate meal times. The production company risks penalties charged by each member of the crew if they break the rules. The IATSE Union Rules and Teamster Work Rules outline the procedure of meals in detail. The main rule is that meals must be served in six-hour intervals. The production company must serve the first meal no more than six hours after the start of the workday. A second meal must be served six hours after the end of the first meal, and so on. If this regulation is not upheld, each member of the crew can charge a penalty to production on his or her time card for specific increments of time over the six hours. The rules also specify which meals can be cold or hot, among other things (see Appendix C on page 218 for the IATSE Union Rules.)

Music videos often supply a cold breakfast buffet on the shoot day(s), including items such as bagels, muffins, and coffee. Although if the budget allows, a hot breakfast is always a terrific way to begin the shoot day on a positive note and goes a long way toward keeping crew morale up. The video production always includes a hot, catered lunch for the crew.

It's not uncommon to have an eighteen-hour shoot day or more. Since meals must be provided every six hours, this means the production company will be required to offer a third meal. If a shoot isn't scheduled to go that long, the production may not have scheduled a third catered meal, in which case petty cash comes to the rescue and the PAs will order from a take out restaurant of the crew's choice. This meal often occurs at the very end of the shoot or during the wrap. Usually, everyone is tired and aching to finish up and get home, so the crew will most likely agree to have a *walking meal*, which means they'll eat while they work rather than sitting down and taking a full break to eat. According to union rules, this is still considered work time and thus a non-deductible meal, meaning that time cannot be subtracted from the timecard. The crew continues to get paid while they work and eat at the same time.

CLIENT AND ARTIST RELATIONS

Keeping the client happy on the set is an important ingredient to having a smooth and successful shoot. A few ways of accomplishing this are:

• Providing good food
• Having a comfortable holding area
• Getting the artist his or her own monitor
• Relaying information
• Troubleshooting
• Making an enthusiastic effort to please

Artist Meals and Craft Service

It always pays to find out during preproduction what kinds of food the artist, client, and key crew members prefer and to serve those items during the shoot. Keeping the artist's trailer stocked with shrimp cocktail, if that's what the artist likes, makes for a much smoother shoot—the cost of the shrimp is minimal compared to that of a discontented artist.

The Artist Holding Area

It's also important to make sure the artist has a clean, comfortable holding area—a place where the artist waits and relaxes between takes. Usually the space will also serve as the artist's dressing and make-up room. Some artists are very particular about their holding area, so it never hurts to do too much rather than too little. Simple touches, such as having fresh flowers in the room, can go a long way toward creating an upbeat atmosphere and starting the day on the right footing.

The Client Monitor

A video monitor should always be set up specifically for the record label so that the video commissioner can see the material as it is shot, which can prevent later problems. When the commissioner oversees a shoot by watching what's being filmed in real time, he or she is essentially approving it. In theory, it takes the onus of what's being shot off the production and places it on the record label.

It's best to have a separate monitor with a director's chair set up specifically for the commissioner in a comfortable yet somewhat out-of-the-way place for a few reasons. First, it avoids crowds gathering to watch the shoot on the commissioner's monitor. Second, it allows the commissioner to concentrate on what's being filmed. Third, it helps to prevent the commissioner from having direct contact with the director.

Information Transmission

It is important that the producer be the sounding board for the client. "The artists and their inner circles are becoming more learned and adept when it comes to the technical and creative aspects of filmmaking," producer Jil Hardin explains, "and their input can be at times contributive and valuable. Ultimately, it is the artists who have the greatest amount at risk and should therefore assert their opinion, as they deem necessary."

The producer must listen to clients and take their concerns seriously. At the same time, the producer must filter what gets passed on to the director. In this way, the client can freely express him or herself without distracting or frustrating the director.

Troubleshooting

Part of the producer's job requires being a skilled troubleshooter. Anyone on the set with a problem comes to the producer for a resolution. For instance, if equipment essential to the shoot did not make it to the set, the producer must locate it and have it brought to the set immediately, while determining whether this will affect the budget, either negatively, in lost time, or positively, if perhaps the error was on the vendor's behalf and a discount can be negotiated.

Enthusiastic Effort

Sometimes the client makes unreasonable, even absurd, requests. It's best for the production team to make every effort to fulfill the client's request when possible, or at least listen intently. Enthusiasm and respect for the client goes a long way in building and establishing connections, which is a large part of client relations: the music video industry runs on such relationships.

PROVISIONS FOR TALENT AND EXTRAS

If the treatment calls for a lot of talent and extras, it pays to have a separate holding area for them. This can include a separate table set up for their craft service and, if possible, separate catering, as well as a place for wardrobe, hair and make-up, and bathroom access. Either the casting assistant, the 2nd AD or the 2nd 2nd AD serves as the talent and extras' link to production, keeping tabs on who has to be ready for which scene wearing which outfit. They keep the 1st AD informed on the talent's status at any given time. The 1st AD lets the person in charge of the talent and extras know when and who is needed, where, and for what. The casting assistant or 2nd AD also distributes the unsigned releases and collects them once they've been signed (see page 111 in Chapter Six for additional information on talent releases).

SAFETY AND PRECAUTIONARY PROCEDURES

The safety of the client, talent, and crew are of paramount importance on a video set. Thus, each shoot must have a first aid kit and fire extinguisher on hand.

While filming, it is extremely important that all technical aspects of the filming process be adhered to, and that afterward, all mechanical information gets transmitted to the necessary people to ensure the well-being of the film throughout the developing and printing process (see Chapter Ten starting on page 186 for more information). The following procedures ensure that the film is handled properly:

• Checking the Gate
• Camera Reports

Checking the Gate

At the end of each take, before the shot is broken down and the crew goes on to the next set up, the assistant camera has to check the *gate*—a piece of metal in the shape of a film frame on the camera—for debris accidentally stuck in it. A piece of hair or other rubbish in the frame will show on the film and ruin the shot. If the AC finds something, the scene must be re-shot before moving on.

Camera Reports

For each can of exposed film, the AC writes a *camera report*. This report covers everything about each specific roll of film, including:

• Which takes were good and which were bad
• What in-camera effects were used
• Special instructions for the lab

The camera reports are vital to knowing everything that has happened to the exposed film. For example, if there was a jam in the camera, it should be detailed in the camera report of the specific roll of film. The lab receives a copy of each camera report so that they know the history of the film on the shoot and so that it can be developed according to the DP's instructions. The production company keeps a copy of each report as well.

DIRECTING THE SHOOT

Directing a music video combines leadership, creativity, and craft, blending intuition and technique. Although creativity can be considered more of an innate gift, craft is an acquired and learned skill that can offer growth through experience.

Music videos are the apex of three interrelated aspects of popular culture: music, film, and image. That said, it's no surprise that most established music video directors tend to emerge from either still photography or filmmaking. Interestingly, very few established directors come directly out of the music industry.

When asked about their on-set responsibilities, many directors stress the following important factors that they say determine a successful director and music video:

• Leading the Entire Team
• Applying Technical Knowledge and Creative Intuition
• Maintaining Focus and Multitasking
• Working With the Artist to Elicit an Appealing Performance
• Telling a Story
• Embracing Spontaneity and Chaos
• Fostering Good Client Relations
• Racing Against the Clock

- Having a Point of View
- Experimenting With the Process
- Collaborating as Part of a Team
- Being Financially Responsible

"Music videos are weird, because directing is the easiest job to do and the hardest job to do well," says director Noble Jones. "You're surrounded by cameramen, art directors, editors, choreographers, hopefully a good artist, some money, and a good producer. You show up; you go, 'Yeah, that's cool.' and 'Aw, he's brilliant,' and that's about it. In the craftsman sense of the word, it's really hard to do well. At the end of the day, you are in a managerial position. You are asset management. They have this much money, this much time, this artist, and this particular day of the year; these are your assets. You have to manage them as best seen fit."

LEADING THE TEAM

The director assumes complete control of the shoot, setting the tone for its creativity as well as functioning as the authority on the set. "I'm here to direct," explains director Matthew Rolston. "That doesn't mean just directing the artist and my cameraman. That means directing every single person on my crew and every single element of the video."

"Being in a leadership role and also a creative role, there are so many things you've got to deal with, so many different situations," says director Little X. "The best analogy is the military structure of the crew. You have to lay out your battle plan for what this video's going to be from the beginning all the way through the end, not halfway through the first verse and chorus. If you don't do it, you're neglecting your duties. As the director, you don't just direct what you're going to shoot, you also direct the energy of the shoot."

What makes a great music video?

"A great video is the perfect unity between the visual aspect and the music—a video that when you watch, you can't imagine how it could possibly be any different because every element is so perfectly aligned. That's a great video."

—Matthew Rolston, Director

"A great music video is one that makes your jaw drop. It should connect the audience to the music, make them fall in love with the artist, and make that artist relevant to their lives, to the point where they have to know the artist, be with the artist, and travel the journey with the artist. That's what a great music video does: it opens the door to let the audience connect with the artist and want to love him or her. On a personal level, as a director, I have different criteria. A great video has to have a new statement about what you can do with filmmaking. What's considered a great video changes from year to year, from decade to decade, because videos, in a weird way, are meant to be disposable. They're meant to sell a record within a very short period of time and capture the public's attention for that moment in time. Even the greatest videos in the world can ultimately look dated. The trick behind a great music video, for a record company, no matter how much bullshit they throw at you, is one that connects with an artist and sells more records. It's as simple as that. Because we're too young of an industry right now to start talking about what is a great, lasting video."

—Joseph Kahn, Director

As in any endeavor, all leaders are different. Each has his or her own technique and approach to leadership. "The people who follow the leader are going to reflect that leader's emotional state and level of commitment and a million other things," explains director Matthew Rolston. "So a big part of my job is to remain clear-headed and fair, and hopefully keep it fun, be kind, and help people get past their fears. There's a lot of fear and performance anxiety. Understanding all those things is part of being a director. When you're in production, the source of almost every problem that can be ascribed to an artist or management or a label is fear, which is not a good place to be coming from creatively."

Director Sanaa Hamri agrees, stating, "Directing is being fearless and always believing in the project and in myself."

APPLYING TECHNICAL KNOWLEDGE AND CREATIVE INTUITION

Directing is a mixture of technical knowledge and imagination. "People think artistic and technical things are different, but it's not true. If you don't technically know what you're talking about, you cannot be the artist you want to be. Da Vinci said you're sailing without a sail," explains director Little X. "You have to have the knowledge. Your inner eye doesn't mean anything if you can't put the camera and lenses the way you want it. So that's really one of the key things I learned about, a director being the constant of the image. Yeah, you've got this DP and that DP and this crew and that crew, but you are the constant of your look and what it is that you do. When you get the combination of a director who knows what he's doing and a great crew and you put those things together, everyone can function properly, because everyone's job is heightened."

Part of what makes the process innate is allowing the director's personality to emanate through the video concept and the individual style. "I think no matter how much any director is controlled or pushed around or whatever," says director Dave Meyers (Missy Elliot's "We Run This" and Kid Rock's "American Badass"), "there's an art to filmmaking that's really precious in that sub-textually your personality as a director comes out in everything that you do." However, the director can hone this natural ability by developing the skill of filmmaking through hard work and practice.

"I think any good director has to draw upon his or her strengths to make their work special," says director Samuel Bayer. "I try to bring into the world of music video the lessons that I learned in art school. I wanted to be a painter. And I still want to control my art. Thus, I am the director of photography on all of my shoots. My hand is the hand that paints the picture, so my hand has to be on the camera; my eye has to be in the lens. I don't want to entrust that to somebody else. When I light the thing, I want to light it my way. I try to make my work living, breathing paintings. I want them to be worlds. Every one of those jobs is a world created specifically for that artist. I use very specific color palettes for my videos, using color theory that is something I learned in art school. It's technical, but it's also instinctual. I shoot from my gut."

MAINTAINING FOCUS AND MULTITASKING

Because each shoot is different, it goes without saying that the director's job on set is very complicated. At any given time, the director may simultaneously have to deal with the DP asking about the lighting; the make-up artist checking to be sure the artist's make-up is satisfactory; the hair stylist wanting to know if the director saw that small piece of hair sticking up in the last shot; the producer relaying a question from the record label; or the AD wanting to discuss the three next set-ups. Everyone on set looks to the director for answers to their questions throughout the entire shoot. It can be very exhausting and exhilarating at the same time.

Directors have to think on their feet and multitask. If they're running out of time, they may have to condense ten shots into five and figure out how that will work while answering all of the questions being thrown at them as well. Creativity, patience, and the knowledge to answer all questions are what make a director great.

WORKING WITH THE ARTIST TO ELICIT AN APPEALING PERFORMANCE

Methods of directing the artist differ, stylistically, depending on the specific director, the genre of music, and the artist. For instance, a hip-hop artist approaches making a video differently from a rock band. The most basic difference being that a hip-hop artist rarely, if ever, shows live instruments being played in the video, whereas a rock band generally does. Also, hip-hop artists usually tend to prefer slick, polished visuals with beauty shots and trendy outfits, whereas rock artists tend toward less gloss and more grit, preferring hard-edged performances and storylines.

The director's goal is to make the artist shine in whatever environment he or she is being portrayed and to bring forth the artist's personae for the audience. To do this, there are various techniques that directors employ, which include:

• Focusing on the Artist's Performance
• Capturing the Artist's Personality
• Teaching Performance Techniques

• Encouraging and Inspiring Uniqueness
• Rehearsing and Bonding with the Artist Prior to the Shoot
• Instructing the Artist to Vocalize Playback
• Keeping the Artist in the Loop
• Turning Limitations into Strengths
• Making the Artist Appear "Cool"
• Securing Coverage
• Planning Ahead When Writing the Treatment
• Composing Shots Mindfully
• Keeping the Pace Moving
• Using One's Best Judgment

Focusing on the Artist's Performance

The artist's performance is almost always a key ingredient of the video, with the exception of videos that do not feature the artist. Consequently, the director focuses considerable attention on this aspect of the shoot, which entails intently watching the artist to find special moments in his or her performance and then capturing and enhancing them through camera angels, coloration, editing, and all of the features of filmmaking that enable the director to manipulate emotion.

"I like directing band or artist performance because I come from the tried and true world of indie rock," explains director Phil Harder. "I try to get the bands into the mood of performing as they would at the encore of a hometown show. Bands really dig that kind of attention, and will work with the director to make it happen. I try to cut through the trendy crap and get to the honest performance. Most of the time, I lock the camera down and let the band do their thing."

Capturing the Artist's Personality

At their best, music videos allow artists more freedom of self-expression than they might get onstage or in a recording studio. This allows a great director to capture the essence of the artist on film—to capture at least one facet of that artist's personality and make it visual.

"I'm really interested in the artist's performance, how they put the song across, and how they sing," says director Matthew Rolston, "so my videos tend to be mostly about the artists, how good they can look, how I can bring a certain visual value or emotional quality to bear, and the way that they're presented that is appropriate for them, is right for that track, and is a way that no one has ever seen them before."

The director helps artists express their personalities on film. "I am vocal with my talent and get the most out of the band's performance to lens," states director Dean Karr. "Being a musician also, I know what to cover, and I know when the band is doing a good job or when I need to cattle prod them into giving more."

Teaching Performance Techniques

Many directors spend time working with the artists, often employing acting techniques to improve their performance for the camera and enhance their visual image and impact.

"There are exercises that I give the members of the band," explains director Noble Jones. "Some guys hide behind microphones. Sometimes it's a matter of weaning them off microphones. I've cleared out complete bands and just worked with the singers. I teach the drummers how to hit, as there's a correct way to hit and there's a more theatrical way to hit drums. Things like that. Understanding eye lines, understanding how to use space, and how to eat up space. A lot of it is how you would talk to any actor about the subtext of a story."

Encouraging and Inspiring Uniqueness

Directors also help artists to further their visual creativity and image. "My main job, I think, as a director, is to take people into directions that they're not naturally inclined to take themselves," says director Marcus Nispel. "You have to give them enough confidence to make them take a leap of faith and say, 'I want to follow him through this dark valley.'"

What do you love about music videos?

"I love that it's a great opportunity for people to try new things. I see videos by Michel Gondry and Cunningham and Spike Jonze and all these guys that are just doing new things every time they make a video. It's refreshing and inspiring."

—Joe Hahn, Director

"I love the collaboration and the community."
—Randy Skinner, Independent Video Commissioner; Formerly Vice President of Video Production; Virgin Records

"[I love] the freedom to do whatever and to experiment without anyone knowing that you're experimenting and that you have incredible flexibility as a music video director. As long as you know what they're expecting, you can try anything. You want to invent a crane? You want to invent a shot? You want to stick the camera on someone's foot? There are no rules, and I love that about the medium. It's a freedom that you really don't have anywhere else as a director. Feature films are very director-driven, but unless you're making a Fellini movie, there are certain rules, and you have got to know how to tell the story. That's what I love about music videos: the freedom."

—Marcos Siega, Director

Rehearsing and Bonding with the Artist Prior to the Shoot

Any kind of bonding that happens between a director and an artist prior to the shoot day helps alleviate tension and nervousness that naturally comes with meeting new people and working together for the first time. At best, there is a comfort level in getting to know someone that may be subtly translated on film. At minimum, once an artist knows and trusts a director through an interpersonal relationship, the director can elicit the performance quicker and more easily, making for a more fun and relaxed shoot that's bound to produce better footage than one that is tense.

"Ultimately, the best videos come out of the best relationships," says director Bryan Barber (Outkast's "Hey Ya!" and Christina Aguilera's "Ain't No Other Man"). "For example, Philip Atwell does great videos for Eminem because he knows Eminem. I do great videos for Outkast because I have a personal relationship with Outkast. Dave Meyers does great videos for Missy Elliot because he knows Missy Elliot. And that's all across the board. The videos that we all love today are the videos that are done by directors that generally know or have some relationship or understanding of the artist."

Instructing the Artist on Vocalizing to the Playback

Directing the artist to sing along to the playback is important. Authentically singing has a different look and energy, as the strain in the throat muscles and the exertion of a live performance cannot be captured through lip-synching alone. Projecting when performing is integral to a powerful performance.

Keeping the Artist in the Loop

Keeping the artist in the loop is essential. While the concept of the video might come from the director, the video itself must center on the artist. The director needs to earn the artist's trust, develop open lines of communication, and avoid misunderstandings.

"I'm always checking in with the band and label to get their input throughout the shoot, and I try to keep them informed on where I'm going next or how the day is planned out," says director Phil Harder. "This keeps everyone involved and avoids a lot of problems."

Turning Limitations into Strengths

If an artist is camera shy—as sometimes happens, particularly with new artists—rolling film on the rehearsal or a practice take without telling him or her can reap excellent results that might not otherwise be achieved. If the artist has a specific quirk, such as looking down or away, a talented director may be able to build on it, changing it from a sore point to a focal point of interest through dynamic camera movements, dramatic lighting, or the like.

"There's a lot of emotion behind what musicians are doing," explains director Noble Jones, "and a lot of struggle to get heard. So with that struggle comes pain, and getting through that pain you get some real good stuff." The director's job is, in part, to figure out how to translate that pain visually so that it's interesting.

Making the Artist Appear "Cool"

The definition of "cool" varies depending on the genre and image of the artist. Whatever cool means to the particular artist must be achieved. Sometimes, for an artist such as Rivers Cuomo, the lead singer of the band Weezer, cool may be presenting the artist as anti-cool. The main point is to "make the artist look good beforehand so there's not an argument later on," explains director Marc Webb.

Securing Coverage

Film can be the cheapest part of the shoot if the great moments are caught; or it can the most expensive, if coverage is lacking and the label is forced to pay for reshoots. When planning the shot list, care must be taken to include close, medium, and wide shots. The director should be proactive by capturing lots of moments, even the ones that may appear offbeat at first. This is particularly important advice for new directors who haven't honed their look and style and who are still experimenting.

Planning Ahead When Writing the Treatment

The treatment should be written in keeping with the artist's persona and comfort level. For example, a director should not write an idea that has the artist acting in the video if the artist is uncomfortable acting on screen. The ideas written in the treatment are what become the video, so the director must make sure they are good ideas and well-thought out so as not to create a difficult situation during the actual shoot.

Composing Shots Mindfully

Shooting dynamic angles to tell the story, enhance the video's overall look, and propel it from average to compelling is the director's goal. In addition, the director must consider how to minimize unappealing shots such as double chins, for beauty shots, or focus on slimming angles, especially for women, as well as beauty lighting such as ring lighting for close-up performance shots.

"It's all about composition," director Samuel Bayer offers. "In music, when you strum

a guitar and hit the wrong strings you get something called a discord, an unpleasant combination of chords. If you hit a real chord, a harmonic sound will come. The same lesson holds true for music videos. The composition of the shots and the color palette can create a harmonic look or a discordant look. I try to create harmonic looks using composition and specific color palettes utilizing color theory."

Keeping the Pace Moving

The director must keep the pace moving to keep the artist's energy fresh. "The director has to create the momentum of the shoot and keep it going," says director Jonathan Dayton of the directing team Dayton Faris. "And then it's just a nonstop parade of quick decisions that you have to have a flash reaction to," agrees Valerie Faris, Jonathan Dayton's wife and co-director. If a shoot begins to drag on, the energy level shifts, which never helps the project.

Using One's Best Judgment

Sometimes the record label or the artist insists on shots that the director knows won't work, and it may be good client relations to shoot them quickly and move on. At other times, the director may just simply refuse. The decision will depend on the stage the director is at in his or her career, the actual shot he or she is being asked to capture on film, as well as a slew of other pertinent factors, such as budgeting and scheduling issues. The director must learn to trust his or her own instincts to handles these types of client requests.

TELLING A STORY

"The most important skill that you have to have as a filmmaker is telling a story," says director Brett Ratner, who went from music videos to making feature films. "In storytelling, there are different aesthetic things. For instance, how did the lighting help me tell that story? When did I go in for the close ups? I wasn't randomly cutting back from a close up to wide shot, and then to a close up to a wide shot. If you watch D'Angelo's 'Brown Sugar' video, it's very cinematic. It feels like a movie. For instance, when D'Angelo does his records sometimes, it sounds like he's really far away, like he does certain music production effects. To capture that feeling visually, I put the camera farther away. I was using distance, which is just what you do in movies. If you want to be right there and intimate, you put the camera closer or you put a little wider lens on it. If someone is watching someone talk, then you move a little farther away with a longer lens in order to give that feeling [of distance] with the lens. So I really worked on that. That was the purpose of music videos."

According to many directors, the element of storytelling is broadly defined. The director shapes every aspect of the video—from location and lighting to camera movement—to best represent the artist, to put his or her personality onto the screen, and to maximize the artist's goals.

"Centralize the artist," suggests director Marc Webb. "The artist becomes the star of the video, but you've got to make that video work. You've got to make that video make sense. And that, to me, is the ultimate goal of the music video. It's got to function. Sometimes you have to sacrifice having eight million close-ups of the singer in order to make the story make sense. And that's a struggle that I frequently run into. In order to make the story work, in order to make a person understand what's happening within the video, you have to cut to somebody opening a door rather than a close-up of the singer singing the song. You have to figure out those priorities.

Snapshots from the Set

"I was shooting a Cash Money video, and all of the guys—they travel in groups of around thirty guys—had come out to California for the shoot. Everyone had gotten the flu, and they were miserable. We were shooting the video, and they just were not feeling it. It wasn't gritty enough for them. So, in the middle of one of the days they said, 'We're not shooting any more.' And I literally pointed across the street to a garbage dump, where there were train tracks and garbage stacked up and mounds of dirt, and I said, 'What if we start shooting over there?' They looked over, they walked over, and they said, 'Yeah, let's start shooting over there.' And we just reinvented the video at that moment across the street."
—Marc Klasfeld, Director

"Often, problems are turned into solutions if a director uses common sense. I turned a blizzard in New York into one of the most interesting things I've shot. It was a music video for the English band Mansun. In the video, Jesus returns to Manhattan, and everyone thinks he's just some crazy homeless person. We shot without snow the first day, and then a blizzard hit overnight. I rewrote the idea to fit the weather. The video ended with Jesus stranded in the cold, freezing his holy ass off and praying to the gods in the middle of a New York blizzard. The actor was really suffering, and it looks quite strange. The streets were filled with four-foot drifts, and the wind blew the snow sideways. I couldn't have asked for better art direction. It's part of the reality of working on location."
—Phil Harder, Director

Usually, I incorporate those, making the artist look good, beforehand, so there's not an argument later on. And I try to be very clear beforehand."

Storytelling allows the director to manipulate the image and perception of the artist through the filmmaking process. "Directors are conscious of the subconscious," explains director Little X. "So the kid at home doesn't know why the red room makes him feel a certain way, but you, the director, should understand why. These are things that we need to be aware of. What's this angle going to do, what's this lens going to do, then what's this color going to do, what does this song mean. This person has brought meaning to this very emotional love song, but the label wants to make him a star."

EMBRACING SPONTANEITY AND CHAOS

The directors who choose to make music videos are a special breed. They must have fire in their bellies, thick skin, and a malleable sense of aesthetics that allows them not to get too attached to one idea. They must always be able to handle the constant change that is thrown their way.

"Music videos do exist in a sort of rock and roll type atmosphere, where you may be shooting something one second and in the very next second you may be shooting a whole different video," says director Marc Klasfeld. "And there's something that's very horrifying about that; and at the same time there's something that's very exciting about that, because when it works, it really works. And there's also something that you can capture in music video that you can probably only capture in a sort of independent feature film because it's so wild like that. *Apocalypse Now* wasn't made in any sort of structured way, and there's only one way to make that movie. Sometimes, with some of these videos—certainly some of the ones that I've made—if I had to struc-

ture it in a very commercial sort of way, it would've never been made. There is something that's very exciting, appealing, and sexy about that chaotic nature of it."

With usually only one day to get the whole project down on film and a month from concept to delivery, the music video world has nothing on Indy Car racing when it comes to speed. Directors must be astute decision makers in this fast paced environment. "My grandpa always used to say 'indecision is worse than wrong decision,'" Jonathan Dayton says. "And onset it's usually more important to make a quick decision than to just wait."

"I think it's important to have the ability to look both at the details, the little things, and the big picture at the same time," director Valerie Faris says. "You always have to be shifting your focus from close-up to the big picture."

"I really love the humanity and the spontaneity of what goes into making a music video," says director Mc G. "I really like being in the field, I like the crew, I like putting my eye in the eyepiece of the camera, I like working with the talent, and I like freezing before the sun comes up. I become disappointed when it's overcast and I was hoping for the sun. I like racing to get all those shots in before the sun goes down. I like it when you have a car sequence and the car won't stop, and you've got to get it down. Your everyday shooting day is unlike anything else. And being a director is really fun, especially when you know what you want to do. It's terrifying—and not fun—and terribly overwhelming when you get caught with your pants down, and I would encourage everybody to avoid that as often as possible. But sooner or later, you're going to get caught not knowing exactly what you want to do in a given situation. You need to be able to think your way out of it. But it's just so fun when you're setting up a shot, putting lenses on the camera, working with a DP you like and with actors who are interested in being the best they can be. [It's exciting when] the band wants to really do something different, something new; or [when] you're trying out a new lighting configuration or a new panavision camera. You're excited about the technological component and thrilled at the intimacy of the performance you're eliciting from the artist. And craft service has got Krispy Kremes, and the wardrobe people need your attention, and everybody's screaming, and you feel very, very alive."

Being at the helm of creative spontaneity as a director is both a rare and fortunate position. "As for the mayhem on set, I'm cool with it," reveals director Joseph Kahn. "If they want to give me hundreds of thousands of dollars to walk on-set and give me so little time that I have to make shit up as I go along, some great creativity is going to pop out of there. It's really good. I've had tons of videos where I've walked on set and because everything's prepped out at the last minute I have to make it up as I go along, like Moby, that's one of them. [With] Eminem, a lot of that stuff is improvised. You lay the groundwork, and it's like jazz. You go in there and you compose it together on the spot. It's a privileged way of playing with other people's money, that's for sure. I liken some of my techniques, because of the mayhem, to jazz playing."

FOSTERING GOOD CLIENT RELATIONS

A music video has two main parts: the music and the video. The inspiration comes from the artist and the artist's music. The director's expertise is in the visual medium. There's also a third part— the guiding force—which is the record label that helps steer both creative parties, keeping them on track and in the same direction regarding the budget, the time frame, and the artist's image.

Developing the music video must be a collaborative process between all three.

"The bands are always cool," says director Phil Harder. "Most of the time the bands have great ideas and give very constructive input into the process, because they know their music and image better than me. Bands like Bare Naked Ladies, Matchbox Twenty, Incubus, and Yellowcard are quite good with giving constructive input."

"The artist is my ultimate boss and who I ultimately respect," explains director Dave Meyers. "They're the ones who created the inspiration that's making me want to create visuals, so I'm interested in hearing their opinions. If they reject something, I'm interested in why. I might learn something. They sometimes see things differently, and I've learned amazing things from these people."

Although the record label's video commissioner represents the artist's best interests and acts on behalf of the artist, there are many times when the director's vision of the treatment may clash with that of the commissioner's. Even though both are working toward a common goal, getting there isn't always smooth sailing.

"Sometimes I get into the crossfire between my creative vision and the label's needs," says director Phil Harder. "I've learned to give in during those contentious discussions and shoot what the label wants, which usually consists of many close shots of the singer's face. I find it's better to shoot too many close-ups for the label; in turn, they give me the freedom to do my thing for the rest of the video. I usually choose what ends up in the edit anyway. If a shot sucks, but the label demands it, I shoot it quickly and let it fall on the editing room floor. On set, I have to bring it all together in the allotted shoot time and avoid the dreaded overtime."

"Most of my struggles come from the label, but the struggles are all for the good of the video," Harder adds. "Difficulties, debates, and struggles are all part of the process of making art, and I think music videos can be an art form."

RACING AGAINST THE CLOCK

One of the biggest struggles on set is having enough time to shoot everything necessary to complete the video. A one-day shoot can run over eighteen hours, and it still can be a race to get all the footage a director wants shot. "Because of the nature of the economics of the music video business," says director Matthew Rolston, "I've done twenty-hour days, which are now illegal and should be. I would say that the stamina of dealing with that and the pressure of it is the greatest hurdle in making music videos."

However, necessity can breed innovation, and music videos often provide the impetus for ingenuity. "When you're shooting, you have to be creative, because there's always something that doesn't happen exactly the way you want it to," says director Joe Hahn. "You have to use your creativity to compromise and create a new scenario that may be better, or may not be better. But you have a specific amount of time to work with, so a lot of that's budgeting your time and just making those decisions on what's the most important thing that's going to make that video great."

This frequently means scaling back and cutting shots throughout the day. "I'm always struggling with the time factor, no matter how small or large the budget," says Phil Harder. "My storyboards usually include way too many shots, but somehow we always mange to finish the job."

HAVING A POINT OF VIEW

Music videos encourage young filmmakers to express their visions while managing the demands of others. That's why so many video directors move on to television or feature film work, like Brett Ratner. "To be a director, you have to have a point of view. I have a very specific point of view. I know what I like, and I know what I don't like. Music video is the greatest medium ever, because you can have so much fun doing it. You can learn and make mistakes at the same time. It's not the end of the world. Like Russell [Simmons] once said to me, 'It's just a video. There's no box office attached to it.'"

Having a strong perspective translated through a visual medium can open the audience up to ideas they never considered before and show them ways to view commonplace ideas differently from what they are used to. "I think the most important thing for a director is having a point of view," says director Marc Klasfeld. "I would rather not watch any technical nonsense and just see somebody with a point of view who pushes me to see something in a different light and learn something new."

"If you come into the music video industry as a director and you say, 'You know what? I want to be the biggest action, blow-up, car-chase director ever,' then try to always do stuff with car chases," says director Sanaa Hamri. "Do action videos. If you want to be a film director that wants to do stripper stories for the rest of your life, then do videos that only have strippers on poles. Have a point of view, because when they [record labels] look at the body of [your] work, they will see what you're about. They'll look at it and go, 'Wow, I have this stripper story, and this director is perfect, because he shoots strippers all day!' See, when I say point of view, I don't care what other people are into. It's not about having a point of view that's morally correct within somebody else's idea; it's about finding out what you want."

EXPERIMENTING WITH THE PROCESS

Music videos allow and encourage experimental filmmaking. The projects are quick from start to finish so that a director can complete several of them within a short period of time. They have less concern for continuity, allowing more creative freedom than in story driven projects, such as feature films. Films are longer and almost always reliant on continuity, so there's not as much leeway for pushing boundaries and trying out different equipment, film stocks, and techniques.

"Ultimately, what's going to make you successful is experimenting," says director Marcos Siega. "One day you're shooting something, and it's so exhilarating when you see the final cut of it, you're just like, 'You know, I'm never going to compromise again.' Up until that point, the compromising is all about learning. But then you're like, 'This is it. This is what works, and I should stick to this.' And for me, that was [Papa Roach's] "Broken Home" video, which is why it's one of my favorite videos. I did compromise after that. I'm just being honest. Sometimes, you do a job for money and you get caught up in people telling you you're great. It happens. It's a pitfall of success. But I think you just find that moment where you're like 'This is me. This is my style. This is what I do.'"

"Music videos have taught me so much," reveals director Marc Webb. "You learn how to make decisions. You learn so many things. All the boring, crappy, weird things, like the difference between a twelve-hour day and a fourteen-hour day, different film stocks, and different cameras—all that shit that you can't really learn except by doing—I've learned in the last four or five years of doing this [directing] day in and day out, which is such a valuable experience in filmmaking."

Shilo, primarily a commercial directing team, enjoys making music videos because of what they describe as the openness to artistic interpretation in the video world. "In general, there are no mandatory product shots or legal disclaimers, so we find ourselves with a great deal of flexibility in creating a compelling story to accompany the music," they explain. "At three minutes or more, they also allow us to develop more complex storylines as opposed to say, a fifteen- or thirty-second television commercial, which can be a bit more limiting."

"I've always put a big influence on how you tell a story visually, so when I say that music video was my film school, I say to any music video, or aspiring director, that it's the one medium where you can really experiment with the style without anyone knowing that you're doing it," reveals director Marcos Siega. "Meaning you could still make a great music video and say, 'I'm only going to use one lens in this video.' No one has to know, because they're not going to come up to you and say, 'What lens are you using?'"

COLLABORATING AS PART OF A TEAM

While the director leads the charge, he or she is not the only one trying to take the hill. No one makes a music video by themselves. The crew, the artist, even the craft service people have their role to play. "Music video is a collaborative art form," says director Matthew Rolston. "Maybe it's a craft rather than an art form. Either way, it involves a lot of people, and as a director you're only as good as the team. So you have to make room for the creativity of the team. Within my leadership I want people to bring me ideas. Lots of them. And I want to learn from everybody involved so that I'm constantly challenging myself and I'm also constantly challenging my crew."

"I'm a very collaborative guy," director Brett Ratner says. "I try to be open-minded to other people's ideas, and I take the best of them and I apply them to what I'm doing. If someone on the street has a suggestion for me, I'm going to take it if it's good. The trick is having the taste level and knowing what's a good idea and what's not a good idea, as well as working with the best people that I could find. Getting the best crews in the world, which would make me look good and I would learn from them. That was really the key. Asking, 'Who did that video? I need to get that person to work with me.' And that's what I was very good at: getting people that I couldn't afford or that were beyond my means. I remember Thomas Cross. He was a big commercial DP. He did some Madonna videos, and I got him to start shooting rap videos for me. So I was always try-

ing to go to the next level. And have fun at the same time—that's important. Not being afraid to fail is a big part of it, too."

"The most important thing is surrounding myself with the right team," explains director Sanaa Hamri. "I'm merely the conductor of an orchestra, but I need the right orchestra to create the most beautiful music. If you don't have the right people around you, you won't be good at what you do."

A major aspect of leadership is communication. A director needs to know how to give the orders, but also how to listen. "The most important skill to learn, above all else, is sensitivity. The ability to communicate with other humans," says director W.I.Z. "When I understood and embraced film as a collaborative medium, I was one step closer to getting what I wanted."

BEING FINANCIALLY RESPONSIBLE

As previously mentioned, as far as the record company is concerned, a music video is a four-minute commercial to market the song and artist. They want to get the most bang possible for their buck. "At the end of the day, I have a responsibility as a music video director to make a commercial," says director Marcos Siega. "I always felt that responsibility was really important. The bands are paying for these things. They're paying for half of it. Record companies put a lot of money into marketing something, and it's because they want to sell records. I'm hired to do a job, which is to make a commercial."

If the video doesn't help bring the song and the artist attention, it certainly wasn't worth the time, effort, and especially the money to the record company. This can reflect poorly on the director. Established directors are acutely aware of their accountability to the performer and the label on both artistic and monetary levels.

"I'm not just making this music video for my sake," says director Mc G. "I've got a real responsibility to this band who've got their whole life dream invested in their first single and their first video. It's really got to work for them, and I can't just be so cavalier as to do my own little art exploration. I have to deliver for them and put them in a position to be successful. There's a lot of money on the line, and at the end of the day they're ultimately paying for it. I always experience a great deal of responsibility in that respect, and maybe that's because I came from the record side first. I wanted it to work for these bands. 'Hey, bands, if you hook up with me, I'm going to deliver for you and you're going to be in a better place because of it. Then you're going to have more opportunities to explore your creativity and so will I.'"

Directors who understand and are concerned with both the art and commerce of a music video and who can execute a video that serves both purposes are highly valued. "You have a responsibility to the artist to make sure that this video is going to air in a way that it's going to sell more records," explains director Joseph Kahn. "So to take some beautiful singer and then do some stupid video where it's just completely all about the director saying, 'What a great director I am,' and the singer doesn't get sold, you just wasted a million dollars of that singer's money, because it comes directly out of their pocket. I have too much suburban guilt to squander someone else's money."

"You can't be a director without being a financial person," Kahn continues. "And the weaker you are at finance, the weaker of a director you're going to be, because this business is not just someone standing at a paint and easel and slapping paint on there. It's moving mountains around mountains of people. It's spending thousands of dollars by the minute and collectively using huge investments. It's the most expensive art form outside of architecture. So you have to have a good financial head on your shoulders in order to achieve, because every time you put a camera somewhere, that costs money."

Budgetary considerations are factored in from the beginning. "You really do conceive with the budget in mind," explains director Marcus Nispel, "rather than conceive and then regret that the budget never really quite works out or compromise it. You just come up with simpler ideas. And you think with two brains," continues Marcus. "Because I own my own production company, I was always one-half producer, one-half director. So on one hand you see what the job inspires, what the track inspires, and on the other hand you think, 'How am I going to get all of this done?' You don't want to go over budget. I did a few hundred music videos, and not one of them went over budget."

WRAPPING OUT

"Wrapping out" has several meanings, which apply at different times during a shoot. It can mean any of the following:

- The completion of filming and removal of equipment from a specific location
- The end of a specific day of shooting
- The completion of the entire production

WRAPPING OUT OF A LOCATION

Wrapping out of a location involves several steps, which include:

- The grips, electrics, and the art department removing all of their gear

- The equipment getting loaded on the truck
- The art department set-ups being deconstructed and removed
- The production support being broken down and packed up
- The catering being cleaned up
- The garbage being thrown out
- The location being cleaned by the PAs

WRAPPING OUT OF A SHOOT DAY

When wrapping the first day of shooting on a two- or three-day shoot, the wrap can be as simple as powering down the lights and everyone leaving with the intention of coming back the next day to finish. The PAs do a general clean-up, putting away craft service and dumping the garbage, but the equipment is left, for the most part, until the next day of shooting, which can then start up again with very little set up.

WRAPPING OUT OF AN ENTIRE SHOOT

When the AD calls out "That's a wrap!" at the end of a shoot, the clean up and clean out is the same as when wrapping out of a location, although on a much larger scale. Everything shifts gear, and the entire crew cleans up and loads out of the location. The production coordinator makes sure to collect all the paperwork needed to finalize the shoot. The artist changes out of his or her wardrobe and leaves. Any additional talent does the same after filling out and submitting time cards. The crew immediately begins breaking down the lights and the set, and packs all the equipment back into the trucks to return to the rental houses. The PAs pack up the production vehicle with the equipment they picked up. The AC puts away all of the camera equipment and gets it ready for return to the rental house. When the crew, art department, and PAs complete the wrap of equipment, they fill out and submit time cards to the production coordinator.

PROCESSING THE EXPOSED FILM

As soon as the shoot is finished, the exposed film is immediately taken to the lab to be processed. The production manager or coordinator will have already called the lab to notify them when and approximately how much film will be dropped off and by what time it needs to be ready for pick-up the following day. The production manager or coordinator gives the AC the purchase order for the lab. The AC uses the camera reports to file the purchase order, returning it to the production manager or coordinator. The purchase order outlines the following:

- All instructions concerning how the lab should process the film
- How many rolls of film were exposed
- The stock number of each roll
- Whether the rolls were all exposed normally or whether they need special treatment, as well as any other pertinent information and instruction

The PO includes a full summary of each individual camera report. Along with the purchase order, the AC will hand over the cans of exposed film, the cans of unexposed film, and the camera reports on each exposed can.

COMPILING A PRODUCTION REPORT

At the end of the shoot, the AD or production manager is asked to compile a brief *production report* detailing the events of all of the shoot days, primarily if there was an accident on the set that necessitates an insurance claim or any other unusual occurrences that should be documented. It's a basic recap of the day for the records. Some production companies require this; others do not.

THE PRODUCTION TEAM'S FINAL ON-SET WRAP PROCESS

The production team collects time cards for the crew and talent and makes sure that a PA delivers the exposed film to the lab. The production manager and coordinator stay on the set until every last detail has been attended to. They make sure that all of the garbage has been dumped and all of the gear-filled vehicles have left. The production team also does one last "dummy check" to make sure nothing has been forgotten or left behind on location. With that, the shoot is officially completed and the production team goes home, ready to reconvene the next day at the production office to do the final wrap of paperwork and usher the music video into the postproduction phase. "My favorite part of the music video process is wrapping the shoot, but before the telecine," says director Patrick Daughters (Yeah Yeah Yeahs' "Gold Lion" and King of Leon's "King of the Rodeo"). "Everyone is hopefully happy and tired, which is the best feeling to have. All of the shots are still dancing around in my head for one last night before they become fixed imagery."

CHAPTER TEN
POSTPRODUCTION AND THE FINAL WRAP

Once the shoot is over, the production company should have all the footage it needs. At this point two processes begin:

(1) Postproduction—also known simply as *post*—in which the raw footage is transformed into the actual music video

(2) Final Wrap, in which the wrap book is pulled together while the loose business ends of the video shoot are tied up

The producer generally oversees both processes. If there is money in the budget to hire a *postproduction supervisor*, he or she will oversee the entire process of finishing the video in postproduction. This entails organizing and communicating the postproduction schedule so that everyone knows where they have to be and when, sending out rough cut tapes and/or DVDs to the appropriate people and obtaining changes and approvals based on them, making sure that everyone has the correct version of the edit, managing the postproduction budget, keeping tabs on all of the postproduction elements (film, DATs, master tapes, offline tapes), and delivering the video on time. The post supervisor fosters communication among all parties and keeps the postproduction process moving in a timely and conscientious manner, paying close attention to budgetary details.

THE POSTPRODUCTION PROCESS

The director focuses entirely on postproduction, having nothing to do with the final wrap. He or she spearheads the postproduction process, carrying the vision from the treatment through the actual shooting of the footage and finally to the edit. Postproduction includes several steps:

- Processing the Exposed Film
- The Telecine Process
- The Offline Edit
- The Online Edit
- Adding Special Effects
- The Final, Mastered Video

The entire process of postproduction, also known as *posting the video*, takes about one-and-a-half to two weeks on average. It can go on longer if the treatment calls for a lot of visual effects, or if the approval process gets delayed or extended due to a disagreement between the label and artist on the rough cut, or simple procrastination about making a decision.

PROCESSING THE EXPOSED FILM

At the end of the shoot, even if it's the middle of the night, the producer makes sure the exposed film gets to the *processing lab*—the laboratory where the film is developed—with all the information needed to properly develop it. At the lab, the exposed film is put through a process that brings forth the latent images from the shoot into a film negative.

Processing Different Types of Film

The type of film used during the shoot determines the processing method. It is most common to use negative film on music video shoots. Negative film, when processed, turns into a film negative with the colors, or black and white values for black and white film, inversed. This type of film must be printed onto a separate spool of film or videotape in order to be viewed as intended. In telecine, the negative images are transferred onto digital videotape to create the positive version of the images.

Some directors choose to use *reversal film*, a film stock created for direct projection, meaning that there is no need to create a positive version of the negative, because it can be projected straight from the original film. Reversal film automatically becomes a positive image after it's exposed and developed, displaying images in their original color and brightness instead of the negative images. It has a narrower range of tones, or *exposure latitude,* that it can accurately capture, but offers vivid, hyper-realistic color saturation. Director Brett Ratner used reversal film for D'Angelo's "Brown Sugar" video to get the rich, vibrant colors. Processing reversal film requires additional steps, including two chemical developers in the process, as opposed to the one developer used in color negative film.

Color negative film generally has better exposure latitude than reversal film, offering a wider, subtler range of color. With negative film, the director and colorist have more room for creativity in the telecine process than with reversal film.

Developing the Film

Developing film from a shoot involves several steps:

- The lab technicians load the film into a continuous processor machine.
- The machine guides the film through a series of timed chemical and water baths set at specific temperatures to allow the image captured on the film to emerge.
- The exposed film is immersed in a developer solution to bring out the latent images.

- The developed film is immersed in a stop-bath to halt the developer action.
- The film is then moved to a hypo solution that fixes the image.
- The fixed film gets another water bath to remove all of the chemicals.
- The machine then dries the film.

The film processing procedure requires careful monitoring of temperature and time, which are crucial factors in determining the final image quality. This becomes especially true when the director of photography has "pushed" or "pulled" the exposure on the film to compensate for difficult lighting conditions or as a creative choice.

PUSH PROCESSING

Pushing the film is a two-part method to compensate for poor lighting conditions—first, during the actual shoot, and next, during the processing. In a situation where the DP is shooting in low light conditions, he or she may elect to shoot film at a higher exposure index than the film's rating. The DP does this by setting the camera for a higher speed film than they are actually using, which is called "pushing" the film.

Cinematic film, which is similar to still camera film, comes in various speeds. The different speeds are expressed technically in ISO numbers. The International Organization for Standardization (ISO) is an international standard-setting group that produces worldwide industrial and commercial standards: the ISO standards. Because the speed of photographic film is measured and determined by ISO standards, it's often referred to as its "ISO number," which indicates light sensitivity and speed. The lower the sensitivity, the lower the speed, which means more light is needed to make an exposure. A film with an ISO of 50 is *slower,* or takes a greater amount of light to expose, than a film with an ISO of 100—in fact, it takes twice as much.

When the DP pushes the film, it allows for lesser amounts of available light to expose the film, and causes it to be underexposed in a very controlled manner. This information gets written into the camera report. When it comes to the lab, the technicians know how to compensate by pushing, or forcing, exposure as they develop the film, in this case by overdeveloping the film, allowing it to remain in the developing solution longer than normal to let the underexposed images develop more fully and produce a denser image.

The downside of the process is that it increases the grain size and contrast, and, for color film, it *desaturates* or washes out the image a bit. A DP can push modern film stocks up one stop with minimal loss of quality, but the loss starts to show if the film needs a two stop push, adding higher contrast, lower resolution, distorted colors, and noticeable graininess. Usually, only negative film will stand this process. If possible, running camera tests to see if the quality loss is objectionable is a good idea; however, music videos rarely afford the time or money to do so.

PULL PROCESSING

"Pulling" the film stock is the exact opposite of pushing it, and also has two components: (1) pulling the film during the shoot and (2) pulling the film during the processing. If, on the shoot, the setting is too bright for the film—a beach on a cloudless day, for example—the DP may pull the film, meaning that he or she will shoot so that the film is overexposed. To compensate, the camera reports will instruct the lab to pull it, or under develop it. Pull processed film often exhibits tighter grain and more saturated colors. The director and the DP might chose to pull the film prior to the actual shoot in order to achieve this effect.

BLEACH BYPASS

The procedure of bleach bypass entails either the partial or complete skipping of the bleaching function during the film processing so that some or all of the silver is left on the negative creating a black and white image superimposed over the color image. The retained silver increases the contrast and grain, while the reduced color desaturates the picture. Director Mark Pellington used this technique in The Fray video "How To Save A Life" to achieve its distinct look.

Once the film is developed and the negative is available, the film goes to the postproduction house for the telecine process. This next process allows the director to explore different looks for the overall video, as well as to sync up the audio to the visual imagery.

What makes a great music video?

"A great video is one that marries the visuals and inspires the song so that you kind of like the song better after you've seen the video. If you heard the song on the radio, you'd be like, 'Eh, it was OK.' But then you see the video and you're like, 'Wow. I love the song.' That's a successful video."

—Sanaa Hamri, Director

"A great video is one that begs to be seen repeatedly. However, I realize this is largely a matter of personal taste."

—Patrick Daughters, Director

THE TELECINE PROCESS

"Telecine is the process of transferring film into an electronic form so that it can be viewed on televisions and computers," explains Company 3 colorist Dave Hussey (Gwen Stefani's "What are you Waiting For?" directed by Francis Lawrence and Lindsay Lohan's "Rumors," directed by Jake Nava). This process, also known as *color correction*, or *film to tape transfer* in colloquial music video conversation, involves three separate yet intertwined aspects:

(1) Color correcting the film images: altering the color balance by modifying the ratio of the printing light values

(2) Transferring the film to digital videotape: manipulating, or correcting, the look of the film while laying it down to the digital videotape

(3) Synching the audio track: simultaneously joining the audio track with the image using SMPTE time code (as discussed on page 149 in Chapter Eight)

Throughout the entire process, everyone has to take great care to get the specific mechanical details, such as film speed and audio speed, right. Otherwise, problems may arise that can make postproduction a long, drawn out, expensive nightmare.

Color Correcting the Film

Similar to the process of retouching a photo in Photoshop, the telecine process lets the director and telecine technician fix the color on the film while creating a positive copy from the film negative to a digital medium. While transferring the film onto this medium—usually digital videotape—the telecine technician, known as the *colorist*, can alter the brightness, color balance, contrast, and many other aspects of the video's look.

"Telecine is very similar to the process of printing a photograph," says Company 3 colorist Tim Masick (Santana, featuring Rob Thomas' "Smooth," directed by Marcus Rayboy and Notorious B.I.G's "Mo Money Mo Problems," directed by Hype). "Different colorists can treat each piece of negative very differently. A nice analogy has been to a piece of classical music: the negative is the score and the color correction is the performance of that score."

Transferring the Film to Digital Videotape

Along with correcting the color, the colorist scans the motion picture film images and converts them to digital videotape by way of the telecine device (see "The Basic Equipment Used for the Telecine Process" later in this section). Film normally runs at twenty-four frames per second (fps), and the standard for video in the US is 29.97 *fields* per second. In video, a field is one of the many still images that comprise a moving picture. They are similar to frames, but have half the vertical resolution and are displayed twice as fast per second. Thus, due to mathematical differences, the transfer of film to videotape would not work—the two would remain out of synch—without employing a technique allowing film to be converted to video. That technique, which creates equality between film's frame rate and video's field rate, is called *3:2 pulldown* (also known as *2:3* pulldown). It is the process of transferring images from film to video by adding fields to the picture. Every other film frame is held for an additional video field resulting in a sequence of three fields/two fields/three fields/two fields for every frame of film, or three fields for every two frames. "Movie frame rates need to be changed in order to get them to play smoothly on television," says The Syndicate senior colorist Beau Leon (Green Day's "Boulevard of

Broken Dreams," directed by Samuel Bayer and No Doubt's "Underneath It All," directed by Sophie Muller).

Syncing the Audio Track

Technical precision during the shoot makes the telecine process far easier. Using the digital slate at the beginning (or end) of a take helps the telecine artist lock together the DAT playback machine's audio and the camera's images by way of the SMPTE timecode. The camera rolls on the slate for the first few seconds of every take so that the time code is visually recorded. Later, during the telecine, the colorist matches the visual timecode on each take with the audio timecode on the DAT tape that was made specifically for the telecine (see page 149 in Chapter Eight), uniting the visuals and the song seamlessly so that the lip-synching is correct.

If there is a technical problem, the telecine technician may have to synch the audio to the video by eye, a frustrating, time-consuming process. In a case like this, it generally makes more sense to have the offline editor sync up the track to the visuals. Not that the process is any less frustrating for the offline editor, but for practical purposes, the offline edit costs a lot less per hour than the telecine, making it much more affordable.

The Basic Equipment Used for the Telecine Process

The basic equipment for the telecine process is as follows:

- The telecine: the device that scans the motion picture film images and converts them to digital videotape or another digital medium
- The color corrector: the device that adjusts the color of the image
- The colorist who works the equipment

The director and the DP have presumably taken the telecine process into account when they actually shot the film, aiming for a look they know they can achieve during telecine. The colorist generally works with an assistant, who puts up the next reel of film when one has been color corrected and transferred. The assistant also changes the videotape or the digital media receiving the image when it's time for a new one. More often than not, the telecine transfers the corrected film image to DigiBeta, a digital videotape of excellent quality, for the master. It may also be transferred to another format for use in loading in the dailies during the offline edit, but this depends upon the needs and equipment of the offline editor.

"There are mainly two types of telecine devices," explains colorist Dave Hussey. "There is a Spirit that uses a CCD and white light to illuminate the film. The other commonly used device is the Rank Cintel, which uses a very high-resolution cathode ray tube (CRT) as a scanning light source. There are also several different kinds of color correction devices that allow you to manipulate the colors and contrast of the electronic signal sent from the telecine. The most popular corrector is the da Vinci. It enables you to control blacks, midrange, and white levels, also all of the color values. Through the use of 'power windows' you can also control specific area's within each film frame."

The Telecine Session Attendees

After the huge crowd at the shoot, the telecine session has a rather exclusive guest list—usually only the director, producer, and, if available, the director of photography, attend. Some label commissioners go to the telecine, and occasionally an artist may show up.

Directors always go to the telecine and usually form relationships with the colorists, who play creative roles in video making process. Directors often rely on colorists for imaginative suggestions.

"One of the most important relationships in a telecine session is that of the director and the colorist," says Hussey. "The director often picks which colorist he wants to work with. The colorist he picks will be the one who 'gets his look.' I have had relationships with directors for ten or fifteen years in some cases, and throughout that time we have been able to continue to come up with new ideas and try new things that keep the work fresh, innovative, and not predictable. I know what the director likes and doesn't like, and he, in turn, doesn't have to spend a lot of additional effort trying to explain what he's looking for."

Although the DP has a standing invitation to the telecine session, he or she cannot always make it—and they often do not get paid to go. Most prefer to go when they can, because if the video looks good it reflects well on them. Having initially interpreted the director's vision of how the video should look, the DP has a technical and creative knowledge of how the film was shot and what was intended when it got to the point of editorial manipulation, so this input during telecine is valuable. "DPs are often very busy and sometimes unavailable for telecine session, but it's great when they can come because they bring their own perspective on how the film would look best," says Hussey. "DPs sometimes push us a little farther than we might have gone otherwise."

The producer usually attends the telecine, mainly to make sure it's moving along and there is no dawdling. A telecine session is expensive—on average, running from four hun-dred and fifty dollars an hour to seven hundred dollars an hour—and going into overtime can drive a project seriously over budget. "Producers need to be very time conscious in telecine," explains Hussey, "and are always good at making sure that the session keeps pushing forward due to the lower budgets for music videos in the past several years."

Producers also keep the flow of communication open between the creative and the client. "I oversee the telecine with the director and make sure that the label knows which way we are making the film look," says producer William Green.

The label's video commissioner and the artist may attend as well, although it's not a necessity. "The label and artist ultimately have the final approval of the music video, so their acceptance of the color look that we have chosen is obviously very important," says Hussey. "The label can also be more detailed in the overall picture of how they want the artists image to be portrayed. Typically, in the case of a newer or first-time artist, labels tend to not want to go as dark and moody as you might with an artist whose look is already known and established. Also, the label is often more familiar with what the artist likes and what has been done in the past regarding their videos. I don't believe telecine is a great place for the artist to be. An artist could get hung up on how they look from a certain angle or shot, when only a small part of it was ever going to be in the video. I believe the director should be given a chance to telecine and produce a cut before getting comments from the artist."

The Role of the Colorist

A good colorist offers creative ideas throughout the process. "When the client comes in, my job is to help them think of options they have not thought of," explains senior colorist Beau Leon.

"There are thousands of colors to work with. I try to open their minds, extend their horizons, and show them what they didn't think of. I like to listen to the music and see the director's concept," says Leon. "You can tell the story by the look, also."

"Telecine work is very much a collaborative effort between the director, director of photography, and their clients," explains Dave Hussey. "A good colorist needs to bring all of these people together to form a consensus on what they are trying to achieve. Good social and conversational skills are necessary. It's important that a colorist inspire confidence among his clients with the work they are doing and have a good aesthetic sense. A colorist needs to be able to look at a shot and come up with ideas on how to make it look great. A colorist needs to be able to interpret what his clients are verbally asking for visually on the screen, and in some cases be able to show them additional ideas which will enhance their work even more."

"Good colorists are the ones who are not afraid to push the button and think outside of the box," Leon adds. "There is nothing that colorist cannot do. In color there are thousands of options and a good colorist knows the right fit."

The Telecine Schedule

The telecine is usually scheduled to take place the night after the final day of shooting. Music videos schedule night sessions because they cost less. The telecine gets underway as soon after the actual shoot as possible—as soon as the production can get the film back from the lab—in order to dive right into the postproduction process.

The amount of time the telecine takes depends on the amount of footage shot, the type of footage shot—for instance, exterior versus interior—and the pace at which the client likes to work. "If you are working on film that was shot interior, this generally moves along quicker," says Dave Hussey. "The lighting tends to be more consistent. In exterior shoots it can take a little longer to correct because you may have the sun going in and out from behind clouds. Also, the amount of audio to sync can affect the amount of telecine time you will need. A general guide for telecine is about three hours of telecine for every hour of film you have shot."

Different colorists use differing formulas to calculate the approximate amount of time necessary per session. "I try to color twelve-hundred feet of 35mm every twenty minutes with additional time to set up the initial look, which takes maybe thirty to forty-five minutes," explains colorist Tim Masick. "It can be quicker with a director I work with frequently, and longer with someone I've never worked with before."

During processing, every foot of film shot gets developed. In telecine, every foot of processed film usually gets corrected and transferred. "The most important reason we transfer all of the footage in music videos is that it helps the editor immensely in choosing shots," Dave Hussey says. "It's much easier for the record label to get excited about the cut of the video if they are looking at the final look of the film. I've known more than one artist that was upset about the way they looked in the flat transfer and couldn't get past that to approve the edit on the video."

In making music videos, it makes sense to transfer all of the film up front. This avoids the need to go back and do a second (or even third) telecine down the line. "Coloring all the film and not just the final video is mostly due to time constraints," says Beau Leon. "Your turnaround time is very short, and there is such a demand that you don't have time to wait to transfer two times. Also, it is very hard to edit a video when you are not able to look at a clean, color-corrected version."

"When I was in the Amazon filming Dave Matthew's 'Don't Drink the Water,' I had to gain the trust of a local shaman, who was taking our expedition up river. He invited me, my producer, and my cameraman into his banana leaf hut, and inhaled a strange tree bark. He pulled all energy from my mates, making them faint, and turned into a bird, flying around the hut, eventually stopping in front of me, where he healed me by extracting bad juju out of all my joints and then vomiting black soot each time. He ended up on my throat and pulled a beautiful clear crystal stone out of my body. Only those who know this type of healing will know what I'm talking about, but it sure as hell wasn't some silly Vegas magic trick. I couldn't believe I was so fortunate to be chosen for this ritual. After that, he led us on the most amazing adventure up the river, which consisted of eating a lot of piranha and bug bites."

—Dean Karr, Director

"I did a video for Nickelback's 'Too Bad,' and the weather made it extremely tough in a specific scene. But we finished it, and everybody was very happy and it got played on MTV a bunch. Fantastic. Soon, thereafter, somebody says to me, 'You know, I think the rain effect you put in that scene is so cheesy and over the top; it's just appalling. Why did you do that?' I said 'I'll tell you why we did that. It's the way the weather was when we were shooting it. We were out in the middle of fucking nowhere, there was a gale, and it was literally pouring rain, and the rain was traveling horizontally across the screen, so we just kept shooting. So, it's for real, pal.'"

—Nigel Dick, Director

After the telecine, the production team or post supervisor makes sure all of the proper elements get to the offline editor in order to begin the editing process. The post supervisor—or producer, if a post supervisor was not hired—is fully responsible for the completion of the video, with the oversight of the executive producer and/or the head of production.

THE OFFLINE EDIT

During the offline edit, the director picks the shots he or she wants to use from all the footage. In concert with an offline editor, they piece the images from the telecine together to reflect the story in the treatment. The editor must be able to strike a balance between cutting to the music and conveying a story. At this point, the video begins to look like a video. "In editing you're trying to just capture the best moments and take away all the shit," says Valerie Faris, of the directing team Dayton Faris.

"'Offline' editing means that you are working with copies of the original source material, and working towards creating the final edited master," explains offline editor Clark Eddy (Marilyn Manson's "Sweet Dreams," directed by Dean Karr and Black Eyed Peas' "Don't Phunk With My Heart," directed by The Malloys). "Typically, offline means that we are working at a lower resolution than we will finish with. Historically, cutting film was done with a workprint. Linear tape systems generally used 3/4-inch dubs, and non-linear systems today use about any format; but generally work at a lower resolution in order to save disk space and render times."

"The shoots can be fun. It depends, but sometimes you aspire to do more than you actually can, and when you're cutting you can get creative again and really find interesting connections," says director Roman Coppola.

Most directors tend to work closely with their editor throughout the offline editorial process. During this process, the editor builds the rough cut shot by shot, using the director's treatment and notes as a map. He or she becomes extremely familiar with all of the footage, picking the best shots and stringing them together in a creative sequence that merges the music and the imagery to tell a story and, hopefully, draw on the viewers' emotions.

"Music video editing is the marriage of the artist's musical message and the filmmaker's visual interpretation to create an emotional connection with the audience," says offline editor Lenny Mesina (Common's "The Corner," directed by Kanye West and Blink 182's "Down," directed by Estevan Oriol). "I edit because I'm extremely passionate about both mediums, film and music. Editing gives me the opportunity to creatively express my interpretation of what the director and musician envision."

Building the Rough Cut

After the telecine, the *dailies*—the color balanced digital tapes containing all of the footage, complete with time-coded audio—get delivered to the *edit bay*. The edit bay is the room where the editing equipment—computers and tape decks—is set up. The editor's assistant or the editor digitizes all of the footage, loading it into the computer in a compressed, low resolution form. A four-minute music video might have around ninety minutes or more worth of dailies to choose from—about a twenty-two-to-one ratio between actual footage shot to footage used. The amount can fluctuate drastically, depending on the project and the specific players, as well as how many cameras were used. A two-camera shoot, with several shots of each angle, generates at least double the amount of dailies. Shooting in high speed (for a slow

motion effect) burns through a lot of film as well. Similarly, if a 2nd unit team was working the whole time the first unit team was shooting, the editor will have all those dailies, too, giving him or her a lot of footage with which to work.

The editor then goes through all the footage, grouping and categorizing it. Each editor has his or her own system for accomplishing this. "I usually load my own footage, as it gives me a chance to get familiar with it," says offline editor Clark Eddy. "Footage loads at real time (at least from tape it does), so there's no temptation to scan quickly ahead. Then I break it down and sort it. It's like painting—the better you scrape and sand and prep, the better the final product will be, and the faster you'll ultimately get there."

"My process begins by listening to the track," says offline editor Lenny Mesina. "I let the music dictate the rhythm of the editing, the mood I want to establish, and then I find the accompanying images in the footage to create a musical and visual flourish."

Usually the director will give the editor notes at the very beginning of the edit, and then give him or her a day or two to piece together a rough version of the video. This is the most creative time for the editor. "I listen for words or sounds that are accented musically in the song; then I pair that particular sound, or sometimes lack of sound, with an image in the film that's conveying a similar emotion," Mesina explains. "Exposing those moments is a subtlety of editing that is often taken for granted or overlooked. I scrutinize every frame to make sure the correct emotion is created by the combination of an image with a specific beat or musical note. Then I eliminate all viable options until the cut feels complete."

"The most important moment in editing is in selecting the material," says editor Nicholas Erasmus (Weezer's "Beverly Hills," directed by

Marcos Siega and All American Rejects' "Dirty Little Secrets," directed by Marcos Siega). "Your cut will only be as good as your selects. I make notes when I select the material so I can remember how I felt about the material the first time I saw it. This is important on a project that may carry on for many months. Other than that, I don't intellectualize what I'm doing. I just react from my gut and go with it. Later on I can look back and intellectualize what I did."

"For most music videos, I multi-clip the performance takes," editor Clark Eddy says, regarding using a process where he can put every clip with the same time code up on his screen in its own frame. "The brilliant thing with this is that it allows you to instantly see what is going on in the other takes at the same sync point of the song. With a fast enough system, you can view sixteen takes at the same time—a lot to watch, but if you know what you're looking for, remarkably your eye can find it. I try to resist the urge to just go through the multiclips and cut from that without exploring all the footage, and I like to work in as many layers as possible, laying down selects from take one on layer one, all the way through to selects from take twenty on layer twenty. This is a great way to come across 'happy accidents.'"

Once a basic structure is in place, the director goes to the edit bay to work with the editor. The director often works with the editor for a day or more from this point forward, tweaking the shots and fine-tuning the timing to realize the vision written down at the beginning of the process in the treatment. "I would say that my loyalties lie with the director, as it's the director's vision that you're working toward completing, and that vision should encompass the desires of the label and the artist," Eddy says. "Some artists have a lot of input; others have minimal. You have to listen to everyone. Everyone has an opinion or a reaction, and 'everyone' is your audience."

The culmination of this process is the rough cut of the video, all the low resolution clips in the right order, synched to the song, but without any of the effects like fades, wipes, or the visual effects that may be needed for the treatment.

The Role of the Offline Editor

Offline editors pay attention to detail and are persistent. "An excellent editor notices the details, the nuances within the performances captured on film, that people might miss. Then they present them in a way that helps enhance the music and makes the audience appreciate the song and video even more," says Lenny Mesina.

"A great editor has the ability to bring much needed objectivity to the filmmakers, who are already very close to a project," Nicholas Erasmus says. "Great editors also need to be collaborative while still defending their point of view, remaining open to new ideas. Having a sense of what makes a great performance is essential, as well as knowing exactly when not to cut the film and just let the moment play out."

"Realizing that there is always more than one way to look at something is key," says Clark Eddy. "And understanding emotion is crucial. Always go with the emotion of a shot or a scene over anything else when faced with decisions. Also, allow happy accidents to happen. Pull selects and slap them together. You never know, something might work better than anything you could have preconceived."

The Equipment Used for the Offline Edit

The most widely used nonlinear editing system by professionals in the film and video industries are Avid and Final Cut. "My Avid is my main piece of equipment—a $55,000.00 Avid Adrenaline with three monitors, a keyboard, a computer, a drive tower, drive storage, and a box that helps it all to interface called an Adrenaline box," says editor Dustin Robertson (Madonna's "Hollywood," Remix co-directed by Mondino and Dustin Robertson and Janet Jackson's "All Nite (Don't Stop)," directed by Francis Lawrence). "I rent digital beta decks when I need them to input and output media, and I work from a home studio, which is nice. I can work when I am inspired to work and not force myself into a facility schedule."

Final Cut has only recently moved into the professional editing spotlight, though for years amateurs favored the program. "I have both Avid and Final Cut, but these days I prefer FCP 5," says Eddy of Final Cut Pro 5. "Once Final Cut figured out multiclipping, I was an instant convert, after thirteen years of editing on Avid. My basic equipment is a dual processor G5 with eight GB RAM and an analog and SDI capture card; a fast RAID; loud and clean speakers; a fourteen-channel mixer; and a client monitor, like a forty-two inch plasma. I work a lot on my laptop as well on location, so a souped-up Powerbook and a portable FW800 drive (a 400 gig fire-wire hard drive) comes in handy."

"With the advances in technology, an editor should always be prepared to work on new editing platforms," Erasmus says, pointing out that "in the editorial realm, technical platforms are irrelevant compared to the talent. The creativity of the artist—editor or visual effects artist—is the most important part of the mix."

The Offline Edit Attendees

Generally, the offline edit involves the editor and the director. The post producer or producer may stop by to see how it's going, to offer up an opinion (if asked), or to drop off or pick up dubs of the rough cut. Rarely do the label commissioner or artist stop by.

The Offline Schedule

"The time it generally takes to complete an offline edit is two to four days for a 'rough cut,' and then two to three days to address label and artists changes and approvals," explains Lenny Mesina. "So it's approximately a one week turn-around for the entire edit." This time frame works only if the client requests only one set of changes. Often, the client asks for more changes and the edit lasts upwards of two (or more) weeks.

The Approval Process

Once the editor and director complete the rough cut, it goes to anyone who needs to approve it. This includes the label's video commissioner and artist(s), but can also involve others, such as the product manager, or the A&R person who signed the artist, or even the president of the record label.

If the production did not hire a post supervisor, it becomes the producer's responsibility to make sure the clients see copies of the rough cut, either by posting it online and directing them to the correct website or by shipping a dub to them. The producer collects the comments and feedback from the clients and sends them to the director and editor. "This is a period that is wonderful, if everyone is happy with the footage, or never ending, if they are not," remarks producer Jil Hardin.

The editor and director make changes to the rough cut based on the comments and feedback from the clients. Once finished, they submit a second rough cut to the clients. Although contractual agreements are usually for two rough cuts prior to the final edit, it is not uncommon for the process to drag on as more rough cuts are requested. "Most of the time, video editing lasts two to four weeks. It depends. I've been on some for only four days, others for four months," says offline editor Dustin Robertson.

According to Clark Eddy, "It seems that people are expecting the process to happen faster and faster these days. Two to three weeks from telecine to *conform* (online) seems to be the average. Usually, I can get a first cut out within a few days, sometimes overnight. Every job is different with different demands, and you have to be adaptable. Music videos are short run projects, and sometimes they require long days or all-nighters."

Once the clients give their final approval on the music video edit, the editor generates an *"EDL,"* or *edit decision list*, which is a digital file listing all the takes used in the offline, in order, with the time each shot appears and instructions as to the transitional timing between shots (quick cut, slow fade, etc). The offline editor generates the EDL, which gets passed along to the online editor with the final, approved rough cut when they schedule the online edit. "Once the final offline master is created and approved and locked," says Eddy, "then the project is conformed, or onlined, at a high or uncompressed and broadcastable resolution." This means the editor and director take the high quality images from the telecine master tapes and make a high resolution duplicate of the lower resolution offline edit.

Advice for Aspiring Directors

"What I gained out of film school is access to the equipment. Now, of course, everybody has the capability of getting a digital camera and editing on all this new technology that's available. So I don't think it's essential or important to go to film school anymore, because you can pretty much get access to all that stuff on your own. I would say the best thing is just to do it, at whatever level or skill you're able to muster. If you have a sister who plays the violin, make some type of video of her, or if you have a friend that's in a band, do something for them. Jump into creating work right off the bat, instead of saying, 'Oh, I should be assistant director.' Just jump right in and learn as you go, and do it at whatever level you can. Start making videos for friends, and then gradually you'll build up a body of work, confidence, and a set of ideas that is a reflection of who you are. Then you can take that and go to work in a more professional way."

—Roman Coppola, Director

"Just do it. Especially now, with computers and cameras, there's no excuse if you aspire to be a filmmaker not to do it. Where there's a will, there's a way. And everyone knows someone with a video camera. Every school has computers now. So I don't even think money's a big concern. Because if you really wanted to, you'd borrow a fucking camera and you'd edit on someone else's computer. If you really want to direct, direct. Just go and direct something. My advice to directors who want to do music videos but aspire to do movies—because there's a difference between a music video director and a feature film director or storytelling director—is don't worry so much about the cool aesthetic. That comes. Just find your voice. Just really think about the story. A director's job is to tell the story, and that gets lost in music videos sometimes."

—Marcos Siega, Director

THE ONLINE EDIT

Online editing is the final stage in the music video production. Once the low resolution offline edit is approved, the images must be reassembled at full resolution using the high quality master tapes generated during the telecine. The editor adds all the visual effects and titles, if relevant, to the video. "The online edit is done as a final polish so that the video, and more importantly the artist, looks as good as possible," explains Ingenuity Engine's postproduction producer Matthew Poliquin. (Pink Spiders' "Little Razorblade," directed by Joseph Kahn, and "Buttonz," by The Pussycat Dolls featuring Snoop Dog, directed by Francis Lawrence). First the video is conformed, and then it is tweaked and cleaned up.

The Video Conform

The first step in the online edit is the video conform. This process usually takes one to three hours, not including cosmetic and visual effects work. The video conform is created using the edit decision list that was generated at the end of the offline edit (see The Approval Process on page 196). The online editor programs the online edit computer to read the EDL, follow its instructions, and generate a copy of the rough cut from the master tapes of the dailies by digitizing the project, this time in high resolution. This high-resolution version, the basic blueprint of the video, is in the home stretch to becoming the final video. Once tweaked and fully onlined, meaning once the online edit video conform has been completed, this version will become the master.

Cosmetic Cleanups and Tweaks

Once the approximately four-minute video is constructed, the director perfects it with the online editor, making sure all the shots have been laid down according to the rough cut. Next, they tackle any cosmetic work, exporting segments of the high quality digital video for air-brushing or using Photoshop to clean up any unruly frames. This can include removing logos that might have snuck onto the set (MTV frowns on such things), removing blemishes, or adjusting any color variations that might have cropped up between takes. At this point, any visual effects shots that had been removed and constructed separately (see Adding Visual Effects on page 199) are re-inserted into the video timeline. Once all of the shots requiring special attention are replaced, the editor and director go through the video once again to smooth out any minor rough spots and tweak any visual effects that might need work.

The Role of the Online Editor

The online editor must have complete mastery over his or her tools—the computer hardware and software systems—have an excellent eye for detail, and be able to work well with the client. He or she assumes a less creative role in the overall process, mainly working as a technician to rebuild the cut supplied by the offline editor, as well as making the tweaks and polishes requested by the director, producer and label.

The Equipment Used in the Online Edit

There are various computer systems used for the online edit. "Some sort of digital media acquisition system will be used for the online edit," says Poliquin. "Examples are the Avid Adrenaline or Nitris, Final Cut Pro with a Black Magic card or Aja card, or Discreet's Flame or Smoke systems. All of those are a combination of hardware and software bundles of all different price ranges."

These hardware/software packages allow the editor to interactively create, composite, and edit highly challenging sequences that merge live action with computer-generated imagery and 3D graphics. Postproduction facilities integrate these systems into dedicated suites. For example, the editorial and visual effects facility Ingenuity Engine has powerful computer systems loaded with software systems, giving the editor as many tools as possible to achieve the desired effects.

ADDING VISUAL EFFECTS

As discussed in Chapter Eight, visual effects refer to artificially creating an image for a film or manipulating the existing image. This broad term alludes to any alterations to film or video images during postproduction, as opposed to special effects, which are done live during the actual filming of the video. Today, visual effects are usually generated by software and computer systems, and they often involve integrating live-action footage, pyrotechnics, and in-camera special effects with computer-generated imagery in order to create environments or scenarios that look realistic but would be dangerous, costly, or impossible to capture on film.

"Effects are done for a myriad of reasons, ranging from safety (making it appear as if the band is skydiving—something that could not be done practically) to budgetary (replacing or enhancing of backgrounds or locations that are in remote or exotic locales, as well as crowd duplication using a small number of extras and copying them to create a crowd of thousands—saving the production quite a bit of money on food and pay for the actors) to impossibility (gravity defying objects, color changing backgrounds, band members climbing out of sinks)," explains Poliquin.

Not only are visual effects common on big-budget videos, they have recently become accessible to the amateur music video director with the introduction of affordable animation and compositing software like Combustion, Maya, Lightwave, After Effects, SoftImage XSI, Boujou, and Flame.

Compositing

Compositing, also called *keying*, is the process of combining several visual layers in order to make a shot look real. *Screen comps*, the images being keyed together, can either be live action or stills, such as photographs or drawings. A common use for compositing is replacing an image on a television, monitor, or other screen in the video. For instance, when shooting the actual video, a shot of a cell phone screen may be left blank in order to key in a different image during the postproduction process.

"Compositing is where all of your elements are put together," says Poliquin. "The elements can be CG [computer generated] or shot elements. Subtleties that a compositor should look out for is correct color, focus, grain, angle of light, reflections, and shadows."

The most popular computer programs used in compositing include Adobe After Effects, Autodesk Combustion, and Apple Shake. The most common compositing techniques used on a music video are bluescreen or greenscreen, and rotoscoping.

BLUESCREEN OR GREENSCREEN

The terms *bluescreen* and *greenscreen* refer to both the screen itself and the visual effects resulting from using a monochromatic colored screen as a background for a scene. The screen is evenly lit by the DP so that there are no shadows on the subjects being filmed in front of it, a necessary technicality for creating the visual effect.

"The artist is filmed against a green or blue screen," explains Poliquin. "Later [during the online edit] the screen is removed and a background/backdrop is put in its place. This could be an entire environment, or something outside a window—making a car look like it's driving down the street, or that a set is an apartment with a grand New York City view."

ROTOSCOPING

Rotoscoping is a technique that involves animators tracing live action movement, frame by frame, for use in cartoons. A classic example of this is A-Ha's video "Take On Me." Today, when keying in elements, each *matte*—layer—can be live action, animated, or computer generated.

COMPUTER GENERATED IMAGERY

Computer generated imagery (*CGI* or *CG*) is the application of computer graphics to visual effects in filmmaking. As computer technology has grown, CGI has become the dominant form of creating visual effects. "CG involves building computer models based on geometry to represent the physical," explains Poliquin. "The models are virtually lighted, textured, and animated to create the desired effect—either something photo real or a product that is considered to be more stylized."

This process allows filmmakers to create a virtual environment. Some feel it frees them from the constraints and variables of real time filmmaking and enjoy the control inherent in creating CG effects. "One of my favorite videos is 'Points of Authority,'" says director Joe Hahn. "That was completely CG. The only involvement of the band was, of course, making the song, and we also had a facial capture session where we did a scan of everyone's face and recreated it in a virtual environment. But that was a great video because I got to basically create a giant battle scene and have robots kill each other. It was kind of like making an action movie. That was also great because we accomplished that whole video in, I think, a matter of six weeks. It was a pretty intense project, but it was good as far as us knowing exactly what we wanted and getting that. Because all the pieces in that video were specifically designed to last the amount of time within that video, there was no excess. Everything you see in that video was made for that video, and there's nothing that you didn't see because you have to create a story and then find out how long each moment lasts and where those moments take place before actually seeing the final product or having a filmstrip to inspire you. All we had to work with was storyboards. It's kind of like sketching before you have a final painting. It was a lot of fun to do."

The most popular computer programs for CGI include Maya and Softimage XSI.

The Visual Effects Designer

Designers are skilled at computer programs used to create complex graphics. They understand modeling and texturing, creating graphics and artwork that enhance the visual environment but are not meant to look lifelike. "Designers are used for things like titles and graphics," says Poloquin. "It is similar to compositing, but the goal is not to make something look real as much as it is to create moving graphics and artwork."

The most popular computer programs for designing include Adobe After Effects, Photoshop, and Illustrator, as well as integration with some CG programs.

The Visual Effects Supervisor

If postproduction effects play a large role in a video, an FX supervisor generally starts during preproduction and works through postproduction, making sure the process is handled correctly at every stage. The FX supervisor works closely with the director to see that everyone understands what they need to do to make sure that the effects come out right, as well as with the DP to see that all the shots are lit, framed, and photographed so that the effects artist can work with them.

"A good visual effects supervisor must be able to adapt immediately to whatever happens or changes on set," says Poliquin. "They must know the ins and outs of what is to happen later in post, what or how things need to be shot on set in order to achieve the desired effect later, and must be able to answer any question that anyone has on set."

The Visual Effects Artist

A visual effects artist is proficient at operating various computer simulator systems to replicate realistic physical or natural phenomenon (explosions, fire, smoke). He or she designs and implements both 3D and complementary 2D effects, as well as has a strong understanding of light, color, composition, and mood. The visual effects artist may be required to partake in the compositing process, so he or she must have a clear understanding of it. "A good visual effects artists must know the software and hardware that he or she is using, manage their time well, and make the client happy," says Poliquin. "They should strive to always outdo or out perform themselves on each job."

Although the computer systems are the tools used, the actual creativity and expertise of the artist is far more important than any amount of hardware or software.

The Visual Effects Schedule

Detailed visual effects can take hours or weeks to create. It all depends on what the treatment calls for. "Sticking to a time table is usually very difficult, as postproduction is the most mercurial part of the process, where the final look, types of effects, and texture is decided," explains producer Oualid Mouaness.

It is not uncommon for postproduction to continue right up to the final deadline. "The most crucial time for the producer and director is in the final hours of the postproduction process," says producer Jil Hardin. "This is where every frame is scrutinized for possible errors or guarantees and hopes of perfection. This is commonly finalized in the middle of the night, or the early hours of the morning after little or no sleep and just before the closed captioned, digital master has to get sent via satellite, or same day shipping, to make an on-air delivery deadline arbitrarily set by a music video channel or an A&R representative of the label."

The shots or sequences that are slated for visual effects are removed and constructed separately from the video conform. Then they are re-inserted into the video timeline at the end of the process to complete the online master.

THE FINAL, MASTERED VIDEO

Once the online editor and director finish the video, they have to *master* it—create a final version of the video from which copies will be made—in the format the contract calls for. The contract also dictates the number of viewing copies—dubs from the master—they must deliver to the label with the final video master. All together, these are known as the *deliverables*. Normally, the label requests two close captioned Digibeta masters and a handful of viewing copies, either on DVD, Beta SP, or VHS. The production company usually keeps one or two Digibetas for their vault, as well.

THE FINAL WRAP

While postproduction is taking place, the production staff completes the final wrap of the video project, which includes:

• Concluding Responsibilities of the Production Team
• Returns and Drop Offs
• Collecting Paperwork and Organizing the Wrap Book
• Actualizing the Budget
• Submitting Overages
• Solving Problems

The wrap usually takes a few days and is almost always completed before postproduction is finished. Post is concluded when the final video master has been approved by the record label commissioner and all of the deliverables have been shipped to the label.

THE CONCLUDING RESPONSIBILITIES OF THE PRODUCTION TEAM

On the day following the final shoot day, the production team makes sure postproduction begins without a hitch, and collects and organizes all the final paperwork pertaining to the project. This includes submitting the time cards to the payroll company after calculating and signing off on them, paying vendors and crew that need to be compensated immediately, and collecting all conclusive information needed for the wrap book and for actualizing the budget.

The production staff helps shepherd the project through postproduction. If a post supervisor is onboard, the production team merely assists. If no money was budgeted for a post supervisor, the production manager and production coordinator focus on the final wrap with the guidance of the producer, while the producer oversees both post and the final wrap.

The producer, upon completing the project, explains all aspects of the project to the head of production, or executive producer at the production company, and passes the wrap book on to them at the very end. It's the responsibility of the head of production or the executive producer, not the freelance producer, to obtain final payment from the label.

RETURNS AND DROP OFFS

The day after the final shoot day is the return day. It's best to have the same two PAs who did pick ups also do returns, since they already know what was picked up from which vendor. Following the same basic procedure as that of the pick up day, the coordinator gives the PAs a list of all the places to drop off the equipment with all the information and paperwork they might need. The PAs take the truck filled with equipment out of the bonded lot in which they parked it the prior night and drive it to the rental houses, returning the equipment.

Usually, the exposed film is taken to the processing lab as soon as the production wraps, and the film is developed immediately so that the telecine can take place the following day. Often, on the return day, the PAs will be sent to pick up the developed film from the lab and deliver it to the postproduction facility where the telecine is scheduled to take place.

COLLECTING PAPERWORK AND ORGANIZING THE WRAP BOOK

The wrap book compiles all of the documents and receipts for the entire project. Every production company has its own format. Among the production coordinator's primary responsibilities, gathering and properly assembling all of the paperwork for the wrap book may be the most important. Accumulating information for the

wrap book and keeping it in order starts at the very beginning of the project, as mentioned in Chapter Eight, at which time the head of production instructs the coordinator how that company organizes its wrap book.

The information in the wrap book falls into two main categories: (1) monetary expenditures, and (2) documentation noting all other transactions, creative information, or pertinent notes, such as contracts, permits, storyboards, etc. Every penny is accounted for on the purchase orders, time cards, and petty cash logs. All other paperwork consists of creative or contractual documents involved in making the video. The wrap book may be set up as follows.

The Production Book

The production book summarizes the basic details of the project and includes a brief overview of it.

Record Label Contracts

The agreement between the production company and the label is the main contract in this section. Also included are other contractual documents or information, such as letters of commitment and/or confirmation and overage documentation. Important correspondence with or about the artist(s) and their management may be filed in this section as well.

The Treatment and Storyboards

Another section of the wrap book includes the treatment, the storyboards, and any other creative documents or renderings such as wardrobe sketches.

The Budget

A separate section contains all iterations of the budget, pertinent correspondence about the budget, and any logs referring directly to the budget.

Purchase Orders

Also included in the wrap book are all of the purchase orders in numerical sequence. Each PO contains all significant information regarding vendors involved in the project, including the company name, address, phone number, website, and contact name. The PO includes the vendor's federal identification number as well. If the vendor is an independent contractor, a social security number will suffice. If the production company is ever audited, they can use these numbers to prove payment to vendors.

The coordinator makes sure that any notes detailing the transaction and payment information between vendors and the production company are written on, or attached to, the purchase order. For instance, the PO should state what was purchased or rented. If a check was issued, the date, amount, and check number are also noted on the PO, and a copy of the check is attached. Generally speaking, one copy of the PO goes to the vendor, one goes in the wrap book, and one goes to the production company's accounting department accompanied by a check request for payment.

Most production companies require hard copies of all bills with final amounts on them attached to the purchase orders. This simplifies the bill paying process later, especially for vendors who get paid directly from the production company's account. When the production staff is long gone, having completed the wrap and moved on to another project, the accounting department must have documentation showing exactly how much was charged and paid.

Some production companies like the insurance certificate for the specific vendor attached to the PO. Other production companies like a separate section in the wrap book for all insurance certificates.

Time Cards

All crew time cards from the payroll company are filed in their own section. After filling out the time card, the individual worker keeps one copy and returns the other two copies to the production coordinator. The production coordinator brings the time cards to the production manager, who calculates and approves each one, and then passes them on to the producer, who must sign each time card.

The coordinator then puts a copy of each time card in this section of the wrap book. The other copy gets submitted to the payroll company, attached to a purchase order. The payroll company calculates the combined amount of all wages, including government taxes and union agency dues that the payroll company pays. A percentage for their fee is added on top of this amount, and they submit a bill with the breakdown of all costs to the production company. The production company cuts a check for one lump sum, noted on the purchase order, for the entire amount to the payroll company, which then sends paychecks out to the workers on the project.

Petty Cash

Each person who receives petty cash during the course of the production neatly tapes all of their receipts to sheets of paper and lists them on a petty cash log, reconciling the money spent for production coordinator. The total of the receipts plus the cash left over should equal the amount of cash requested and received. If additional money was spent, the individual's petty cash log should reflect the out-of-pocket expenditure and what the production company owes the individual. All remaining petty cash is turned in to the production coordinator. The coordinator puts together an integrated petty cash log that combines everyone's petty cash expenditures.

Talent and Casting

Another section of the wrap book contains the talent releases, along with photos of the talent and any additional casting information considered pertinent.

Location

In addition, all location releases, location permits, and parking permits are filed in the wrap book. Location information, such as driving directions or specific rules and regulations about a particular location, may be included here as well.

Additional Documentation/Miscellaneous

A final section of the wrap book includes the call sheet, the production report (if one was generated), the camera reports (unless they are attached to the PO for the film lab), missing and damaged (M&D) reports (if applicable), and any additional, important paperwork.

ACTUALIZING THE BUDGET

At the end of the project, the production manager or producer inputs all of the purchase order amounts into the complete purchase order log, all of the crew time cards into the complete crew payroll log, and all of the petty cash logs into one complete petty cash log. The final amounts from each of these three records are automatically transferred into the Point Zero bid, creating the *actualized budget*. This gives an accurate record of how much money was genuinely spent on each line item, and whether the production went over or under budget.

Throughout the production process, the producer and/or PM keeps a rough, working tally of how much they spend, but during the final wrap they get the actual figures. However, since the final wrap is done before they complete postproduction, they still have to estimate the editing costs. Since the preproduction costs and shoot costs are accurate at this point, the actualized budget is a pretty close estimate of the final expenditure of the project. Once postproduction is finished and the video is delivered to the record label, the producer, the head of production, or the executive producer at the production company plugs in the precise post figures to get the actual cost assessment to determine whether they made a profit or took a loss on the music video.

SUBMITTING OVERAGES

If overages were accrued on the project, the producer pays special attention to them during the wrap. Generally, the label wants them treated separately from the originally contracted budget. "When there are overages, part of the final wrap procedure is breaking down and supplying the label the back up to show that the money you have asked for is the money you have spent," explains producer William Green.

The producer and PM have to provide paperwork indicating what the overage money was for and where it was applied. This money is included in the actual budget for the production company's needs. However, if the record company has agreed to pay the production company for these expenses, they must be broken out for the label's needs.

SOLVING PROBLEMS

The production team also handles any M&D claims, insurance claims, and any other problems that may have arisen on the project. Problems are dealt with on a case-by-case basis. The only real consistency is in dealing with insurance claims. If the production faces a sizable missing or damage problem, or a substantial insurance claim, the production company needs to consult their insurance broker immediately and follow his or her directions to avoid further problems or costs.

Once the final wrap is complete, the production manager and production coordinator have finished their commitment to the production company and can move on to their next project. The producer follows the project through to final delivery, if no production supervisor was hired. If there is a production supervisor, the producer proceeds to the next project. Once the music video is completed and delivered to the record label, the director has finished his or her commitment. Everyone involved can move on to the next project, and the cycle begins all over again.

ACKNOWLEDGMENTS

I am filled with gratitude and appreciation for all those who helped make this book possible. Thank you, Hank Bordowitz, my manuscript consultant, for all of your editorial work and valuable input. Thank you, Bob Nirkind, my editor. Your attention to detail in reviewing the information contained within these pages and your professionalism have made this project what it is. Jim Fitzgerald, my agent, thank you for your support and patience. Jim Laakso, thank you for the detail and speed with which you transcribed the many interviews. Dean MacKay, thank you for years of detail-oriented concentration, loyalty, and persistence in the face of music video production problems. Thank you for bringing the visual portion of this book to life through your photographic expertise.

Thank you to all of the people whom I interviewed (please see Expert Testimonials and Contributors on pages 13–16). Your candid disclosures are the core of this book. Nicole Ehrlich, Jill Kaplan, and Jeff Panzer—you three went above and beyond in your support of this project. You are appreciated, and I hope to have the opportunity and honor to repay the favor.

Thank you, Denise Roy, for your expert opinion, advice, and friendship throughout the entire book writing process; from the creative to the business aspects, your input and guidance were integral. Were it not for you, I don't think this book would have seen the light of day. Thank you, Jane Kagon and Pascale Halm at UCLA Extension Department of Entertainment. The two of you planted the seed and supplied the sunlight and water that enabled this project to grow and take shape.

John Traina, thank you for years of practical support and loyalty in the toughest production situations. Hayley Mortimer, your guidance reaches far and wide. Many thanks for helping me structure and keep my focus, both with this project and with the bigger picture aspects of my life. Nicholas Erasmus, thank you for years of creative and personal encouragement, support, and honesty. Lisa Beth Kovetz, thank you for all of the creative brainstorming and support from a fellow author. Tara Howley Hudson, thank you for the continual reminder to live, to speak, and to write my own truth.

Mom and Dad, thank you for teaching me that I can achieve anything, that nothing is out of my reach, and that with hard work and persistence, anything is possible.

And thank you, Mark D'Agostino, my supportive, loving, and understanding husband. Because of you, I strive to be better in every capacity of life. Throughout this project, I worked harder because of you. Your own personal fire to succeed has profoundly influenced me, and I will be forever indebted to you for inspiring me to excel.

APPENDIX A.

THE MAIN BUDGET—THE POINT ZERO BID: TOP SHEET AND PRODUCTION COST SUMMARY

(pages 1 and 2 of 8)

MUSIC VIDEO
PRODUCTION COST SUMMARY

Bid Date:		Bid Name:	
Production Co.:		Record Label:	
Address:		Address:	
Telephone:		Phone:	
Fax:		Fax:	
Job Nº:		Contact(s):	
Contact:			
Director:		Artist:	
Producer:		Title(s):	
DP:			
Art Director:		Management:	
Editor:		Address:	
Pre-Production Days:			
Build & Strike Days:	Hours:	Phone:	
Pre-light Days:	Hours:	Fax:	
Studio Shoot Days:	Hours:		
Location Days:	Hours:	Delivery Date:	
Location(s):		Delivery Format:	
Shoot Date(s):			

SUMMARY OF ESTIMATED PRODUCTION COSTS			ESTIMATED	ACTUAL
1	Pre-production & Wrap Costs	Totals A & C		
2	Shooting Crew Labor	Total B		
3	Location & Travel Expenses	Total D		
4	Special Props & Related Expenses	Total E		
5	Studio & Art Department Costs	Totals F, G, & H		
6	Equipment & Related Expenses	Total I		
7	Stock, Develop and Print	Total J		
8	Miscellaneous Costs	Total K		
9		A to K		
10	Director / Creative Fees	Total L		
11	Insurance			
12	Production Fee			
13	Sub-total	Production		
14	Talent & Talent-related Costs	Totals M & N		
15	Post Production Costs	Totals O & P		
16	Sub-total	Talent and Post		
17	Other			
18	Other			
19	Other			
20				

Contracted Total			GRAND TOTAL			
Contingency Day						

COMMENTS

Budget Tier to the next level will include any & all add'l costs (i.e. higher crew rates & benefits, etc.) associated w/ this higher tier level.

Prod Co

Bid Name

	PRE-PRO & WRAP	Days	Day Rate	Overtime Hours			ESTIMATED	ACTUAL
A	LABOR			1.5	2.0	5.0		
1	Line Producer							
2	Assistant Director							
3	Director of Photography							
4	Camera Operator							
5	1st Assistant Camera							
6	2nd Assistant Camera							
7	Camera Loader							
8	Helicopter Pilot							
9	Cam Mount Tech							
10	Asst Cam Mount Tech							
11	Gaffer							
12	2nd Electrician							
13	3rd Electrician							
14	4th Electrician							
15	Grip/Electric Drivers							
16	Key Grip							
17	2nd Grip							
18	3rd Grip							
19	4th Grip							
20	Sound Mixer							
21	Boom Operator							
22	Playback							
23	Crane Op							
24	Crane Tech							
25	Asst Crane Tech							
26	Camera Car Driver							
27	Still Photographer							
28	Script Supervisor							
29	Home Economist							
30	Asst Home Ec							
31	VTR Operator							
32	Set Security							
33	Storyboard Artist							
34	Teleprompter Op							
35	Generator Operator							
36	Animal Wrangler							
37	Location Mgr/Scout							
38	Production Supervisor							
39	2nd AD							
40	First Aid							
41	Craft Service							
42	Firemen							
43	Policemen							
44	Transportation Captain							
45	Teamsters							
46	Caterer							
47	Asst Prod Supervisor							
48	Prod Assts							
49								
50								
						Sub-total A		
						PT/P&W		
						TOTAL A		

APPENDIX A. (pages 3 and 4 of 8)

Prod Co
Bid Name

B	SHOOTING LABOR	Days	Day Rate	Overtime Hours 1.5	2.0	3.0	ESTIMATED	ACTUAL
51	Line Producer							
52	Assistant Director							
53	Director of Photography							
54	Camera Operator							
55	1st Assistant Camera							
56	2nd Assistant Camera							
57	Camera Loader							
58	Helicopter Pilot							
59	Cam Mount Tech							
60	Asst Cam Mount Tech							
61	Gaffer							
62	2nd Electrician							
63	3rd Electrician							
64	4th Electrician							
65	Grip/Electric Drivers							
66	Key Grip							
67	2nd Grip							
68	3rd Grip							
69	4th Grip							
70	Sound Mixer							
71	Boom Operator							
72	Playback							
73	Crane Op							
74	Crane Tech							
75	Asst Crane Tech							
76	Camera Car Driver							
77	Still Photographer							
78	Script Supervisor							
79	Home Economist							
80	Asst Home Ec							
81	VTR Operator							
82	Set Security							
83	Storyboard Artist							
84	Teleprompter Op							
85	Generator Operator							
86	Animal Wrangler							
87	Location Mgr/Scout							
88	Production Supervisor							
89	2nd AD							
90	First Aid							
91	Craft Service							
92	Firemen							
93	Policemen							
94	Transportation Captain							
95	Teamsters							
96	Caterer							
97	Asst Prod Supervisor							
98	Prod Assts							
99	Runners							
100								
					Sub-total B			
					PT/P&W			
					TOTAL B			

Prod Co

Bid Name

C	PRE-PRODUCTION & WRAP EXPENSES	Amount	Rate	x	ESTIMATED	ACTUAL
101	Car Rentals					
102	Air Fares					
103	Per Diem					
104	Scout Expenses					
105	Pre-pro Expenses					
106	Prep Trucking					
107	Taxi Service					
108	Office Rental					
109	Office Phones					
110	Office Supplies					
111	Research					
112	Working Meals					
113						
			TOTAL C			

D	LOCATION & TRAVEL EXPENSES	Amount	Rate	x	ESTIMATED	ACTUAL
114	Location Fees					
115	Permits					
116	Car Rentals					
117	Van Rentals					
118	Production Motorhomes					
119	Parking, Tolls, and Gas					
120	Production Trucking					
121	Camera Trucking					
122	Other Trucking					
123	Customs					
124	Excess Bags					
125	Air Fares					
126	Per Diem					
127	Air Fares					
128	Per Diem					
129	Breakfast					
130	Lunch					
131	Dinner					
132	Other Meals					
133	Car Service					
134	Taxi Service					
135	Kit Rentals					
136	Weather					
137	Gratuities					
138	Craft Service					
139						
			TOTAL D			

E	SPECIAL PROPS & RELATED EXPENSES	Amount	Rate	x	ESTIMATED	ACTUAL
140	Special Props Rentals					
141	Special Props Purchases					
142	Picture Vehicles					
143						
144	Picture Animals					
145						
146	Makeup Effects					
147						
148						
149						
150						
			TOTAL E			

APPENDIX A. (pages 5 and 6 of 8)

Prod Co
Bid Name

F	STUDIO RENTAL & EXPENSES	Amount	Rate	x	ESTIMATED	ACTUAL
151	Rental For Build Days					
152	Build OT Hours					
153	Rental for Pre-Lite Days					
154	Pre-Lite OT Hours					
155	Rental for Shoot Days					
156	Shoot OT Hours					
157	Rental for Strike Days					
158	Strike OT Hours					
159	Power Charges					
160	Dressing Rooms					
161	Studio Parking					
162	Studio Security					
163	Stage Manager					
164	Stage Phones					
165	Climate Control					
166	Trash Removal					
167						
				TOTAL F		

G	ART DEPARTMENT LABOR	Prep Days	Shoot Days	Day Rate	Overtime Hours 1.5	2.0	3.0	ESTIMATED	ACTUAL
168	Production Designer								
169	Art Director								
170	Set Decorator								
171	Lead Person								
172	Set Dressers								
173	Prop Master								
174	Asst Props								
175	Scenics								
176	Effects								
177	Stage Electric								
178	Teamsters								
179	Art Coordinator								
180									
							Sub-total G		
							PT/P&W		
							TOTAL G		

H	ART DEPARTMENT EXPENSES	Amount	Rate	x	ESTIMATED	ACTUAL
181	Set Dressing/Prop Rentals					
182	Set Dressing/Prop Purchases					
183	Paint					
184	Signage					
185	Hardware					
186	Special Effects					
187	Outside Construction					
188	Art Trucking					
189	Art Equipment					
190	Art Supplies					
191	Art Kit Rentals					
192	Art Phones					
				TOTAL H		

Prod Co

Bid Name

I	EQUIPMENT & RELATED EXPENSES	Amount	Rate	x	ESTIMATED	ACTUAL
193	Camera Rental					
194	Sound Rental					
195	Lighting Rental					
196	Grip Rental					
197	Generator Rental					
198	Crane Rental					
199	VTR Rental					
200	Walkie Talkie Rental					
201	Dolly Rental					
202	Camera Car Rental					
203	Aerial Equipment Rental					
204	Production Supplies					
205	Expendables					
206	Mobile Phones					
207	Steadicam Rental					
208						
209						
210						
			TOTAL I			

J	STOCK, DEVELOP AND PRINT	Amount	Rate	x	ESTIMATED	ACTUAL
211	Purchase Filmstock					
212	Develop Filmstock					
213	Print Filmstock					
214	Videotape Stock					
215						
216						
			TOTAL J			

K	MISCELLANEOUS COSTS	Amount	Rate	x	ESTIMATED	ACTUAL
217	Petty Cash					
218	Shipping					
219	Office Phones					
220	Messengers					
221						
222	Special Insurance					
223	Loss, Damage, Repair					
224	Outstanding Deposits					
225	Production Services					
226						
			TOTAL K			

L	DIRECTOR/CREATIVE FEES	Amount	Rate	x	ESTIMATED	ACTUAL
227	Director Prep					
228	Director Travel					
229	Director Shoot					
230						
231						
232						
233						
			Sub-totaL I			
			PT/P&W			
			TOTAL L			

APPENDIX A. (pages 7 and 8)

Prod Co

Bid Name

M	TALENT & RELATED LABOR	No.	Prep Days	Shoot Days	Day Rate	Overtime Hours 1.5	2.0	3.0	ESTIMATED	ACTUAL
234	Principals									
235	Principals									
236	Principals									
237	Principals									
238	Principals									
239	Extras									
240	Extras									
241	Extras									
242										
243	Key Makeup									
244	2nd Makeup									
245	3rd Makeup									
246	Key Hair									
247	2nd Hair									
248	3rd Hair									
249	Key Stylist									
250	2nd Ward Asst									
251	3rd Ward Asst									
252	Teacher/Welfare									
253	Choreographer									
254	Asst Choreographer									
255	Stunt Coordinator									
256	Security									
257	Teamsters									
258	Caterer									
259	Craft Service									
260	Band Tech									
261										
								Sub-total M		
								PT/P&W		
								TOTAL M		

N	TALENT & RELATED EXPENSES	Amount	Rate	x	ESTIMATED	ACTUAL
262	Air Fares					
263	Per Diem					
264	Car Service					
265	Casting Dir & Expenses					
266	Rehearsal Studio					
267	Dressing Rooms					
268	Catering / Craft Service					
269	Makeup / Hair Expenses					
270	Wardrobe Expenses					
271	Wardrobe Expenses					
272	Band Instruments					
273	Talent Agency Fees	20%				
274	Talent-related Crew Agency Fees	20%				
275						
276						
			TOTAL N			

214

Prod Co

Bid Name

O	POST PRODUCTION LABOR	Amount	Rate	x	ESTIMATED	ACTUAL
277	Post Supervisor					
278	Asst Post Supervisor					
279	Post PA's					
280	Director Post Fee					
281						
				Sub-total O		
				PT/P&W		
				TOTAL O		

P	POST PRODUCTION EXPENSES	Amount	Rate	x	ESTIMATED	ACTUAL
282	Off-line Edit					
283	Off-line Load					
284	Off-line Stock					
285	Off-line Other					
286						
287	Digital 2D Animation					
288	Digital 3D/Modeling					
289	Digital Rotoscoping					
290	Digital Compositing					
291	Digital Stock					
292	Digital Other					
293						
294	Music					
295	VO/ADR					
296	Sound Effects					
297	Sound Design					
298	Audio Mix					
299	Audio Stock					
300	Audio Playback Elements					
301						
302	Film to Tape Color Correction					
303	Tape to Tape Color Correction					
304	Telecine Neg Clean					
305	Telecine Stock					
306	Telecine Other					
307						
308	On-line Conform					
309	Character Generator					
310	Closed Captions					
311	Color Camera					
312	On-line Stock					
313	Edited Master					
314	Clones					
315	Dubs					
316						
317	Standards Conversion					
318	Digital Transmission					
319	Stock Footage					
320	Animation					
321	Film Editing					
322	Opticals					
323	Negative Cutting					
324	Lab Work Other					
325	Tape to Film Transfer					
326	Post Shipping/Messengers					
327	Post Working Meals					
328						
329						
				TOTAL P		

APPENDIX B. *VIDEO TREATMENT*

Jack Johnson
"Sitting, Waiting, Wishing"
By The Malloys

The video will be a single take shot entirely in reverse (with Jack singing and playing the song backwards). When it airs, it will be played back in reverse so that Jack will appear to be singing normally, but everything happening around him will be in reverse. However, we are not doing a video that matches the lyrics. We will play off the notion that when bad things happen in reverse, they actually can be seen as good.

The following description will be how the video will be seen when it airs, as opposed to how it is shot—which is exactly the opposite.

Fire hoses are spraying backwards as Jack comes flying into a chair that sits in the middle of a disheveled white room. The water turns off, and we see that he is wet with various food substances (cake, eggs, tomatoes, etc.) that are splattered on his skin and clothing. Smoke is dissipating from the room.

From the water hoses spraying him offscreen, we start to show all the things that happened for Jack and the room to get to this point. Surrounding Jack are a bunch of fireworks (Roman candles, cherry bombs, flowers, and other medium-sized fireworks). They are going off in reverse, and the sparks are going back into the box where all these fireworks were lit. When they all go out, we see the trail of fire leading off screen that ignited all the fireworks.

From the fire being lit, we see a box of fireworks being thrown from offscreen around the floor, where Jack was playing.

On the white wall directly behind Jack, framed pictures containing various images, which appear to be puzzle pieces to a larger picture, begin assembling behind him on their own.

At this point, Jack's guitar is smashed, except for the neck. In reverse we see the camera go in for a close-up. It goes in really tight, so tight that it pushes jack off his chair, drives him into the back wall, and smashes him and his guitar. Jack picks himself up and puts his chair back in the middle of the room, where he continues singing the song.

Jack then begins to get pelted by cake, eggs, and tomatoes that fly off him and offscreen. This happens in reverse for about 10 seconds.

Behind Jack, it starts to become clear that the various framed pictures behind him are forming the larger image of his album cover for *In Between Dreams*. The final missing picture frame needed to complete the overall image flies from offscreen into Jack's hands. He places the framed picture in the middle of the group of assembled pictures to finalize the album cover.

Jack then walks toward camera and jumps into the air, throwing his feet up above his head and catching them on a bar where he suspends upside down (half of his body will be onscreen and half offscreen). He finishes the last line of the song and then pulls himself up and out of frame. We are left with the very clear image of Jack's album cover on the back wall created by the assembled, framed pictures.

Media
SERVICES

Your Payroll & Software Solution!

New York: 212-366-9390
Los Angeles: 310-440-9600

Work Rules - IATSE - MVPA Music Video Production Agreement

Term of Contract		12/1/05 - 11/30/2009
Contracted Day		8 consecutive hours
Contracted Workweek		Any 5 or 6 consecutive days of 7
Calls	Day/Night	Anytime Time Begins at Set Call Time
	Partial Day	No Except Travel days - Actual hours up to 4 hours @ 1x - No benefits
		No minimum call for "wrap only" crew.
Overtime	1.5x	9-12hr., 6th day
	2x	7th day, Holidays, After 12hrs.if over $500K budget. After 14 elapsed hours if under $500K budget.
	Increments	
Turnaround	Daily	10 hours On all work assignments
Penalty	If rest is short	Base or OT rate when released plus 1X for invaded hours.
Meals	Intervals	6 hr. intervals 1st meal no earlier than 3 hrs. except for early call crew provided w/ND Breakfast.
	Lengths	1/2 - 1 hour
	Penalties	1st 3/4 hr or fraction - $8.00
		2nd 3/4 hr and each additional - $12.00
	Second Meal	May be deducted if it is outside minimum call and 6 hrs after preceding meal period.
	Extensions	1st may be extended 15 min. to complete set up 2nd may be extended 30 min. to complete set-up or wrap.
	Walking Meal	Non-Deductible Breakfast may be provided crew called in early. Then first meal due with regular crew.
		Second meal may be a non deductible walking meal so long as there is opp. to eat and within 3 hrs of Wrap.
Production Zone		>Within a circular 45 mile zone from intersection of City Hall for designated production centers*
Location Rules		*See: Wage Rates - IATSE - MVPA Music Video Production Agreement*
Work time/Travel Time Provisions		Travel Days -pay for up to 4 hours. NO benefits paid.
Cancellation of Cal		By 3pm - prior non work day By end of prior work day By 6PM if called for weather
		Penalty - Work Day - 8 hrs pay Travel Day - 4 hrs pay Wrap Only - No penalty
Minimum Staffing		>No Minimum Staffing - "...staffing practices ... consistent with general past practice in music video
		production industry." "...practical interchangeability within production crafts."
		>Covers "... classifications traditionally covered by IATSE..." Excludes office clerical, PA's or guards.
		>Star requested Hair, Make-up or Wardrobe are exempt from agmt., but may become members.
Payment of wages		Consistent with state laws
Hazardous Work		No special provisions
Jurisdiction		Throughout US, Puerto Rico and US Virgin Islands.
Pension Health & Welfare		**Under $55,000 Budget** - No benefit payments due
		Over $55,000 Budget
		For work in LA Co. or hired in LA Co. to work elsewhere: Current MPIPH rates H&W:$3.2975 per hour for
		all hours worked or guaranteed plus IAP: 5% of scale straight time rate.
		For Camera or Post Production hired outside LA Co.: $8.2660 per hr.+ $0.75 p/d + 4.5% of Scale
		1/22/2006: $8.4486 per hr. plus 5% of Scale plus $.75 per day
		For Las Vegas projects: Pension 8% of gross, health: $25.00 per day.
		For New York*, SF Bay Area, Detroit, Illinois, & Wash. DC.
		$55,001 - $300K budget: $48 per day (12/1/06: $51 per day) (12/1/07: $54 per day) (12/1/08: $57 per day
		$300,001 - $500K budget: $68 per day (12/1/06: $71 per day) (12/1/07: $74 per day) (12/1/08: $77 per day
		Over $500,001 budget: $78 per day (12/1/06: $81 per day) (12/1/07: $84 per day) (12/1/08: $87 per day
		* NY Execpt L52 & L161 same as Camera and Post Production - above.
		For all other areas: $47 per day (12/1/06: $50 per day) (12/1/07: $53 per day) (12/1/08: $56 per day)
Holidays		Memorial Day Independence Day Day after Thanksgiving New Years Day
		Labor Day Thanksgiving Day Christmas Day
Union Security		>Existing employees covered by agreement will become members of IATSE after 30 days employment
		>Preference of employment: First consideration to those referred by local unions.
Scale Rates		*See: Wage Rates - IATSE - MVPA Music Video Production Agreement*
Notes		>Producers must be direct signatory to full agreement. No letters of adherence.
		>Covers production of Music Videos only.
		>Must notify union of each production in writing. Penalty:As of12/1/06 Advance one budget tier.
		Penalty effective with 4th violation in 18 months.
		>IATSE or crew may appoint a Job Steward for each production. IATSE may have reasonable access to set.
		>Must provide a crew list within five days of request.
		>After 30 days work in two years employees can be put on Industry Experience Roster.
		>Scope of Agreement - Where employer has no effective control of portions of pre and post production work
		covered or assigned, then employer shall not be liable under agreement. Employer not prevented from
		sub-contracting when does not have facilities or equipment or employees skilled in required work.
		>Intent is to conform w/music video industry practices and not diminish work opportunities for union members
		>Recognize jurisdiction over music videos made by traditional means for any medium including Internet.
		>Internet music videos by non-traditional means to be negotiated, all but wages & work rules apply.
Phone Numbers		MVPA - 213-387-1590 IATSE: NY 212-730-1770, LA 818-905-8999

Media SERVICES™

Your Payroll & Software Solution!

New York: 212-366-9390
Los Angeles: 310-440-9600

Wage Rates - IATSE - MVPA Music Video Production Agreement

WAGE RATE RULES	
Budget	
$0 - $55K - Agreement not applicable	
$55,001 - $300K - As negotiated.	
$300,001 - $500K - $19.67 per hour (+3% 12/1/06, 07, 08)	
Over $500K - Per LA AICP/IATSE Rates >>>>>>>>>	

PRODUCTION ZONES	
Alaska	Anchorage
Arizona	Phoenix, Tucson
California	Sacremento, San Diego
Colorado	Denver
Florida	Miami (incl. Palm Beach, Dade & Broward counties), Orlando (incl. Winterhaven & Lakeland), Tampa (St. Petersburg & Clearwater)
Georgia	Atlanta
Hawaii	Honolulu
Louisiana	New Orleans
Maryland	Baltimore
Mass.	Boston
Michigan	Detroit
Minnesota	Minneapolis & St. Paul
Missouri	St. Louis
Nevada	Las Vegas
New Mexico	Albuquerque & Santa Fe
N. Carolina	Charlotte & Willimington
Ohio	Clevland
Oregon	Portland
Penn.	Philadelphia & Pittsburgh
Pureto Rico	San Juan
Tenn.	Nashville
Texas	Austin, Dallas, Ft. Worth, Houston & San Antonio
Utah	Salt Lake City
Virginia	Richmond & Washington DC
Washington	Seattle

LOCATION RULES

In Production Zones:
> Report to locations within zone unless access difficulties, the transportation provided.
> Local Hire if employee lives within 45 miles of location.

For Nearby Location, outside Production Zone:
>Mileage - Curr. IRS Rate ($0.405) per mile from perimeter of "zone" to reporting place and return.
>Travel outside zone paid as allowance at 1X rate not to exceed 1hr per day and is not included in rest period.

Overnight Locations:
> Work time from set call to set dismissal.
> Transport to be provided.
> Rest periods calculated Portal to Portal.
>Housing or housing allowance to be provided on overnight locations.

IATSE-AICP 2004 Commercial Production Agreement Wage Rates*

Classification		10/1/2005	(8 hours)		
Dir. of Photography	Hourly	84.59	676.75		
Camera Operator	Hourly	51.78	414.22		
1st Camera Asst.	Hourly	37.46	299.69		
2nd Camera Asst.	Hourly	34.41	275.30		
Camera Loader/Utility	Hourly	29.44	235.50		
Sound Mixer	Hourly	57.78	462.26		
Boom Operator	Hourly	39.00	311.97		
Sound Utility	Hourly	39.00	311.97		
VTR/Video Playback	Hourly	39.00	311.97		
Key Grip	Hourly	36.26	290.05		
2nd Grip	Hourly	32.48	259.81		
Dolly Grip	Hourly	33.63	269.04		
Grip	Hourly	30.99	247.94		
Entry Level Grip	Hourly	27.13	217.04		
Lighting Gaffer	Hourly	36.26	290.05		
2nd Electrician	Hourly	32.48	259.81		
Dimmer Operator	Hourly	31.71	253.71		
Electrician	Hourly	30.99	247.94		
Entry Level Electrician	Hourly	27.13	217.04		
Property Master	Hourly	36.26	290.05		
2nd Prop	Hourly	31.71	253.71		
3rd Prop	Hourly	29.71	237.64		
Costume Designer	Weekly on Call	2044.54	Daily on Call	490.59	
Key Costumer	Hourly	33.78	270.27		
2nd Costumer	Hourly	32.07	256.59		
3rd Costumer	Hourly	29.38	235.00		
Entry Level Costumer	Hourly	23.39	187.13		
Key Make Up Artist	Hourly	41.27	330.18		
2nd Make Up Artist	Hourly	35.13	281.07		
3rd Make Up Artist	Hourly	31.84	254.70		
Key Hair Stylist	Hourly	40.94	327.54		
2nd Hair Stylist	Hourly	35.91	287.25		
3rd Hair Stylist	Hourly	30.61	244.89		
Script Supervisor	Hourly	30.28	242.26		
First Aid	Hourly	28.29	226.35		
Craft Service	Hourly	26.28	210.20		
Art Director	Weekly on Call	2885.12			
Asst. Art Director	Weekly on Call	2159.23			
Set Decorator	Weekly on Call	2203.41	Daily on Call	521.92	
Lead Set Dresser	Hourly	31.71	253.71		
Set Dresser	Hourly	29.71	237.64		
Construction Coord.	Weekly on Call	2143.75	Daily on Call	507.16	
Propmaker Foreperson	Hourly	36.42			
Propmaker	Hourly	31.71			
Paint Foreperson	Daily on Call	427.21	291.37		
Painter	Hourly	31.71	253.71		
Lead Scenic Artist	Hourly	47.00			
Scenic Artist	Hourly	42.50			
Special EFX Foreperson	Hourly	36.42	253.71		
Lead Effects	Hourly	33.63	375.99		
Effects	Hourly	31.71	339.98		
Studio Teacher/Welfare	Hourly	39.38			

Marine Coords, boat handlers & operators if not covered by another union.

Wages "As Negotiated"

If Employed: (Daily rate = 1/5 of 5 day rate)

Prod. Accountant	5 Day "On Call"	2157.09
Prod. Office Coordinator	5 Day "On Call"	1294.90
Asst. Prod. Accountant	5 Day "On Call"	1222.95
Asst. Prod. Office Coord.	5 Day "On Call"	767.39
Art Dept. Coordinator	5 Day "On Call"	767.39

APPENDIX D. *TEAMSTER RULES AND GUIDELINES FOR MUSIC VIDEO PRODUCTION*

New York: 212-366-9390
Los Angeles: 310-440-9600

Work Rules - Local 399 Teamsters - <u>MVPA</u> - Music Videos - Los Angeles

Term of Contract		1/1/2006 - 12/31/2007
Contracted Day		8 consecutive hours
Contracted Workweek		Any 5 or 6 consecutive days of 7
Calls	Day/Night	Not mentioned
	Partial Day	Travel Days - Actual hours up to 4 hours at Straight Time - 4 hours benefits paid.
		Wrap Only - No minimum call
		Drop offs & pick ups of covered vehicles: Minimum call 4 hours
		Split shift replacements - Minmum call 4 hours *Prior shift min. 8 hours*
		No minmum call for location mangers and scouts
Overtime	**1.5x**	9-12hr., 6th day
	2x	After 12hrs., 7th day, Holidays
	Increments	
Turnaround	Daily	9 hours Overnight Locations - 8 hrs.
Penalty	If rest is at least 8 hrs.	1x for invaded hours
	If rest is at least 6 hrs.	Premium rate for invaded hours
	If rest is less than 6 hrs.	Premium rate for day until 9 hour rest period is provided.
Meals	Intervals	6 hr. intervals 1st meal no earlier than 3 hrs. except for early call crew provided w/ND Breakfast.
	Lengths	1/2 - 1 hour
	Penalties	1st hour or fraction - $8.00
		2nd 3/4 hr and each additional - $12.00
	Second Meal	
	Extensions	1st may be extended 15 min. to complete set up 2nd may be extended 30 min. to complete set-up or wrap.
	Walking Meal	Any second meal, excluding NDB, may be a non-deductible walking meal
Studio Zone		>Within a circular 45 mile zone from intersection of Beverly Blvd. and La Cienega Blvd. in Los Angeles
		> Mileage paid from perimeter of zone at IRS rate (Currenty $0.485 per mile)
Overnight Location Rules		>Per Diem allowance and housing or housing allowance to be provided.
		>Transportation provided or mileage paid to/from overnight locations
		>Worktime set call to set dismissal with transportation to/from daily locations
		>Rest periods calculated portal to portal.
		>Local Hire if live within 45 miles of production location - No housing, per deim or mileage need be paid.
Worktime/Travel Time Provisions		Travel Days - Actual hours up to 4 hours at Straight Time - 4 hours benefits paid.
		Transport of production vehicles to location at applicable minimum calls.
Cancellation of Call		By 3pm of prior non work day or end of prior work day
		By 6pm if for inclement weather
		Penalty: Wk Day: 8hrs pay; Drop off/pick up/split shift Day: 4hrs pay, Travel days per travel day rules
Operations/Staffing		<u>**For budgets with "Production Budgets" (exclude Post-Production & Talent costs):**</u>
		>**Under $50,000** - Agreement does not apply
		>**Over $50,000** - No min staffing requirements, but covered equipment and functions must be staffed if used.
		<u>Covered equipment/functions:</u> All vehicles requiring Class A or B License

15 or more Passenger Vans	Drivable Generators	
Motorhomes	Prod. Trailers	
Water Trucks	Catering Trucks	
Hydracranes (5 ton or more)	Specialty Vehicles	Production Vans (400 Amp Gen min.)
10 Ton Trucks	Chapman Cranes	Camera Cars
Fuel Trucks	Car Carriers (4 vehicles or more)	
Honeywagons	Highway Buses (38+ Pass. Incl. Driver)	
Location Scouts and Managers		

> Staffing consistant w/industry practice. Employees may work in more than one category in a day, but must be paid at higher category for entire day.
> **Over $300,000** - Location Mgr must be hired for non self-contained locations. "Self-Contained" locations include: Studio Lots, Warehouses, Stages, Filming Ranches and other locations with off street parking.
> **Over $300,000** - Shuttling of Crew on shoot days only is covered work. Does not apply to agency, talent, or label and does not preclude use of PAs to make runs to and from set.
> **Over $300,000** - Minimum one Transportation Captain - Can not be a Driver/Grip or Driver/Electrician etc., or be required to operate specialized equipment, or work simultaneously on two or more productions.
   Exception if there are four or fewer Production Vehicles driven by company employees.
    Production Vehicles are: All vehicles requiring Class A or B License, 15 or more passenger vans,
    motorhomes, houscars, catering trucks, camera cars, cube trucks and subcontracted vehicles.

Operations/Staffing	> **General**
Continued	>Preference of Employment (Roster) does not apply to drivers of "Special Equipment" such as
	Chapman cranes, camera cars specialty picture vehicles, prod. Vans and hypenate drivers.
	>Preference of Employment (Roster) waived for one driver specifically requested by artist or label.
	>Motorhomes covered if orginating or operating in Hawaii, LA , Orange or Ventura Counties, or
	San Francisco, SanDiego or Las Vegas studio zones.
	> Outside above zones teamster to be employed to drive motorhomes/housecars in following
	counties, if available for local hire: Alemeda, Contra Costa, Kern, Marin, Monterey, Napa, Riverside
	San Berardino, San Diego, San Francisco,San Luis Obispo, San Mateo, Santa Barbara, Santa
	Clara, Santa Cruz, Solono, Washoe (Nevada) and Yolo
	> Not required to transport drivers to distant location to drive motorhomes/housecars.
	> Drivable Generators (200 AMP+ bolted to truck) driven at Class B rate.
	> 1 Driver/Cook of each drivable mobile kitchen covered at Class A rate. Assistants not covered.
	> Vehicles towing trailers originally manufactured with three axles are covered.
Payment of wages	>No special provisions, but CA law requires payment on same schedule as staff. Penalties are high.
Hazardous Work	No special provisions
Jurisdiction	California, Hawaii and Nevada
Pension Health & Welfare	> $3.3975/hr plus 5% of scale to MPIP Idle Days: 4 hours of contributions
	> Location Managers/Scouts P&W based on::
	Partial week = 12 hours per day Five day week = 60 hours
	Six day week = 67 hours Seven day week = 75 hours
	>For production budgets less than $500,000 calc rate for IAP is $15 per hour.
	>With permission of L399 - Local hires may have P&W go to local trust funds at these rates or less.
Holidays	New Years Day Memorial Day Thanksgiving Day and day after
	Independence Day Labor Day Christmas Day

Scale Rates

Under $50,000 Prod. Budget, Agmt does not apply

Production Budgets $50,000 to $300,000 rates individually negotiated.

Budgets over $300K	1/1/05	Budgets over $500K	1/1/05	Rates increase 3%
Classification:	Per Hour	Classification:	Per Hour	on 7/1/06 & 7/1/07
Captain	27.00	Captain	32.20	
Driver - Class A Vehicle	23.47	Driver - Class A Vehicle	27.92	
Driver/Cooks	23.47	Driver/Cooks	27.92	
Driver - Class B Vehicle	21.76	Driver - Class B Vehicle	25.85	
Camera Car Driver	27.00	Camera Car Driver	32.20	
Prod. Van Driver/Opr	27.56	Prod. Van Driver/Opr	32.88	
Chapman Crane Opr	27.00	Chapman Crane Opr	32.20	
Motorhome Drivers	21.76	Motorhome Drivers	25.85	
Drivable Generator	21.76	Drivable Generator	25.85	
Loc. Mgr/Scout (per day)	475.00	Loc. Mgr/Scout (per day)	500.00	

Notes	>Covers Music Videos shot in any form. Non-traditional forms to be negociate
	>Producers must be direct signatory to full agreement
	>L399 may appoint one stewad for each productio
	>Where Employer has no effective control portions of pre and post production, they not cover
	>Employers not prevented from subcontracting for services consistent with industry practic
	>No use of non-covered equipment to deliberately avoid terms of agreeme
Phone Numbers	Local 399: 818-985-7374 MVPA: 213-387-1590

THE AUTHOR

Lara has produced or directed over 100 music videos, commercials, feature films, short films, documentaries, live broadcasts, and DVDs. She has worked with artists such as Mary J. Blige, Whitney Houston, Tom Jones, Harry Connick Jr., Aaliyah, Missy Elliot, Salt-n-Pepa, Branford Marsalis, Boyz II Men, Jermaine DuPri, Al Jarreau, P. Diddy, the Notorious B.I.G., K-Ci & Jojo, Teddy Pendergrass, and Smokey Robinson, among many others. Several of her videos were nominated and won awards.

After learning the music video business as a freelance production manager and producer in the early 1990s, Sean "P. Diddy" Combs asked her to establish and oversee his production company. Subsequently, Lara started Bad Boy Films in 1994 and, at that time, was Executive Producer of all Bad Boy Records' music videos. In 1995, Lara opened her own production company, 361 Degrees, and began directing as well as producing music videos. Soon thereafter, she expanding into commercials, short films, feature films, documentaries, live broadcasts, and DVDs.

Lara taught the class "Music Video Production" at UCLA Extension Department of Entertainment, giving students a working familiarity with the process of making music videos from both the business perspective and the creative perspective. In December 2003, she traveled to Cuba as part of a UCLA Extension Program filmmakers' delegation.

Lara received a B.A. from Smith College in Northampton, MA, and studied jazz and rock-n-roll at the Berklee College of Music in Boston, MA. She currently lives in New York City with her husband.

PHOTOGRAPH BY BETSY BELL

INDEX